Children of "Red Atlantis"

The Development of Federal Indian Policy

1735 through the Indian Reorganization Act

James P. Lynch

HERITAGE BOOKS
2011

HERITAGE BOOKS
AN IMPRINT OF HERITAGE BOOKS, INC.

Books, CDs, and more—Worldwide

For our listing of thousands of titles see our website
at
www.HeritageBooks.com

Published 2011 by
HERITAGE BOOKS, INC.
Publishing Division
100 Railroad Ave. #104
Westminster, Maryland 21157

Copyright © 2011 James P. Lynch

Other books by the author:

*By "theire free act & deed": Connecticut's
Land Relationship with Indian Tribes, 1496–2003*

*Gideon's Calling: The Founding and Development of the
Schaghticoke Indian Community at Kent, Connecticut, 1638–1854*

*"our ancient & Loving ffriends": The Town of Southampton, New York's
Relationship with the Shinnecock Indians, 1628–1920*

All rights reserved. No part of this book may be reproduced or transmitted in any form or by any means, electronic or mechanical, including photocopying, recording or by any information storage and retrieval system without written permission from the author, except for the inclusion of brief quotations in a review.

International Standard Book Numbers
Paperbound: 978-0-7884-5285-7
Clothbound: 978-0-7884-8680-7

This research is dedicated to Erhard Konerding, Government Documents Librarian, Olin Memorial Library, Wesleyan University, Middletown, Connecticut.

Long time valued friend and associate, without whose professional assistance, and expertise over the past thirty years this research would not have attained fruition.

Table of Contents

Introduction..9.

Chapter 1.
The Concept of Tribal Sovereignty......................................17.

"a people distinct from others": Tribal Sovereignty............24.

"as mere domestic communities": Plenary Authority.........29.

Chapter 2.
American Indian Policy, 1735-1850....................................33.

"All the Indians with whom our colonies have any connections": A Unified Indian Policy, 1735-1776............34.

"Treating with, and making purchases": The Early Nationalist Period, 1777-1789 ....46.

"the Indians possess the natural rights of man...": The Era of the Indian Trade and Intercourse Acts, 1790-1834 ....57.

"the State of Maine is in accordance with the Constitution" :Veazie v. Moor ....72.

Chapter 3.
The Process of Federal Recognition of Indian Tribes ....76.

"...in Congress assembled": The Constitution and the Recognition of Indian Tribes ....78.

President Jackson's Westward Removal ....87.

Chapter 4.
"…mere domestic communities" The March 3,
1871 Congressional Proviso ....96.

"generally it is the power of the Senate to decide"............97.

"that no tribe of Indians shall hereafter be acknowledged"100.

Intent ....102.

Chapter 5.
Under the Plenary Control of Congress.............................104.

"The Indians hold the relation of wards…"......................104.

"The plan is obviously a wise and humane one"...............106.

Chapter 6.
Working Towards the "Dawes Act" ....117.

"No general law exists" ....117.

"in atonement for what we have inflicted" ....120.

"There is nothing more dangerous to an Indian reservation
than a rich mine"..122.

"the road our fathers walked is gone."...............................125.

Chapter 7.
Dawes..127.

"most everyone seems to have been enthusiastic about
Allotment - except the Indians"..127.

"No measure could be devised more efficient" .... 129.

"The passage of the Dawes bill closes the 'century of dishonor' " .... 130.

"The child must become a man" .... 135.

"breaking up the tribal mass" .... 136.

"That where any Indian not residing upon a reservation" .. 138.

"discontinuing guardianship of all competent Indians" ...... 144.

"That whenever it shall be made to appear" .... 145.

"by reason of age, disability or inability." .... 149.

"Experience has demonstrated…" The "Heff" Fix 152

Citizenship .... 158.

Chapter 8.
The Advent of Red Atlantis: The Indian
Reorganization Act of 1934 .... 162.

"They must be aided for the preservation of themselves" .. 166.

"…illy digested emotional attacks" .... 170.

"The Whites can take care of themselves, but the Indians need someone to protect them" .... 172.

"commanding the imagination of Indians and Congressman alike." .... 180.

Visions of Red Atlantis .... 199.

"making Reds of the Indians" .... 201.

Approval at Any Cost ....204.

"there was some change in punctuation" ....209.

Taken to the Woodshed ....213.

Atlantis Sinking ....221.

Atlantis' Inundation ....226.

"edging towards termination" ....230.

"the United States has not yet discharged its obligation to the Indian" ....232.

"Congress can expect no constructive advice and assistance from the Bureau of Indian Affairs" ....233.

To "…take his place in the white man's community on the white man's level" ....236.

Chapter 9.
Summary ....246.

Introduction

In 1934, then Commissioner of Indian Affairs John Collier stated that his purpose for creating the Indian Reorganization Act was to create a socialist-based "Red Atlantis" out of those Indian groups that voted to participate in and reorganize under the Act. Collier's efforts epitomized the zenith of federal paternalism both as a policy governing the American Indian as well as the promotion of a socialist-based ideological agenda. Red Atlantis was to become its metaphor.

Federal Indian policy, like most similar national polices, followed national ideological and political trends. Yet during the time period covered by this writing (1735-1953) there occurred one seminal event that forever altered the nature of Federal Indian policy. With the insertion of a simple sixty-four word "proviso" into the Indian spending authorization bill for 1872, Federal Indian policy was virtually turned on its head. Congressional "commerce" with Indian tribes was supplanted by congressional "plenary" authority over them. Tribes henceforth would be, in the eyes of Federal Indian policy, "mere domestic communities." This change solidified the advent of a paternalistically-based policy over reservation-bound tribes and individual Indians over whom the Federal government asserted legal jurisdiction. Tribes would no longer be recognized as sovereign entities, but would instead be dependent "domestic communities." This simple proviso was to set in motion a chain of events in Federal Indian policy that was to lead to the Indian Reorganization Act of 1934, that most expansive expression of federal paternalism over Indian tribes and individuals. In the eyes of the Act's creators, these Indian "communities" served as guinea pigs in a socialist-inspired experiment whose participants would become the children of "Red Atlantis."

Within its historical context, the longest, most stable American Indian policy predated the founding of the Republic. It was a product of English foreign policy emanating out of the Royal Board of Trade and Foreign Plantations and continued, as we shall see, through 1871. This policy can be viewed as being threat-driven, that is, those independent sovereign tribes inhabiting the frontiers had the recognized capability to threaten the very survival of the colonies and provinces of North America.

In retrospect, American Indian policy as it pertains to federally recognized Indian groups can be viewed as having four distinct policy eras. These eras are themselves reflections of societal, political, and ideological changes occurring in American society. They are characterized as: the era of tribal sovereignty; the era of paternalism and assimilation; the era of termination, and the present-day era of self-governance and neo-sovereignty. For purposes of this writing neo-sovereignty can be defined within the context of Justice John Marshall's *Cherokee v. Georgia* opinion that tribes residing under federal jurisdiction are "domestic dependent nations" that may possess some of the attributes of being a sovereign political entity, but are not sovereign in their own right. It will be argued below that sovereignty itself is, historically and legally, an absolute term.

The colonial-era policy of treating with Indian tribes as political sovereigns was first formulated in 1735 and was consistently applied in England's American colonies and provinces through the American Revolution. This policy was continued largely intact by the newly emergent American government, principally through the efforts of President George Washington and his Secretary of War, Henry Knox. The 1790 Indian Trade and Intercourse Act was for all intents and purposes, the continuation of former English policy enacted into federal law.

This steady policy continued with the enforcement of the Supreme Courts "Marshall Trilogy" decisions until 1871, wherein, as noted earlier, with the insertion of a simple "proviso" into the 1872 Indian Appropriation Act, the foundation of Federal Indian policy was forever changed. A policy heretofore based upon government-to-government relationships via treaty enactments evolved in the post-civil war years into one of a paternalistic-based government-ward relationship. From this point onward Federal Indian policy began its see-saw journey based upon the currents of national ideological reformist-driven change. What were the enabling factors that convinced Congress to enact this proviso and for President Grant to sign it into law? The 1871 proviso emerged from what may be called a "Perfect Storm" of national financial constraints, agitation from civic and religious groups to Christianize, and therefore, in their view to civilize the Indian, and the realization by Congress that circa 1871, the Federal government was no longer dealing with sovereign political tribal entities. The result was the advent of a complete reversal of an Indian policy that predated the Republic's founding. It became the imposition of a ward status upon American Indian tribes that were subject to federal jurisdiction.

In support of this position, in 1886 the United States Supreme Court affirmed that there exists but two sovereigns within the United States, the national government and the states. The following year Congress enacted the "Dawes" Indian allotment act. This legislation resulted from the confluence of three factors: the ward-ship status of Indian tribes, the assimilative-based reformist and civilization efforts, with federal support, by civil and religious philanthropic organizations, and the national economic imperative of land and mineral acquisition and railroad rights of way of, and through, Indian reservations. The amending of the 1887 Dawes Act in 1890 allowed the leasing of allotted Indian lands to non-Indians, which in conjunction with ill-advised and inconsistent assimilation strategies in large part doomed the efforts of Dawes.

The abject failure of Dawes culminated with the advent of the Wheeler-Howard or Indian Reorganization Act of 1934 (IRA). Contrary to accepted interpretations of the intent of this Act, its authors did not intend to stimulate the reconstruction of Indian tribes. Instead, its intent was to take the Dawes Act in a new direction wherein the goal of reservation-based land allotment was focused upon the individual. The goal was now focused upon the creation of collective Indian communities, that is, to create socialist-structured, economically and judicially self-sufficient, self-governing, collective communities that in time would assimilate into the mainstream of American society, thus ending federal responsibility and oversight of these reorganized Indian communities. The desired end result of IRA was the termination of federal services to and responsibilities to and over these Indian communities. These socialist communities would in turn provide a new model for American society to emulate. As Commissioner of Indian Affairs John Collier noted, the ultimate purpose of the Indian Reorganization Act was that it *would usher in a socialist democracy to replace the chaos of capitalism*....[1] The Indian Reorganization Act was a social experiment wherein the Indian was the laboratory guinea pig.

---

[1] Philip, Kenneth R. 1999, *Termination Revisited: American Indians on the Trail to Self-Determination, 1933-1953*:4, University of Nebraska Press, Linclon.

What emerged from this process was a quest for self-governance and neo-sovereignty, a quest that to this day is still subject to the paternalistic attitude of the Department of the Interior, and the plenary powers asserted by Congress.

Thus, England's colonial-era policy was to treat with independent Indian tribes, tribes whose loyalty was crucial to the survival of England's North American empire. Such tribes were considered by Crown authorities to be sovereign nations, capable of acting independently by carrying out their own diplomatic policies with multiple European powers, siding with various governments when it was in their best interests, and most importantly the latent military threat that they represented. Usually such tribes did not normally seek out the English to treat. Most of the time it was the English authorities who sought out these tribes. Apart from those tribes intricately involved in the fur trade, most Indian tribes did not need the European nations as much as the European nations needed the tribes in their repeated struggles against one another for North American and European dominance.

At the heart of this policy was the recognition of a tribal sovereignty. Sovereignty, or the act of having independent or self-governing power or authority, is a concept that is at the heart of current Federal Indian policy and Federal Indian law. The United States government first established federal recognition of Indian tribes on the basis of whether a tribe was, or was not a sovereign political entity. Congress, during the later nineteenth and twentieth centuries judged whether an Indian tribe was to be considered such a sovereign nation. In order to receive such recognition an Indian tribe had, according to the Federal government, had to possess an independent tribal government, free of outside political dominance. In addition such Indian groups had to possess a non-ceded tribal land base over which their authority was recognized.

Upon meeting these two criteria, Congress, as the sole enactor of Indian affairs, would allow the creation of a government-to-government relationship. This relationship would be signified by a treaty negotiated by the Executive branch, subject to confirmation by the Senate. Within this treaty were conditions, specified rights and obligations pertinent to the parties involved. The sole concern of the United States government in entering into these treaties was the maintenance of peace, especially with those independent Indian nations along the ever-expanding western frontier.

At this time, the Federal government envisioned the Mississippi River as the western boundary of the new Republic. Lands to the west of this river were considered "Indian country." The Louisiana Purchase and the war with Mexico changed this perspective. With the acquisition of southwestern territories, such as California and Texas, the national aspiration was to become a coast-to-coast nation. Territories became states. Former independent Indian nations disintegrated or dispersed leaving in their wake tribal remnants, which in many cases came under state jurisdiction. Fewer and fewer Indian tribes remained independent sovereigns.

After the Civil War, the growth of westward expansion accelerated as did the cost to a financially strapped Federal government as it tried to pay down the huge war debt and restore the economies of the devastated southern states. In addition were the ever-growing costs of treaty obligations with Indian tribes. At this time (circa 1871) the Federal government realized that the remaining Indian tribes were no longer sovereign nations as defined by both Congress and the Supreme Court. These tribes now resided on land under federal jurisdiction and thus were subject to the jurisdiction of either federal or state laws. Those under federal jurisdiction were now under the authority of Indian agencies run by various governmentally-appointed religious organizations and churches. They were no longer politically independent. Only the terms of existing treaties between Indian tribes and the Federal government maintained the façade of existing tribal sovereignty. They were reduced to "mere domestic communities." The era of congressional treaty-making with Indian tribes had ceased. The policy of congressional assertion of its plenary powers and institutionalized paternalism over these same entities had begun.

Such a radical change in Federal Indian policy, fostered by well-intentioned religious and progressive philanthropic groups, led to the advent of a federal policy of detribalization and individual land allotment. Congress no longer recognized tribes as independently sovereign, its new role was to paternalistically govern over these national wards. This policy turned out to be an abject sociological and anthropological failure.

Taking advantage of this policy failure, liberal-progressive leadership within the Department of the Interior developed a new, ideologically driven approach to national Indian policy that was to become commonly known as the "Indian Reorganization Act." It was, as noted above, a socialistic experiment created by the leadership within the Interior Department. The Indian tribes and individuals who subscribed to this Act were the government's guinea pigs. The intended result of this Act was to produce gradually assimilating, self-governing Indian communities, a "Red Atlantis." It was, according to its author to serve as a template for the transformation of American society from its capitalist structure to a socialistic society based upon the writings of a Russian count and a communist theorist. Like its predecessor, it also failed to achieve its goals, but its impact remains imbedded in Federal Indian policy and a subject of Court litigation to this very day.

This book's goal is to depict and analyze the progressive development of Federal Indian policy beginning with the association between the colonies and provinces of pre-revolutionary America, through the early confederation and federalist stages of national political development (era of sovereignty), and the paternalistic and later socialistic stages of policy evolution (era of paternalism-assimilation) and lastly, the advent of the era of termination. Each stage occurred not in isolation from the preceding policy era, but was, as we shall see, was derived from it. It culminated with the recognized failure of the Indian Reorganization Act and the advent of a federally Congressionally-sanctioned termination policy.

Chapter 1.

The Concept of Tribal Sovereignty.

The question of what constitutes tribal sovereignty remains to be settled by the highest court in the land, the United States Supreme Court. It is a paradox to have both Federal Indian policy and Federal Indian law built upon a concept that has not been definitively defined or articulated. Federally recognized Indian tribes are referred to as being sovereign, yet these same sovereign tribes are said to be subject to the absolute plenary powers of the United States Congress. In his recent Supreme Court opinion (2004) in *US. v. Lara*,[2] Supreme Court Justice Clarence Thomas described Federal Indian law, the foundation of Federal Indian policy, as "schizophrenic." On the one hand, he noted, the law argues tribal sovereignty, on the other, Congressional plenary authority.

The net effect of the sovereignty issue has seemingly been the creation of a United States containing many so-called "sovereign" tribal nations, *Imperium in Imperio*, sovereigns within a sovereign, "a house divided," to borrow President Lincoln's much-used phrase, wherein Indian tribal members have superceded, or conversely, have ceded many of the civil rights available to the ordinary non-tribal American citizen.

---

[2] United States v. Billy Jo Lara, 541 US 193 (2004)

To understand the dimensions of this problem it must be recognized that within all cultures and language groups, in response to the dynamics of socio-cultural change through time, word meanings oftentimes change in response to changes occurring within a social or political environment. In today's era of political correctness word meanings change as quickly as a March breeze.

It is one of the primary tasks of ethno-historical enquiry to understand the contextual, cultural, social, and ideological setting of a group or society under study at different points in time. Only then can sound analytical judgments be made in regard to the historical and anthropological record of a particular era.

For example, in our governing charter, the Federal Constitution, we find in Article 1, Section 8 of the "commerce" clause, "To regulate Commerce with foreign Nations, and among the several States and with the Indian Nations." Commonly, in the present day, "Commerce" is understood to mean, "an interchange of goods or commodities…" Commerce as understood by the original framers of the Constitution was "interaction or political relations." The implications of these different understandings of the word commerce, especially in Federal Indian law, a body of law not based upon enacted statutes, but upon the building blocks of legal precedent or construction by jurists at particular points in time with varying historical understandings can be significant. This is especially true if the term is interpreted by its then contemporary connotation and not by the understanding held by the original framers of the Constitution. The concepts of original context and intent are paramount to both the historian and jurist.

The word sovereignty, or the understanding of its meaning' faces the same dilemma. Is sovereignty, historically an absolute concept, or is it' in a contemporary setting' a matter of degrees such as limited sovereignty, semi-sovereignty, inherent sovereignty?

As an example, on November 6, 2006, the State Department's Bureau of International Information Programs released an official statement regarding the "...unique sovereign status as 'domestic dependent nations' of Indian tribes,"[3] a contradiction in terms perhaps? This release stated in part that,

> American Indian tribes are considered "domestic dependent nations" within the United States. As such, they retain sovereign powers over their members and territory except where such powers specifically have been modified by U.S. law.

This statement is a serious contradiction in terms. Can Indian tribes be "dependent" and "sovereign" at the same time? It is akin to a doctor telling his or her female patent that she is only a little bit pregnant. Either one is or isn't.

Foundational to our understanding of the development of Indian policy is the notion of sovereignty, or precisely the notion of tribal sovereignty. What is sovereignty? What has it meant historically? To begin with let's take a look at the concept of sovereignty within its historical context.

In the fourteenth century, the French philosopher Jean Bodin in his 1576 writing "Six Books of the State" revolutionized political thinking when he successfully argued that the state had to acknowledge one source of authority. This authority or sovereignty was limited only by divine sanction, (*potestas*) that is, the concept of *dominium* wherein all property rights and sovereignty are derived from God's bestowal of grace. Later Protestant reformists, such as Martin

---

[3] The Washington File, November 6, 2006, Bureau of International Information Programs, United States Department of State. (http://usinfo.state.goPv/).

Luther, John Huss, and John Calvin forcefully argued this point. They cited the New Testament Book of Romans[4] as providing the scriptural legitimization for dominium by grace and absolute sovereignty,

> Let every Soul be subject to the Higher Powers; for there is no Power but of God, the Powers that be are Ordained of God. Whosoever therefore resisteth the Power resisteth the Ordinance of God : and they that resist, shall receive to themselves Damnation.

In ancient Greece, governmental dominium was dominated by the tri-parte political philosophy of Aristotle. This model combined elements of democracy, aristocracy, and monarchy as the ideal form of equally shared governmental power. It was described as the *perfecta communitas*, or the perfect community.[5] This notion was supplanted by the Roman concept of *imperium romanum*, or imperial executive authority[6]. This model was represented by the Roman concept of *vinculum societatis*,[7] literally, the links of a chain which bound society together. In the aftermath of Roman imperialism, the Roman Catholic Church and its political off-spring, the Holy Roman Emperor replicated this imperial model under the concept of *Monarcha Universalis*[8] whereby they dominated and exerted a supranational *"dominium"* over Christian Europe. By the fifteenth century or the time of the "Age of Discovery" of the Americas, national rulers were gaining the political upper-hand over the Pope and Emperor on the one hand, and the local feudal lords and princes on the other. Thus *monarchia* supplanted *imperium*.

---

[4] Chapter13, verses 1, 2
[5] Pagden, Anthony, 1995, <u>Lords of all the World: Ideologies of Empire in Spain, Britian, and</u> France :12, Yale University Press, New Haven
[6] ibid:13
[7] ibid:22
[8] ibid:43

In contrast, Bodin's writings heralded the advent of the notion of the divine right of the King or sovereign. Thus national political leadership was considered absolute. It was sovereign over all else and independent of any other secular power. As Bodin stated "Sovereignty is the absolute and perpetual power of the state, that is the greatest power to command." As early as 1715, we find the term "sovereignty" denoting *"A territory under the rule of a sovereign or existing as an independent state"*[9]. By 1750 this notion of sovereignty began to assume a more secular meaning. The Swiss diplomat, Emer de Vattel in his highly influential political writings[10] stated,

> Every nation which governs itself, under whatever form, and which does not depend on any other Nation, is a Sovereign State. Its rights are, in the natural order, the same as those of every other State.

These rights and sovereignty were in turn recognized under the legal concept of the *jus gentium*, or the "Law of Nations".

Sir William Blackstone, in his "Commentaries on the Laws of England" defined law as "a rule of civil conduct prescribed by the Supreme power in a state, commanding what is right and prohibiting what is wrong." Within this context, Blackstone, following Bodin, further declared, "there is and must be a supreme, irresistible, absolute, uncontrolled authority, in which the rights of the sovereign reside."

The powers inherent in sovereignty are unlimited. Sovereignty is by definition indivisible. The sovereign authority can delegate authority to sub-governmental entities. This was especially so in feudal England with its vast baronial estates and

---

[9] The Shorter Oxford English Dictionary on Historical Principles, Vol. II, Third Edition, Oxford, 1950, The Clarendon Press.
[10] Vattel, Emer de, The Law of Nations or Principles of Natural Law, trans. Charles G. Fenwick, 1902, Washington, Carnegie Institution, Book 1, Chap 1, s.4,:11

self-functioning judicial systems such as the Courts Baron and Leets. Yet a Lord and his landed estate existed only at the pleasure of the sovereign. Here we do not find divided sovereignty. The presence of a contradictory sovereignty within sovereignty or *imperium in imperio*[11] could not and did not exist, as ultimate sovereignty rested with the Crown. Thus the very term sovereign denoted "a supreme repository of power, a political unit possessing or held to possess sovereignty." Sovereignty in turn denotes a "supreme power especially over a body politic, a controlling influence."[12] Sovereignty is thus an absolute term. This notion is of critical importance to our study.

Why this short history lesson you might ask? This development of the notion of sovereignty as an absolute concept is prologue to our main focus. By the time of the American Revolution the concept of sovereignty as an absolute had been accepted in English jurisprudence. By extension, this understanding of the absolute nature of sovereignty was accepted within England's North American colonies and provinces.

In the aftermath of the American Revolution, the Continental Congress attempted to dilute sovereignty's absolutist political paradigm via the Articles of Confederation. Congress did so by placing the states as co-equals to the central government. As we know, it was a total failure. In contrast, the English Philosopher John Locke (1588-1689) had, in his 1690 "Two Treatises of Government", argued the notion of a "social compact." Within the parameters of such a compact, the individual voluntarily ceded any notions of a perceived sovereignty to the national government for the good of the whole body politic. As

---

[11] See McDonald, Forrest, 2000, States Rights and the Union: Imperium in Imperio, University of Kansas Press, Lawrence.
[12] Webster's Third New International Dictionary, 1986, Merriam-Webster Inc, Springfield, Massachusetts.

Locke noted, "The great and chief end, therefore, of men's uniting, and putting themselves under government, is the preservation of their property."

In return, the sovereign guaranteed to protect the rights accorded to the individual as stated in their respective compact. Thus our federal charter which created not a democracy, but a representative republic, guarantees to all who surrender their individual sovereignty to the republic to have the natural inalienable rights to "life, liberty, and the pursuit of happiness." According to Locke, without this compact man would live in a "state of nature" wherein man would be a sovereign unto himself doing what is necessary for his own self-interest, an anarchistic "war of all against all" as described by Thomas Hobbes (1632-1704) in his 1651 "Leviathan." Seemingly this was the situation with the former colonies united under the Articles of Confederation. Instead, Locke argued man must live under a government according to the "law of nature. The only way one divests himself of his natural liberty and puts on the bonds of civil society is by agreeing with other men to join and unite in a community", which governs on the basis of reason and experience. According to Locke, at the core of this sovereign government is a law- or compact-enacting legislative body. This legislature is the supreme sovereign power to which all other political bodies, especially the executive, must be subordinate. The compact is the source of, and defining document of sovereignty.

The framers of our compact, the Federal Constitution were deeply affected by Locke's writings. Like Locke, the original framers were wary of arbitrary executive power and government by decree. Thus, the powers of sovereignty were vested in an elected law-making legislative body, Congress. This legislative body's powers were defined and limited by the sovereign compact, the Constitution.

" a people distinct from others.": Tribal Sovereignty

During this same time period the new republic had to address its relations with other 'sovereign' nations. Some were distant while others abutted on her boundaries. Amongst these were the independent sovereign Indian tribes with whom the republic had to initiate government-to-government relations. Under the "commerce" clause of the Federal Constitution[13] "commerce" was understood by the original framers of the Constitution to mean "interaction or political relations," not only commercial enterprise[14]. Congress alone was charged with the regulation of Indian affairs. That instituted a policy, a "Federal Indian policy", in order to facilitate the tribal "commerce" requirement imposed upon Congress by the Constitution. It is upon this sole requirement that current Federal Indian policy traces its legitimating lineage.

Congress was also responsible for the interchange of affairs between sovereign foreign governments, that is, the creation of government-to-government relationships that were signified by the enactment of a treaty. A treaty is simply a statement of rights, responsibilities, and obligations between sovereigns that defines the nature of their relationship.

Who were these tribal nations? In his 1832 *Worcester v. Georgia* Supreme Court opinion Justice John Marshall defined the term Indian Nation simply as,

---

[13] Article I, section 8
[14] Shorter Oxford Dictionary on Historical Principles, 2vols, 1953 ed. Oxford University, Claredon Press. As early as 1587 "commerce" was commonly understood to mean, "To hold intercourse and communication, associate with."

... a people distinct from others.[15]

Yet in this same opinion Justice Marshall went on to say that,

> The Indian nations have always been considered as distinct, independent political communities...

In its 1901 Supreme Court decision, *United States v. Montoya*, the Court added a further clarification to Justice Marshall's 1832 definition,

> The word "nation" as ordinarily used presupposes or implies an independence of any other sovereign power more or less absolute, an organized government, recognized officials, a system of laws, definite boundaries, and the power to enter into negotiations with other nations.[16]

In defining the term "nation", a definition of sovereignty was also rendered by the Court, "an organized government, recognized officials, a system of laws, definite boundaries," and most importantly, "the power to enter into negotiations with other nations."

A most disturbing aspect of the Montoya definition was an ambiguous statement, one that was to mislead later jurists and legal experts, "...sovereign power more or less absolute." This statement seems to imply, without any preceding historical or legal foundational support, the presence of degrees of sovereignty. Montoya also erroneously postulated that,

> The North American Indians do not, and never have, constituted "nations" as that word is used by writers upon international law, although in a great number of treaties they were designated as "nations" as well as tribes.

Montoya was in error on both accounts. During the last quarter of the 18th century and during the first quarter of the 19th, many of these independent tribes,

---

[15] United States Supreme Court, Worcester v. Georgia, 1832, 31 US. (6 Pet.) 515. Justice Marshal's opinion.
[16] United States Supreme Court, United States v. Montoya, 180 US 261, February 1901.

especially those bordering on the new republic, were recognized by the United States via treaty. These tribes also simultaneously entered into treaty relationships with other sovereign countries such as Great Britain, France, and Spain. The Six Nations Iroquois were one such example. Following the writings of Emer de Vattel, these "treaty tribes" were, as Justice Marshall noted in his *Worcester v. Georgia* opinion "independent", that is, they were not dependent on any other nation, as opposed to those who became subject to federal or state jurisdiction whom Justice Marshal described as "domestic dependent nations"[17]. Such "independent" sovereign tribes, as Montoya noted, had "the power to enter into negotiations with other nations."

Prior to 1871, the United States and its predecessor sovereign Great Britain recognized certain Indian tribes as sovereign nations via the establishment of treaty relationships. There was no question that the Federal government recognized such tribes as sovereigns. That is, the Federal government recognized those political units possessing their own independent governments and possession of non-ceded tribal land bases. Going back to the 1832 *Worcester v. Georgia* decision, Justice Marshall noted the conditions necessary for a tribe to be considered recognized as a sovereign,

> ...the several Indian nations as *distinct political communities, having territorial boundaries, within which their authority is exclusive, and having a right to all the lands within those boundaries*, which is not only acknowledged, but guaranteed by the United States (emphasis added)

In fact, in 1830, Congress declared,

> ...a State or nation cannot exist, except in connection with territory, the single consideration of the nature of the title under which the Indian tribes

---

[17] Cherokee Nation v. Georgia, (1831), 31 US. (5 Pet.) 1.

occupy their reservations, is decisive of the extent of their separate political privileges[18]

Both Congress and the judiciary recognized that the nature of a political relationship between these recognized treaty tribes and the United States was changing. Tribes that were once independent and sovereign transformed into dependent wards of a state, subject to its jurisdiction. Within this sovereign-ward relationship we find the beginnings of the Indian trust relationship. Many treaties enacted between the Federal government and still independent tribes contained language by which the Federal government assumed a protectorate function over the lands and Indian peoples affected by the treaty. Essentially these treaties were saying, we will protect you and your lands if you acknowledge your dependency to us. With the ratification of a treaty with such language, a tribe ceased being sovereign and became a dependent ward via a protectorate-trust relationship. In other instances tribes simply became politically and socially dysfunctional in the face of strong acculturative forces. That particular realization led Justice Marshall to declare,

> But if a contingency shall occur which shall render the Indians who reside in a State incapable of self government either by moral degradation or a reduction of their numbers, it would undoubtedly be in the power of a State government to extend to them the aegis of its laws. Under such circumstances, the agency of government, of necessity must cease.[19]

The oftentime overlooked 1852 US. Supreme Court opinion in *Veasie v. Moor*, discussed below affirmed this state of affairs by noting that federal policy concerns were, up till this time, only with those Indian tribes on the borders of the Republic with whom the United States might come into conflict.

---

[18] "Report of the Committee on Indian Affairs", February 24, 1830; Removal of Indians, U.S. House of Representatives, 21st Congress, 1st Session; Report #227.
[19] <u>Worcester v. Georgia</u>, 1832, 31 US. (6 Pet.) 515. Justice McLean's concurring opinion.

By 1830 Congress noted the transitional process from sovereign to dependency was well under way,[20]

> This transition from the practice of conciliating by treaty, to that of controlling by regular laws, has taken place, it is believed, with all the tribes in the old States, except Georgia; and in some of the new, as in Maine...

In 1871 Congress also recognized that this change or transformation from sovereign nation to dependent ward was so pronounced that it concluded it was unwarranted to further recognize tribes as sovereign entities was unwarranted. Representative Armstrong of Pennsylvania stated,

> While I hold that all treaties duly made and ratified by the Senate to be inviolable, I believe it to be fully competent for Congress to declare that this Government will not in the future recognize any foreign State or Power whom they may choose to designate, and where further recognition is in their judgment inimical to the national interests. Much more may they withdraw our recognition of the national character of a people in the anomalous condition of an Indian tribe...

> ...that the relation of the Indian tribes to the United States and their condition is continuously changing, and nations of Indians might have been so recognized years ago may now be well regarded as having deteriorated to such an extent as to justify the adoption of this declaration on the part of Congress.[21]

Simply put, what Congress enacts, Congress can also rescind. It was this changing or evolving political relationship between many of these recognized treaty tribes and the Federal government that led Congress to cease the

---

[20] U.S. House of Representatives, 21st Congress, 1st Session; Report #227.
Report of the Committee on Indian Affairs, February 24, 1830; Removal of Indians.
[21] "Congressional Globe", Senate Debates, Third Session, Forty-First Congress, Part III. Senate Debate, Indian Appropriation Bill, Armstrong Amendment, March 1, 1871.

recognition of Indian tribes as sovereigns by simply denying itself the right to recognize such relationships. Armstrong continued by stating, [22]

> that no tribe of Indians shall hereafter be acknowledged as an independent tribe, and treated with as such…

The declaration Representative Armstrong was referring to was an amendment or proviso he sponsored that passed unopposed in both houses of Congress on March 3, 1871. It was attached to the 1872 Indian Appropriations Act[23] This amendment stated,

> No Indian nation or tribe within the territory of the United States shall be acknowledged or recognized as an independent nation, tribe, or power with whom the United States may contract by treaty; but no obligation of any treaty lawfully made and ratified with any such Indian nation or tribe prior to March third, eighteen hundred and seventy-one, shall be hereby invalidated or impaired.[24]

For once and for all, the Federal government ceased to recognize Indian tribes as being sovereign. At this time it must be understood that tribal recognition by Congress equated to recognition of a sovereignty status. The terms of existing tribal treaties would still be honored by the Federal government, but no longer would these tribes be considered sovereign because their lands and people were now under the jurisdiction of the Federal government. Congress did so by simply refusing to further recognize any Indian group as such or to continue to recognize those pre-1871 treaty tribes as sovereign. The nation's treaty-based obligations to tribes would still be honored but they were now dependent communities under

---

[22] "Congressional Globe", Senate Debates, Third Session, Forty-First Congress, Part III.
Senate Debate, Indian Appropriation Bill, Armstrong Amendment, March 1,1871
[23] US. Congress. "An Act making appropriations for the current and contingent Expenses of the Indian Department, and for fulfilling Treaty Stipulations with various Indian Tribes, for the year ending June thirty, eighteen hundred and seventy-two, and for other Purposes:…",41st Congress, 3rd sess. March 3, 1871.)
[24] currently codified under 25 USC 71, sec. 2079.

federal wardship. This was historically-speaking the pivotal point where the basis of Federal Indian policy was radically altered by Congress and President Grant.

"…as mere domestic communities": Plenary Authority

Prior to 1871, Congress did not exert any direct legislative control over recognized sovereign tribes. Congress only asserted its legislative authority over those tribes that had ceded their political independence and lands via treaty enactments and remained in US territories on federal lands. Indians residing within a state were, as Justice Marshall pointed out, under state jurisdiction. After all, the Constitution mandated that Congress alone was charged with the regulation of Indian affairs. Congress was responsible "for commerce, the regulation of affairs between sovereign governments", that is, a government-to-government relationship that was signified by the enactment of a treaty. After the enactment of the 1871 amendment, Congress began to assert absolute plenary[25] powers over all Indian tribes that came under federal jurisdiction. In Charles Royce's 1896 report on Indian land cessions he addressed the implications of the 1871 amendment,

> The effect of this act was to bring under the immediate control of the Congress the transactions with the Indians…[26]

The era of congressional plenary authority had begun.

So where did Indian tribes stand in relation to the notion of sovereignty? First, there is nothing in the historical record from the Revolution to 1871 that indicates that the Federal government recognized anything but absolute sovereignty as propounded by Jean Bodin in the fourteenth century. The Federal

---

[25] "Plenary": "Of full scope or extent; complete or absolute in force or effect". The Shorter Oxford Dictionary on Historical Principles, Third Edition, Vol. II, 1950, Oxford, Clarendon Press.
[26] Eighteenth Annual Report of the Bureau of American Ethnology to the Secretary of the Smithsonian Institution; 1896-97 Indian Land Cessions in the United States compiled by Charles C. Royce :641.

government never articulated a doctrine of Indian or tribal sovereignty *vis a vis* the Federal government. There was never a situation of *imperium in imperio,* that is, a sovereign tribal state existing within a sovereign national state. These sovereign treaty relations with independent Indian tribes were, as Veazie v. Moor affirmed, external to the state.

As will be discussed below in Chapter 2, in its 1852 affirmation of an earlier Maine court opinion, the United States Supreme Court in its Veazie v. Moor decision[27] articulated which tribes were addressed by the Constitution's commerce clause,

> ...the Constitution manifestly refers to independent tribes with which the general government may come in conflict; not to those small remnants of tribes scattered over the country, which are under state jurisdiction and guardianship.

Either an Indian tribe was sovereign and independent according to the criteria set by the Federal government or it wasn't. When a tribe was either conquered or had voluntarily ceded its independence to the Federal government it became inconceivable that such a tribe could be considered a sovereign co-equal.

Some tribes may have had some of the characteristics of a sovereign state, but they were not considered sovereign. In its *Cherokee Nation v. Georgia* decision[28] the U.S. Supreme Court clearly did not recognize differing degrees of sovereignty when it noted that the Cherokee had some of the attributes of sovereignty, but were not sovereign and therefore lacked the standing as a sovereign as to sustain a

---

[27] Samuel Veazie and Levi Young v. Wyman B. S. Moor, 55 US. 568 (1852)
[28] 31 US 515 (6 Peters) 1832

suit before that federal court. Second, after 1871 the political status of Indian tribes was in the words of the 1871 Amendments House sponsor,

> ...as mere domestic communities, with whom we may contract, but only with the approval of Congress."[29] (emphasis added)

In conclusion, the Federal government in the matter of Indian policy considered sovereignty to be an absolute concept following the dictates of earlier English and medieval law. When Indian tribes failed to retain this absolutist standard, the nature of the Federal-tribe relationship changed from one based upon a government-to-government relationship to one of federal-ward.

---

[29] The Congressional Globe containing The Debates and Proceedings of the Third Session Forty First Congress Embracing the Laws passed at that Session 1871. Debate on House of Representatives Resolution 502: To Restrain the making of Treaties with Indian Tribes, March 1, 1871.

Chapter 2.
American Indian Policy 1735-1853

Many land claims bought by Indian tribes claiming to be sovereign political entities, especially among those tribes within the northeastern region (New England, New York, and Pennsylvania) were based upon supposed violations of Federal Indian law, most notably, claimed violations of the Indian Trade and Intercourse Acts (Non-Intercourse Acts). What was the nation's Indian policy at the nations inception? What was the original intent of the Indian Trade and Intercourse Act? Was this Act a continuation of earlier Indian policy, or was it a new policy enacted by a newly emerging nation?

In this chapter the historical development of antecedent colonial era policies pertaining to trade and intercourse with independent sovereign Indian tribes will be examined. This chapter culminates with a frequently overlooked 1852 Supreme Court decision. This was a decision that clearly defined and articulated the limits, not only of the application of the Trade and Intercourse Acts, but also the extent of federal authority regarding Indian tribes.

The concepts contained in these early attempts to regulate intercourse with these sovereign tribes were foundational to later federal acts. The intended application of the Indian Trade and Intercourse laws was not directed towards remnant Indian groups residing in the northeastern states such as Maine, Massachusetts, Connecticut, and Rhode Island and most of those settled states east of the Mississippi River. This chapter also questions the historical soundness of several Federal Supreme Court decisions regarding the applicability of the Federal Indian Trade and Intercourse Acts, especially in the eastern states.

"All the Indians with whom our colonies have any connection": A Unified Indian Policy 1735-1776

The origins of a unified American Indian policy began in England's southern colonies. The colonies of North and South Carolina faced continual threats from independent Indian tribes in the region, in particular those of the Cherokee and Creek tribes. The tension between the colonies and these two tribes was generated, in part, by the Spanish authorities in Florida and the French who occupied portions of present-day Alabama and Mississippi. Both of these tribes allied themselves with both these counties at various times. Of more immediate consequence were the actions of unscrupulous independent colonial traders who dealt with these tribes as well as the constant encroachment upon tribal territories by a growing population of Irish and Scot immigrant settlers.

These tensions were further increased when, in 1732, the colony of Georgia was formed from part of South Carolina. Georgia's southern and western boundaries were ill defined. As a result, Georgia began to claim jurisdiction over portions of tribal lands. This problem was to persist until 1834. The original land claims made by Georgia led to an almost continual state of tension with independent sovereign tribes in the region. Other colonies faced similar problems, typically caused by traders and land speculators. Georgia's problem was not unique. All of the frontier colonies faced the same challenge of tribal hostility to colonial expansion into their respective territories. Yet the colonies themselves could do little to address the problem given the fact that England's policy, as implemented by the Royal Board of Trade and Foreign Plantations, was, prior to

1756, to fully encourage frontier expansion without consideration of consequences for the colonial populations.

As early as 1714, the colony of Virginia attempted to address the trade problem by enacting a law prohibiting unauthorized traders from trading with Indian tribes.[30] Virginia, as a non-chartered colony, enacted its laws subject to Royal approval. At the request of the Commissioners of the Board of Trade, the King's Privy Council rescinded this law. The Council felt that this law impinged upon acts of the English Parliament, which held that all English subjects had the right to trade with Indians. Similarly, the Province of New York, between 1720 and 1729, enacted ten such laws to govern trade with the Indians. The King's Privy Council voided all ten laws. In 1738, the colony of South Carolina tried to restrain trade with the Cherokee tribe, with whom the colony had ongoing trade-based problems. Like her sister colonies and provinces, South Carolina enacted laws to control the problem, but these were met with objections by the mercantilist-oriented Board of Trade.[31]

That same year, as a result of continual trade- and expansionist-related problems with the tribes and a growing realization by the Crown of the severity of these problems, the Board, with the concurrence of the Privy Council, appointed Edmund Atkin, a merchant of Charleston, South Carolina as a councilor to King George III of England for Indian affairs in colonial America.[32] Atkin, as a merchant, had extensive knowledge of the Indian tribes of the region. He was also a vigorous defender of English interests in the colonies, especially against French

---

[30] Dickerson, Oliver.1912, American Colonial Government 1696-1765:241. Cleveland: Arthur H. Clark
[31] ibid 1912: 242
[32] Jacobs, W., 1954, The Appalachian Indian Frontier, The Edmond Atkin Report and Plan of 1755. University of Nebraska Press

attempts to lure southern Indian tribes sympathetic to the English into their fold. As a result, Atkin also had a very strong interest in the regulation of Indian trade.

The northern colonies were experiencing similar trade and land related difficulties with the region's independent tribes, especially in New York and Pennsylvania. The British were especially sensitive concerning their relationship with the Six Nations Iroquois. Sir William Johnson was appointed as the Crown's direct representative to the Iroquois Nation. Johnson's primary task, as was Crown policy, was to keep the Iroquois from allying themselves with the French. In 1753, the governor of New York was instructed by the Commissioners of the Board of Trade and Foreign Plantations not to allow individuals to purchase lands from the Indians. Such purchases thereafter could only be made by public treaty.[33] In addition, the Board, with the concurrence of the Privy Council, prohibited any province (which did not include chartered colonies such as Connecticut, Massachusetts, and Rhode Island over whom the Board had little control) from making land grants "within its own undisputed boundaries, if such lands were included in an Indian reservation created by treaty."[34]

May of 1755 marked the height of the French and Indian War. At this time, the Lord Commissioners of Trade and Plantations requested that Atkin, who had been the King's councilor to England for 18 years, prepare a report and recommendations pertaining to the relationships and trade that existed between the colonies and those sovereign independent Indian tribes recognized by the English authorities. He was also directed to produce a plan for managing such affairs. The principal intent of this report was to devise a scheme to maintain the loyalty of those tribes the English government recognized in light of French

---

[33] O' Callahan and Fenrow.1889, New York Colonial Documents. Vol. 7:478-479. State of New York, and, Prucha, Francis. 1984, The Great Father. Vol. 1:22. University of Nebraska Press
[34] Dickerson, Oliver.1912, American Colonial Government 1696-1765:343. Cleveland: Arthur H. Clark:

efforts to undermine this relationship. It would also reduce the points of tension between these tribes and the colonies by the control of trade and the regulation of acquisitions of Indian lands.

In his 1755 report, Atkin identified those independent Indian tribes the colonies regarded as such, and with whom they carried on a recognized political (government-to-government) relationship. These tribes were considered independent sovereign nations, possessing non-ceded lands that were not subject to the jurisdiction of any colony or foreign government. He described them as follows,[35]

> All the Indians with whom our colonies have any connection at present in North America, may be considered under two Divisions. In the first are to be comprehended, from Nova Scotia to Virginia inclusive, the Five or they have been lately called, the Six Nations (Mohawk, Sennikas, Onondagas, Oneydoes, Cayugas, and Tuscaroras) next to N. York, with their dependents (the Susquehannas, Delawares, Shawanoes, and other tribes) on the back part of Virginia, Maryland & Pennsylvania, and the Indians bordering on New England, commonly called, in regard I suppose to those others, the Eastern Nations.

In his report, Atkin suggested to the Lord Commissioners of the Board of Trade and Foreign Plantations "…that private individuals should have no contact with the Indians, especially in connection with land purchases…" He recommended that all Indian affairs should be under the general direction of a superintendent[36] Atkin's recommendations to the Board were as follows:

---

[35] Jacobs, W., 1954 The Appalachian Indian Frontier, The Edmond Atkin Report and Plan of 1755:41. University of Nebraska Press
[36] Jacobs, W., 1954 The Appalachian Indian Frontier, The Edmond Atkin Report and Plan of 1755:XXIV, :77-89. University of Nebraska Press

Plan of a general Direction & Management of the Indian Affairs throughout North America, under one uniform Regulation of their Commerce, for retrieving & establishing the British Interest among the Indian Nations & thereby the future Security of our Colonies against the Designs of the French...

...That all the Indian Nations or tribes be divided into two Districts; the Northern District from Nova Scotia to Virginia inclusive, comprehending the Six United Nations of N. York with their immediate Dependents chiefly on the waters of the Ohio, & those commonly called the Eastern Indians, or any others to the Westward; And the Southern District of North Carolina, South Carolina, & Georgia, comprehending the Cherokees, all the other Nations, particularly the Catawbas, Chicasaws, Creeks, & Chactaws, living independent of each other...and to the westward thereof as far back at least as the Mississippi.

...That two fit Persons, who are already personally acquainted with the Indians and their Affairs, be appointed by his Majesty...

...The principal Articles whereof on the part of the Indians to be...

...2d That they shall not admit any English Trader to Traffick among them without producing a Licence for it by the Kings Authority, as after mentioned...

...6. That they [the independent tribes] shall not sell Lands to any of the Kings subjects, but to his Majesty only. In consideration of which, the Condition on his Majestys part in the said Treaty to be.

...That one fit person, having some Knowledge or accquaintance with Indian Affairs, be deputed by the Governour & Council of each Province to accompany & assist the said Commissioners General, at their annual Visitations of each Nation, or at the General Meetings of the Indian Chiefs in their respective Districts; who may represent the several Provinces or Colonies to the Indians, subsequent treaties made...Licences to Traders,

...1. To prohibit all Persons living in the colonies, to go and Trade in any Indian Nation, without a Licence from one of his Majesty's Commissioners duly obtained. Or to deal with any Indians whatever within the Settlements, other than such as are always resident therein...

Atkin's report was submitted to and approved by the Commissioners on the Board of Trade and Foreign Plantations and the King's Lord Privy Council. His report provided the basis upon which the future organization and structure of the relationship between the Crown and the independent Indian tribes was to be formulated.

No New England Indian tribes or groups were mentioned as being part of this proposed new relationship as they had by this time ceded their lands to the New England colonies and were subject to English law. This relationship was first publicly stated in King George's Royal Proclamation of 1763. The pertinent sections include,[37]

The Proclamation of 1763 by King George II

"And whereas it is just and reasonable, and essential to our interest and the security of our colonies, that the several nations or tribes of Indians with whom we are connected, and who live under our protection, *should not be molested or disturbed in the possession of such parts of our dominions and territories as, not having been ceded to or purchased by us, are reserved to them, or any of them*, as their hunting grounds; we do therefore, with the advice of our Privy Council, declare it to be our royal will and pleasure…

…that no Governor or commander in chief of our other colonies or plantations do presume for the present, and until our further pleasure be known, to grant warrants of survey or pass patents *for any lands beyond the heads or sources of any of the rivers which fall into the Atlantic Ocean from the west or northwest; or upon any lands whatsoever, which, not having been ceded to or purchased by us as aforesaid, are reserved to the said Indians, or any of them*

And we do further declare it to be our royal will and pleasure, for the present as aforesaid, to reserve under our sovereignty, protection, and dominion, for the use of the said Indians, all the land and territories…lying to the westward of the sources of the rivers which fall into the sea from the west and northwest as aforesaid; and we do hereby strictly forbid, on pain of our displeasure, all our loving subjects from making any purchases or settlements whatever, or taking possession of any lands above reserved, without our special leave and license for that purpose first obtained…

…And whereas great frauds and abuses have been committed in the purchasing of lands of the Indians, to the great prejudice of our interests, and to the great dissatisfaction of the said Indians…that no private person do presume to make any purchase from the said Indians of any lands

---

[37] Commanger, H. 1954 ed., <u>Documents of American History</u>:48-49. New York: Appleton-Century-Crofts

reserved to the said Indians within those parts of our colonies where we have thought proper to allow settlement; *but if at any time any of the said Indians should be inclined to dispose of the said lands, the same shall be purchased only for us, in our name, at some public meting or assembly of the Indians to be held for that purpose by the Governor or commander in chief of our colony respectively where they shall lie*...[emphasis added]

The King's Proclamation declared a boundary (roughly following the Appalachian Mountain chain) between the colonies and Indian country. This boundary was laid out and submitted to the Commissioners of the Board of Trade and Plantations in 1767 for their approval, which was granted.[38]

What is significant to this writing are the basic concepts advanced in King George's proclamation. Though claiming overall title by right of discovery, the Crown acknowledged the sovereignty of those Indian tribes that had yet to politically cede, or whose lands were still held by natural right not being purchased by the English. Only the Governor or Commander-in-Chief had the authority to do so, and only by an agreed upon treaty with the tribe in question. Herein lies the concepts that were later to be expressed in the Indian policy of a young Republic under the name of the Indian Trade and Intercourse Act.

The boundary line with Indian country expressed in the Royal Proclamation was formalized by Sir William Johnson, the King's northern Indian Superintendent, in a treaty with the northern Indian tribes on November 5, 1768, via a deed executed at Fort Stanwix, New York. This document was titled "Establishing A Boundary Line Between The Whites And Indians, Of The Northern Colonies." A map prepared in 1768 depicted the boundary's northern terminus just to the west of Fort Stanwix, traveling south to the upper reaches of the Delaware River, then westward joining the Ohio River at Kittaning. The New

---

[38] Farrand, M.,1905, "The Indian Boundary Line." <u>American Historical Review</u>. 10 (July 1905): 782-791.

England colonies were clearly outside of the demarcated boundaries of Indian country and were not subject to the proclamation.

The 1763 Proclamation also continued the operations of both a northern and southern superintendent of Indian affairs. Sir William Johnson and Edmond Atkin respectively, also called for the regulation of Indian trade with recognized Indian tribes and prohibited obtaining non-ceded lands within the Indian country as defined in the King's 1763 Proclamation.

It is important to note that Sir William Johnson, appointed by King George III as superintendent of Indian affairs in the Northern District, never visited or met with any purported leaders of any New England Indian group. In a letter to the Board of Trade and Plantations dated April 15, 1756, the nearby colony of Connecticut's Governor Thomas Fitch wrote the following regarding the Indians residing within the Colony. Fitch made it clear that "…one half dwell in English families and the other half in many small clans in various parts of the Colony,…"[39] The colony of Connecticut, not having any tribes within her boundaries, never felt the necessity to appoint a deputy for Indian affairs to assist Johnson.

At this point in time, in contrast to neighboring New York, there were no non-ceded lands reserved to any Indian tribes within the context of the words of the King's Proclamation. When the King's 1763 Proclamation was issued, all lands lying within the borders of Connecticut, for instance, had been lawfully obtained by conquest, conveyance, or by simple abandonment. All existing Indian reservations that were situated upon colony title- owned lands were usufructory in nature. The Colony affirmed this state of affairs to the Commissioners of Trade

---

[39] Connecticut Colonial Records, Vol.10:624.

and Plantations in 1774[40] when it stated the right of pre-emption for all Indian lands within the colony had been exercised via "...purchase..." or "...conquest..." With the exception of the 1638 Treaty of Hartford ending the Pequot War, no other treaties were entered into by the colony with any Indian tribes. Connecticut did not have a western or northwestern boundary that was affected by the King's Proclamation.

In addition, trade restrictions did not apply to Indians residing within settled areas. In fact, Johnson noted the difference between tribes residing in Indian country and those within the jurisdiction of a colony. In a 1767 letter from Johnson to the Earl of Shelburne, a commissioner of the Board of Trade and Foreign Plantations, he noted,[41]

> I should acquaint your Lord that the Wappingers and Stockbridge Tribes, with many others residing east of the Hudson's River or in the New England Governments are upon a very different footing from the rest, being through length of time become Domesticated, and as they are now surrounded by the White Inhabitants,... The majority have submitted to the laws, and as it is long, since they were possessed with any extent of Country....

In that statement, Johnson defined those factors necessary for an Indian tribe to be considered independent by both colonial and English authorities. First, the tribe was politically independent by not being under colonial jurisdiction. Second, the tribe possessed its own non-ceded land base. In a 1773 letter to the Governor of New York,[42] Johnson further described these "Domesticated" groups as tribal "remnants".

---

[40] Connecticut Colonial Records, Vol.14:497
[41] O' Callahan E. B, 1861 <u>Documents Relative to the Colonial History of the State of New York</u>, v. III: 891-894. Weed Parsons Albany
[42] ibid.1861: 458-459

Johnson was not concerned about these New England remnant groups. In his November 1763 report on the "Present State of the Northern Indians", [43] Johnson stated that among those Indian tribes that he was responsible for, none were from New England. The only New York tribes mentioned were the tributary refugee Indian groups of the Six Nation Iroquois. He mentions several tribes in Canada (including the St. Francis Abenaki), in the Ohio region, the Miami's, Chippewa, Ottawa, those around Lake Michigan, the Illinois and Sioux—all independent sovereign tribes residing on the peripheries of the colonies.

In July 1764, the Commissioners of the Board of Trade and Foreign Plantations proposed a plan to William Johnson titled: "Plan for the Future Management of Indian Affairs". Though the plan was never put into effect, it is very descriptive and yields significant insights relevant to later federal Indian laws. According to the Board,[44]

> The Plan has for its object the regulation of Indian Affairs both commercial and political throughout all North America, upon one general system, under the direction of Officers appointed by the Crown, so as to sett aside all local interfering of particular Provinces, which has been one great cause of the distracted state of Indian affairs in General it is judged expedient in the execution of this plan that North America should be divided into two districts each having one Chief Agent or Superintendent the first difficulty which occurs in the consideration of the plan, is how to ascertain the limits of each district…

---

[43] cited in, O'Callahan, E.B. 1889, The Documentary History of the State of New York. Vol. I.:26-30 State of New York, Albany

[44] O' Callahan E. B, 1861 Documents Relative to the Colonial History of the State of New York, v. VII:: 634-636. Weed Parsons Albany

This problem, the creation of a boundary line between the colonies and the frontier Indian tribes, was resolved by establishing a line of demarcation between the two districts where the Ohio River flows into the Mississippi River. The next issue to be addressed was establishing the identities of the Indian tribes in both districts to whom this plan would apply. The northern district is of direct concern. In their letter to Johnson, the Commissioners commented,

> ...You will observe however that we have added to the tribes contained in the list you have transmitted to us those which inhabit the Border of New England and Nova Scotia, which Tribes must be comprehended in the Northern District...

The Board's plan also contained two sections that would have had a significant impact on the colonies,

> ...4th That all Laws now in force in the several Colonies for regulating Indian Affairs or Commerce be repealed...
> ...43rd That no purchase of Lands belonging to the Indians whether in the name and for the use of the Crown or in the name and for the use of the proprietors of Colonies be made but at some general meeting at which the principal Chiefs of each tribe claiming a property in such lands are present....

The plan contained a list of the Indian tribes that the Crown considered to be independent tribes of consequence assigned to the Northern District. These were tribes with whom the colonies carried out a significant trade relationship and from whom at some distant time the English desired to peacefully acquire land. The Commissioners were only concerned with the tribes that "bordered New England". A "Map of the Frontiers of the Northern Colonies"[45], prepared four years later by Johnson's son, Guy, who later succeeded his father as the Indian Agent, clearly showed the Indian country frontier to be in mid-New York beginning just east of Oneida Lake.

---

[45] Sullivan, James, 1928, Papers of Sir William Johnson. v. VI.:450. State University of New York, Albany

In regulating the trade with these tribes the plan called for the establishment of a chain of 11 Northern District trading posts where all commercial activities would take place. None of these was located in proximity to any of the New England colonies. Oswego, New York was the closest post.

The content of this plan makes it clear that the English government did not consider New England as being involved in any "Indian Affairs" with those independent tribes recognized as such by the Crown.

Given that the plan was never put into effect, the governors of each of the colonies were prohibited by Royal edict from purchasing non-ceded lands in the western portion of the territories reserved by the King for the independent sovereign Indian tribes. This was the sole prerogative of the Court-appointed regional administrators, such as William Johnson. The colonial governors were allowed to purchase, via open treaty, non-ceded Indian lands within their respective borders to which they held pre-emptive rights. Individuals were prohibited from purchasing any Indian lands whatsoever unless designated to do so by a colonial or provincial government at the direction of the Crown's Indian agent.. The numerous treaties enacted between New York and Pennsylvania with independent Indian tribes not subject to colony jurisdiction residing within their colonies during this period attest to this. In Connecticut, for example, all lands within the boundaries of the colony, not including what became known as the disputed "Western Reserve" or "Illinois country", were or had previously been ceded to and placed under the jurisdiction of the colony's government. Connecticut explicitly stated this fact in a response (October 2, 1774: "Answers to the Board of Trade") to a 1774 inquiry from the Commissioners of the Board of Trade and Plantations in London,[46]

> ...Thus the greatest Part of this Colony was purchased and obtained for great and valuable Considerations, and other Parts thereof gained by Conquest, and with much Difficulty, and at the only Endeavours, Expence, and Charges of Persons thereby interested in the plantation of *Connecticut,* in *New-England,* and their Associates...

Clearly, the focus and intent of Indian policy enacted by English authorities was upon those tribes on the northern and western frontiers who were not under English control or whose allegiance was critical to the English authorities. The English government was not concerned with remnant tribes remaining in the colonies. Lands to be obtained from sovereign tribes residing external to the set boundaries of a province or colony were the sole prerogative of the Crown-appointed Indian agent. The lands belonging to sovereign tribes still residing within the bounds of a province or colony could be purchased by that entity's governor. In all instances such acquisition of Indian title or right had to be done via an open treaty with the subject tribe's leaders.

"Treating with and making purchases...":The Early Nationalist Period: 1777-1789

During the American Revolutionary War, the Continental Congress initiated a national Indian policy that dealt with issues relating to Indian affairs. Of paramount importance to the new nation, and the central focus of this policy, were efforts to have the independent sovereign Indian tribes join with and assist the war effort, or at the least, work to keep the tribes neutral during the conflict.

---

[46] Connecticut Colonial Records,Vol.14:497. October 2, 1774, Answers to the Board of trade.

During this conflict the Continental Congress treated these tribes as sovereign nations.[47] Treaties of peace as well as cessions of land held by sovereign tribes, were conducted via treaties by the new government on a nation-to-nation basis. although individual colonies continued to treat with such independent Indian tribes, Congress, during July of 1775, initiated the national Indian policy depicted above. By doing so, Congress also expanded upon the English-created model by increasing the number of Indian superintendents and their respective departments from two (northern and southern) to three by adding a "Middle Department."

In 1777, an additional Indian agent was appointed by Congress to manage the affairs pertaining to the "Indians, in Nova Scotia, and the tribes to the northward and westward thereof."[48] Tribes subject to state jurisdiction or remnants residing within a state were not under the jurisdiction of any Indian department. During this time the pre-existing view concerning the non-independence of Indians living within a colony, under its legal jurisdiction, was maintained (see Johnson 1767 quote above).

George Washington, as Commander in Chief of the Continental Army, had extensive tribal-related experiences in the Ohio Valley. He was adopted into the Seneca-Iroquois Wolf clan and given the adoptive name *"Conotocarious"*, "Town Taker or Destroyer" by the Seneca sachem Tanacharison during the French and Indian War.[49] The memories of this intense war-time experience left a life-long impression on the young Virginia militia colonel, a future president and

---

[47] Prucha, Francis. 1984, The Great Father. Vol. 1:31. University of Nebraska Press
[48] Ford, Worthington C. et al, 1904-37, Journals of the Continental Congress, 1774-1789 22:34. Washington, D.C.
[49] Jackson, D., ed. 1976, The Diaries of George Washington. Vol. 1:172. Charlottesville: University Press of Virginia

Commander-in-Chief. During the Revolutionary War, General Washington noted,[50]

> In Respect to the Proceedings of the Commissioners for raising two Companies of the Mohikander and Connecticut Indians, they appear to me not to answer the Views of Congress, as I presume they live within the Government of Connecticut and are to be considered in the same light as its inhabitants

Thus Washington, as President of the United States, was to be instrumental in further developing national Indian policy including the initial Indian Trade and Non-Intercourse Act. He viewed Indians living within and under state jurisdiction as not being subject to national Indian policy. Congress thought likewise. During May 1782, Congress issued two resolutions on the matter,[51]

> *Resolved,* That the sole right of superintending, protecting, Treating with, and making purchases of the several Indian Nations *situate and being without the bounds of any of the Different states in the union,* is necessarily vested in the United States in Congress assembled, for the benefit of the United States, and in no other person or persons.
> *Resolved,* That no person or persons, citizens of these United States, or any particular State in the union in their separate capacity, can or ought to purchase any unappropriated lands belonging to the Indians *without the bounds of their respective states,* under a pretense whatsoever. [emphasis added]

It becomes obvious that Washington's and Congress' focus concerning Indians was not upon those residing as remnants among the colonies. Instead their concerns were directed towards the western frontier. This policy followed the one previously established by the Crown. In 1783 Washington further stated,[52]

---

[50] Fitzpatrick, John, ed. 1939. The Writings of George Washington. Vol. 5: 172. Washington, DC. Government Printing Office.
[51] Ford, Worthington C. et al, 1904-37. Journals of the Continental Congress, (JCC)1774-1789 22:230-231, Washington, DC.
[52] JCC 27:139-140.

The Settlmt. Of the Western Country and making a Peace with the Indians are so analogous that their can be not definition of one without involving considerations of the other.

In 1783, Congress reorganized the structure of Indian affairs. Positions for four agents, formerly called superintendents, were created. Of particular interest was the post of agent for the northern department. As noted below, his area of responsibility, as designated by Congress, was the area of northern Maine, then still part of Massachusetts and the surrounding tribes.[53]

> ...That there be four Agents appointed for the transaction of affairs with the Indians in the different districts—*one for the eastern district comprehending all the tribes under the general denomination of the Penobscot Indians;* one for the northern district, comprehending the six nations, and the nations depending on them; one for the western district, comprehending all the tribes under the general denomination of the western Indians...(italics added)

Congress appointed John Allan to this post. In the process, Congress defined his area of responsibility within the Eastern Department,[54]

> ...The United States in Congress assembled to John Allan Esqr. Greeting We reposing special trust and confidence in your patriotism fidelity and abilities have reappointed and by these presents do reappoint you to be our Superintendent of Indian Affairs in the *Eastern Department* and do authorize and empower you to take charge of the affairs of the United States of America *to the eastward of Connecticut river* agreeably to such instructions as have been or hereafter may be given to you for that purpose.[emphasis added]

The comment defining "eastward of Connecticut river" must be considered within the perimeters of the eastern district as described on page 264 in the

---

[53] JCC 24:264.
[54] JCC 24:379.

"*Journals of the Continental Congress*" (cited above). Additionally, maps depicted in the "Handbook of American Indians" [55] should be consulted in regard to the historical placement of the Penobscot and the location of the Connecticut River in this northern New England region. When viewed together, the intent of Congress is clear in regard to the boundaries of the Eastern Department. The comments regarding the Connecticut River as an eastern departmental boundary were referring to the upper reaches and source of that river in the Maine/northern New Hampshire region that bordered on the historical tribal areas of those tribes "under the general denomination of Penobscot." Later court findings (State v. Newell 84 Maine 465) agree with this,[56]

> Sec. 874. Col. John Allan was appointed by Congress in 1777 "agent for Indian affairs in the *eastern department*" and held that office till 1784. He was instructed to visit "*the tribes of Indians of Indians, inhabitants of St John and Nova Scotia*" and by threats, persuasions, and arguments of various kinds to convince them that it would be better for their interests not to take part against the United States in the war then raging. *He made his headquarters at Machias and assumed a general supervision over the various tribes of Indians from the St. John to the Penobscot.* [emphasis added]

In 1777, a draft of the Articles of Confederation was submitted to Congress, and after significant debate concerning the rights and powers of the states, the Articles of Confederation were approved by the Continental Congress. The Articles did not come into effect until 1781, due to the resistance of Maryland concerning federal ownership of the western lands.

<u>1782, Articles of Confederation and perpetual Union between the States of New-Hampshire, Massachusetts-Bay, Rhode Island, and Providence Plantations, Connecticut, New-York, New-Jersey, Pennsylvania,</u>

---

[55] Trigger B., ed. 1979, Vol. 15. Smithsonian Institute,: 59,:138
[56] <u>Digest of Decisions Relating to Indian Affairs</u>, HR 538, 56th Cong., 2nd sess., Vol. 1: 135.

<u>Delaware, Maryland, Virginia, North- Carolina, South-Carolina and Georgia.</u>

Article I. The Stile of this confederacy shall be "The United States of America
Art. II. Each state retains its Sovereignty, freedom and independence, and every power, jurisdiction and right, which not by this confederation expressly delegated to the United States in Congress assembled…
Art. IX. The United States in Congress assembled, shall have the sole and exclusive right and power of…*regulating the trade and managing all affairs with the Indians, not members of any of the states*, [italics added] provided that the legislative right of any state within its own limits be not infringed or violated…. [emphasis added]

Noteworthy within the text of this document is Article IX, which continued Congress's role in Indian affairs. At the same time, the statement limited the authority of Congress to those tribes who remained independent, not subject to the jurisdiction of any state, "not members of any of the states."

This view conformed to Washington's comments stated above, that Indians under or subject to the laws of a state, or under the state's jurisdiction, were not governed by federal law. It also followed colonial precedent concerning remnant Indians residing within a colony. In addition, Article II clearly supports the jurisdictional limitation stated in Article IX. The exclusionary statement cited in Article IX included the same pre-revolutionary colonial concept that Indians residing in a colony submitting to the laws of the colony were not independent tribes, but were considered remnants under the colony's direct jurisdiction.

A resolution enacted by the Continental Congress shortly after the publication of the Articles of Confederation clearly depicted the intent of Congress and anticipated Justice John Marshall's 1831 *Cherokee Nation v. State of Georgia* opinion,[57]

> ...*Resolved,* That the sole right of superintending, protecting, treating with, and making purchases of the several Indian nations situate *and being without the bounds of any of the different states in the union,* is necessarily vested in the United States in Congress assembled, for the benefit of the United States, and in no other person or persons whatever within the said states.
> *Resolved,* That no person or persons, citizens of these United States, or any particular State in the union in their separate capacity, can or ought to purchase any unappropriated lands belonging to the Indians without the bounds of their respective states, under any pretence whatsoever...
> [emphasis added]

Twice within this resolution, Congress stated that it clearly intended that Article IX of the Articles of Confederation apply only to Indians residing outside the bounds of any state. First, Congress had the "sole right" to administer the Indian affairs of those tribes "...situate and being without the bounds of any of the different states..." and second, only Congress had the authority to make purchases of any "...unappropriated lands belonging to Indians without the bounds of their respective states..." Both statements implied that the authority of Congress in relation to Indian affairs ended at a state's boundary. An analysis of the preceding congressional resolution, within the context of Article IX of the Articles of Confederation, clearly supports this understanding.

Further support of the limitation of federal authority in regards to Indian affairs was the issuance of the Ordinance of 1786 (*An Ordinance for the Regulation of Indian Affairs*). This document also included the "...not members of any state..." limitation as well as clearly stating that the authority of the

---

[57] JCC 22:230-231.

Superintendent of Indian Affairs for the Northern Department applied to Independent tribes residing *"westward"* of Hudson's river,[58]

> Whereas the safety and tranquillity of the frontiers of the United States, do in some measure, depend on the maintaining a good correspondence between their citizens and the several nations of Indians in amity with them...
> *Be it ordained by the United States in Congress assembled,* That from and after the passing of this ordinance, the Indian department be divided into two districts, viz. The *southern*, which shall comprehend within its limits, all the nations in the territory of the United states, who reside southward of the river Ohio; and *northern,* which shall comprehend all the other Indian nations within the said territory, *and westward of Hudson river* ...
> [emphasis added]

Connecticut, by continuous example, contained no "unappropriated" Indian lands within her borders, nor was the State located within the jurisdictional area of either of the two superintendents. Connecticut was geographically located *east* of Hudson's river.

For example, Connecticut continued to apply acts and laws regarding Indians enacted during the colonial area without any challenge from the Federal government. Two such acts," *An Act concerning Purchasers of Native Rights to Land* and *An Act for Well Ordering and Governing the Indians in this State; and Securing their Interest"*, are cited below and demonstrate the state's jurisdiction over Indians residing within her borders circa 1786,[59]

> This Assembly observing many Difficulties and Perplexities arising in this Government, by Reason of many Purchases of Land made of Indian Titles,

---

[58] American State Papers: Documents Legislative and Executive of the Congress of the United States, 1786-1815. Vol. IV.:1007- 1010.
[59] Acts and Laws of the State of Connecticut in America. 1784 ed.: 113 (first enacted May 9, 1717

without the preceeding Allowance, or Subsequent Approbation of this Assembly.
Which to remove:
It is hereby Enacted and Declared by this Assembly, and the Authority thereof, That not title to any lands in this Colony can accrue by any Purchase made of Indians, on the Pretence of their being Native Proprietors thereof, without the Allowance or Approbation of this Assembly.

And it is hereby Resolved, That no Conveyance of Native Right, or Indian Title, without the Allowance or Approbation of this Assembly, as aforesaid shall be given in Evidence of any Man's Title, or pleadable in any Court.

Be it enacted by the Governor, Council and Representatives, in General Court Assembled, and by the Authority of the same, That it shall be the duty of the Civil Authority and Select-man of such Towns wherein are any Tribe of Indians, to take care that they are well acquainted with the Laws of the State, made for punishing such immoralities as they may be guilty of; and make them sensible that they are liable to the Penalties in case they transgress the Laws...[60]

Both laws demonstrate that from 1702 up to 1786 the colony/state of Connecticut exerted complete and unchallenged legal jurisdiction over the persons and lands of Indian tribal remnants residing within the state. No independent sovereign tribes remained within her boundaries.

These colonial era acts were never called into question by the Board of Trade and Foreign Plantations, that reviewed all colony laws[61], nor were they called into question by either the Continental Congress or the President of the United States, nor were they challenged in any federal court.

---

[60] Acts and Laws of the State of Connecticut in America. 1784 ed.: 101 (first enacted in 1702)
[61] Dickerson, Oliver. 1912, American Colonial Government 1696-1765,:225. Cleveland: Arthur H. Clark

The following year (1787) Congress noted,[62]

> ...The laws of the State can have no effect upon a tribe of Indians or their lands within the limits of the state so long as that tribe is independent, and not a member of the state...

In a July 1789 report to the Congress from Henry Knox, Secretary of War Knox echoed the comments of Congress when he stated,[63]

> ...It would reflect honor on the new government and be attended with happy effects *were a declarative law to be passed that the Indian tribes posses the right of the soil of all lands within their limits respectively* and they are not to be divested thereof but in consequence of fair and bona fide purchases, made under the authority, or with the express approbation of the United States...
> ... No individual state could with propriety complain of invasion of its territorial rights. The *independent nations and tribes* of indians ought to be considered as *foreign nations, not as the subjects of any particular state each individual state will retain the right of pre-emption of all lands within its limits*, which will not be abridged. *But the general Sovereignty must possess the right of making all treaties on the execution or violation of which depend peace or war...*
> ...Although the disposition of the people of the States to emigrate to the *Indian Country* cannot be effectually prevented, it may be restrained and *regulated.*
> It may be regulated by postponing new purchases of Indian territory, *and by prohibiting the Citizens from intruding into Indian Lands...*
> ...As the population shall increase, and approach the *Indian boundaries,* Game will be diminished, and new purchases may be made for small considerations- This has been and probably will be the inevitable consequence of cultivation.
> It is however painful to consider *all the Indian tribes once existing in those States, now the best cultivated and most populous, have become extinct.* If the same causes continue, the same effects will happen, and in a short period the idea of the Indian on this side of the Mississippi will only be found in the page of the historian... [emphasis added]

---

[62] JCC 33:458
[63] Abbot, W. ed. 1993, *The Papers of George Washington. Colonial Series.* Vol. 3,: 134-139., June-September 1789 University Press of Virginia

Knox acknowledged that only independent tribes and nations should be considered sovereign entities, in other words, tribes not subject to state or federal political or legal jurisdiction and holding non-ceded lands to themselves. Those tribes were recognized as being sovereign entities. In addition, each state had the right of preemption to any non-ceded Indian lands within its respective borders. Connecticut at this point in time had neither.

During November of that same year, Knox received a letter from a group of commissioners attempting to enter into a treaty of peace with the Creek nation. Their previous mission had been a failure. In addition, they were unable to achieve a similar agreement with the region's Choctaw and Chickasaw tribes. In order to achieve peace with the Indian tribes, the committee suggested the following to Secretary Knox in November 1789,[64]

> ...We made our Communications to the Creek Nation, and they have refused to conclude a Treaty of Peace with the United States...
> ... we respectfully suggest- *That some uniform Plan of granting Permits to those who may be employed in the Indian Commerce, should be established by the Supreme Authority of the United States...* [emphasis added]

The problem being addressed was, and always had been, the frontier relations between the independent sovereign Indian tribes and the United States. Those states whose western borders extended beyond the current frontier boundary claimed their traditional preemptive rights to such lands. Non-regulated frontier

---

[64] DePauw, G., ed. "Documentary History of the First Federal Congress 1789-1791." _Senate Executive Journal and Related Documents_. 2: 36-240.

land speculators, who were the major cause of conflict with independent Indian tribes,[65] whose activities were often aided and abetted by state officials, made purchases of tribal lands from individual Indians that were not agreed upon by their tribal leaders. The problem also applied to non-regulated trade. While some of the privately owned trading companies were respected concerns, others engaged in practices that only further increased tensions along the frontiers.

After the formation of the United States, Indians residing within a state's jurisdiction, subscribing to the laws of that particular state and not in possession of a non-ceded land base were not the concern of the Federal government. Following a practice that extended into the early colonial period, Indians in Massachusetts, Connecticut, Rhode Island, New Jersey and Delaware for instance were considered to be subject to the jurisdiction of that particular colony or state. On the other hand, independent sovereign tribes residing on non-ceded lands on the peripheries of New York, Georgia, the Carolina's, and Pennsylvania were protected by federal Indian laws.

Thus we find that early Federal Indian policy continued to follow that established by England. The focus and intent of this new country were still the maintenance of peaceful relations with those independent tribes on the western frontier who posed both a political and military threat to the Republic. On the other hand, those Indians residing within a state who acknowledged its legal jurisdiction were not considered politically independent tribes, possessing their own tribal lands. Such tribal remnants may have continued to manage their own internal political affairs, but they were not sovereign entities.

---

[65] JCC 33:457

" the Indians possess the natural rights of man": The Era of the Indian Trade and Intercourse Acts: 1790-1834

After Secretary of War Henry Knox received and considered the Commissioner's November 1789 Creek report cited earlier, he submitted his own thoughts to President Washington in a January 1790[66] letter pertaining to the maintenance of peace on the frontier,

> ...That the Indians possess the natural rights of man, and that they ought not wont only to be divested thereof cannot be well denied. Were these rights ascertained, and declared by law- were it enacted that the indians possess the right to all there territory which they have not fairly conveyed, and that they should not be divested thereof, but in consequence of open treaties, made under the authority of the United States, the foundation of peace and justice would be laid.
> The individual States claiming or possessing the right of pre-emption to *territory* inhabited by the indians would not be materially injured by such a declarative law, the exercise of their right would be restrained only, when it should interfere with the general interests-Should any State having the right to pre-emption desire to purchase *territory,* which the indians should be willing to relinquish, it would have to request the General Government to direct a treaty for that purpose, at the expense however of the individual State requesting the same.
> But as indian Wars almost invariably arise in consequence of disputes relative to boundaries, or trade, and as the right of declaring War, making treaties, and regulating commerce, are vested in the United States it is highly proper they should have the sole direction of all measures for the consequences of which they are responsible...

In voicing his thoughts to President Washington, Secretary Knox did not indicate any concerns regarding Indians residing within a state under its legal jurisdiction. His only concern centered upon those states having preemptive rights to purchase *"territory"* inhabited by Indians. Connecticut's pre-emptive rights to

---

[66] Abbot, W., ed., 1993, The Papers of George Washington: Presidential Series. Vol. 4:529-534 September 1789-January 1790,. Charlottesville: University Press of Virginia.

lands within the Western Reserve located in the Illinois territory was one such example, that is, independent sovereign tribes in possession of land that bordered on the frontier. According to Knox those states could exercise that right, but they had to do so through the Federal government.

That same month, January 1790, Knox pleaded that,[67]

> ...The general state of the western frontiers, and of the indian department will require the serious attention of Congress...
> ...Independent of the Creeks, representations have been received from almost *every part of the frontier extending along the south of the Ohio*, stating the depredations of the indians...*Hence the importance of the administration of indian affairs being conducted by fixed principles established by Law, and which published should be rigidly enforced...*
> The obligations which the United States owe their own dignity require that while the unenlightened tribes of Indians are treated with justice and humanity, that an arrangement should exist from them a correspondent conduct. [emphasis added]

In response to Secretary Knox's entreaties concerning the state of affairs with the Indians on the western frontier and with strong support from President Washington, Congress passed, in 1790, the first of the Indian Trade and Non-Intercourse Acts ("An Act to regulate Trade and Intercourse with the Indian Tribes"),[68]

> Section 1. *Be it enacted by the Senate and House of Representatives of the United States in Congress assembled*,
> That no person shall be permitted to carry on any trade or intercourse with the Indian tribes, without a license for that purpose under the hand and seal of the superintendent of the department or of such other person as the President of the United States shall appoint for that purpose; ...And no such other person shall be permitted to carry on any trade or intercourse

---

[67] Abbot, W., ed., 1993, The Papers of George Washington: Presidential Series. Vol. 5:76-79, January-June 1790. Charlottesville: University Press of Virginia.
[68] Acts Passed at a Congress of the United States of America MDCCXCI:197-198.. Washington DC

with the Indians without such license as aforesaid. No licence shall be granted for a longer term than two years. *Provided nevertheless, That the President shall make such order respecting the tribes surrounded in their settlements by the citizens of the United States, as to secure an intercourse without license, if he may deem it proper...*

Sec.4. *And be it enacted and declared,* That no sale of lands by any Indians, or any nation or tribe of Indians within the United States, shall be valid to any person or persons or to any State, whether having the right of pre-emption to such lands or not, unless the same shall be made and duly executed at some public treaty, held under the authority of the United States...

Sec. 7. *And be it further enacted,* That this act shall be in force for the term of two years, and from thence to the end of the next session of Congress and no longer. (emphasis added)

Section 4 clearly followed the recommendations made by Secretary Knox in his January 4, 1790 letter to President Washington as quoted above. In this initial version of the Trade and Intercourse Act, a state's preemptory rights to lands held by "...a nation or tribe of Indians..." could only be executed via the executive branch of the Federal government, either the Superintendent of War or a presidential appointee as noted in Section 1. Based upon Knox's letter to Washington, it would appear that a "...nation or tribe of Indians..." meant those independent sovereign Indian tribes or nations holding a non-ceded land base, having an independent political leadership, and either residing on frontier lands adjoining a state or on lands upon which a state had a legal claim. It did not consider Indian tribal remnants within a state as subjects of this Act.

Following the enactment of this law, President Washington, in August 1790, requested the following from Secretary Knox, [69]

---

[69] Fitzpatrick, John, ed.,1939, The Writings of George Washington from the Original Manuscript Sources 1745-1799, Vol. 31: 91. Washington DC: Government Printing Office.

...I therefore request that you will cause such business, within your department, as may be necessary to receive the aid or approbation of the President, submitted to me as soon as its nature will permit; particularly Regulations for trade and intercourse with the Indian tribes, agreeably to the Act. And information and opinions on the following points.
Whether any other, and what steps shall be taken with them to restrain their hostilities.
Whether the order given, and measures adopted, are adequate to the Peace of the Western Frontiers? If not, what further is to be done for this purpose?
Upon the expediency and policy of a proclamation forbidding encroachments upon the Territory of the Indians or treating with them contrary to the Law lately passed.
Instructions for the Governor of the Ceded Territory [Georgia] So. Of the Ohio. Where ought the Governor to reside? [emphasis added]

The contents of this correspondence made the focus and intent of the 1790 Act explicitly clear. Its application was intended to address the situation on the "Western Frontiers," in the "ceded Territory," and "upon the territory of the Indians." Although it was not specifically stated in the 1790 Act, correspondence from the bill's primary sponsors (Washington and Knox) prior to and immediately after its passage demonstrates the intent of the legislation.

On October 25, 1791, in his third annual address to Congress, President Washington reiterated these points. One can easily discern within his address the major points he and Secretary Knox had discussed prior to the 1790 enactment concerning the need for a uniform law on the frontier,[70]

...In the interval of your recess due attention has been paid to the execution of the different objects which were especially provided for by the laws and Resolutions of the last Session.

---

[70] ibid. Vol. 31:396-398

> Among the most important of these is *the defense and security of the Western Frontiers. To accomplish it on the most humane principles was a primary wish.*
> Accordingly, at the same time that treaties have been provisionally concluded, and other proper means used to attach the wavering, and to confirm in their friendship, the well disposed tribes of Indians; effectual measures have been adopted to make those of hostile description sensible that a pacification was desired upon terms of moderation and justice...
> ...It is sincerely desired that all need of coercion, in future may cease; and that an intimate intercourse may succeed; calculated to advance the happiness of the Indians, and to attach them firmly to the United States. In order to this it seems necessary: That they should experience the benefits of an impartial administration of justice. *That the mode of alienating their lands the main source of discontent and war, should be so defined and regulated, as to obviate imposition, an,, as far as may be practicable. Controversy concerning the reality, and extent of the alienations which are made. The commence with them should be promoted under regulations tending to secure an equitable deportment towards them...* [emphasis added]

In 1984 the Jesuit scholar, Father Paul Prucha, concurred with the conclusion that the Indian Trade and Intercourse Act applied only to the frontier setting. In the first volume of his major study on federal-tribal relations he noted,[71]

> The trade and intercourse laws were necessary to provide a framework for the trade and to establish a licensing system that would permit some control and regulation, but this was merely a restatement of old procedures. The vital sections of the laws were in answer to the crisis of the day on the frontier, and the provisions pertained to the tribes of Indians with whom the nation dealt as independent bodies. Neither President Washington nor the Congress was concerned with the remnants of tribes that had been absorbed by the states and had come under their direction and control. The laws sought to provide an answer to the charge that the treaties made with the tribes on the frontiers, which guaranteed their rights to the territory behind the boundary lines, were not respected by the United States. The laws were not primarily "Indian" laws, for they touched the Indians indirectly. The legislation, rather, was directed against

---

[71] Prucha, Francis. 1984, The Great Father. Vol. 1:94. University of Nebraska Press

lawless whites and sought to restrain them from violating the sacred treaties...

As an example, Connecticut's only Indian-related interaction with the Federal government during the period from 1789-1892 occurred during May of 1789 in regard to the region known as the Western Reserve in the Illinois country that was part of the patent made by King Charles II in 1662 to Connecticut Colony. A committee was appointed to,[72]

> ...make Sale of the Lands belonging to this State lying West of the State of Pennsylvania.... make enquiry whether any Treaty is expected to be made, or the Natives are to be Collected for the Purpose of making a treaty with the Congress of America...to give the earliest information to his Excellency the Governor that Proper measures may be taken to extinguish the Claims of the Natives to the Western Lands belonging to this State.

Connecticut, by virtue of her 1662 Charter from King Charles II held a recognized pre-emptive right to lands in the Illinois country. Connecticut, recognizing the requirements posited within the Trade and Intercourse Act, sought federal participation in a public treaty with the Indians there to obtain the Indian or native title to the state's pre-emptive lands in order to sell them.

In contrast, during October 1792, the Connecticut General Assembly authorized the sale of 33 acres of land owned by three Schaghticoke Indians in Derby, Connecticut.[73] The Federal government did not challenge the legality of this sale. The three were state wards and a small remnant of an earlier Indian community.

---

[72] Public Records of Connecticut, 1789-1892:15 (PRC)
[73] PRC. 1789-1892: 523-524

These two actions clearly demonstrate the frontier focus and application of the 1790 Trade and Intercourse Act. Connecticut acknowledged that only Congress had the authority to acquire the lands of independent sovereign frontier Indian tribes. Yet within the settled boundaries of Connecticut, "remnants" of Indian tribes surrounded by "white settlements" were under state jurisdiction. The state could sell such Indian-owned lands without federal approval.

Given that the legislative life of the 1790 Act was for only two years, Congress, in 1792, began a renewed debate on the issue. The House of Representatives, in the following resolution, "Protection of the Frontiers", January 1792) expressed its position on the future regulation of "trading" and "intercourse" between whites and Indians on the frontier,[74]

> The House resolved itself into a Committee of the Whole House on the bill for making further and more effectual provision for the Protection of the frontier of the United States…
> …Let us occupy posts in the vicinity of the enemy, let them be properly garrisoned and well provided, and the business is done. These will afford an opportunity of trading with the friendly tribes, and will prevent all intercourse between the whites and the Indians except under proper regulation….

The result of this legislative process was the enactment of the 1793 version of the Indian Trade and Intercourse Act. This enactment superseded the 1790 Act. What was implied by both past and present practice, but not explicitly stated in the 1790 Act, was clearly stated in Section 13 of the 1793 version of the Trade and Intercourse Act. This new section echoed Article IV of the 1782 Articles of

---

[74] Debates and Proceedings in the Congress of the United States, "Protection of the Frontiers." Volume III, 1791-1793: 337-356.

Confederation, the principle difference being the additional proviso concerning the presence of settlements of American citizens,[75]

> *Be it enacted & c.*, That no person shall be permitted to carry on any trade or intercourse with the Indian tribes without the license under the hand and seal of the Superintendent of the Department or of such other personas the President of the United States shall authorize to grant licenses for that purpose...
>
> ...Sec.3. *And be it further enacted*, That every person *who shall attempt to trade with the Indian tribes, or shall be found in Indian country*, with such merchandise in his possession as are usually vented to the Indians, without lawful license, shall forfeit all the merchandise offered for sale to the Indians, or *found in his possession in Indian country*...
>
> ...Sec.8. *And be it further enacted*, That no purchase or grant of lands, or of any title or claim thereto, from any Indians, or nation or tribe of Indians, within the bounds of the United States, shall be of any validity, in law or equity, unless the same be made by a treaty or convention entered into pursuant to the Constitution...
>
> ...Sec.13. *And be it further enacted*, That nothing in this act shall be construed to prevent any trade or intercourse with Indians living on lands surrounded by settlements of the citizens of the United States, and being within the jurisdiction of any of the individual States...
>
> ...Sec. 14. *And be it further enacted*, That all and every other act and acts, coming within the purview of this act, shall be and are hereby repealed.
>
> Sec.15. *And be it further enacted*, That this act shall be in force for the term of two years, and from thence to the end of the next Congress and no longer. [emphasis added]

---

[75] The Debates and Proceedings in the Congress of the United States, 2nd Cong., October 24, 1791-March 2, 1793. (also Annals of Congress, v. III).

Section 3 of the 1793 enactment of the Indian Trade and Intercourse Act made a direct reference to activities in "Indian country" that is, an area or region not under federal or state jurisdiction wherein tribal sovereignty was accepted as fact. This further affirmed the intended area of application of the Trade and Intercourse Acts. Additionally, the all important state exclusionary clause, which acknowledged a state's right to hold intercourse and trade with Indian communities within a state, which was Section 13 of the 1793 Trade and Intercourse Act, now became Section 19. The major difference between the 1793 and 1796 versions was the inclusion in Section 1 of an exact frontier boundary line between settled lands and Indian country. The northern portion of this frontier boundary was designated as follows,[76]

> An Act to Regulate Trade and Intercourse with the Indian Tribes, and to preserve Peace on the Frontiers, May 19, 1796.
>
> *Section 1. Be it enacted by the Senate and House of Representatives of the United States of America in Congress assembled,* That the following boundary line, established by treaty between the United States and various Indian tribes, shall be clearly ascertained, and distinctly marked, in all such places, as the President of the United States shall deem necessary, and in such a manner as he shall direct, to wit: Beginning at the mouth of Cayahoga river on Lake Erie, and running thence up the same, to the portage between that and the Tuscaroras branch
> of the Muskingum; thence down that branch to the crossing place above Fort Lawrence; thence westerly to a fork of that branch of the Great Miami river, running into the Ohio...
>
> ...Sec. 19. *And be it further enacted,* That nothing in this act shall be construed to prevent any trade or intercourse with Indians living on lands surrounded by settlements of the citizens of the United States, and being within the ordinary jurisdiction of any of the individual states...

---

[76] U.S. Congressional Documents and Debates, 1774-1873, 4th Cong., 1st sess., Ch. 30.

Of significant importance is the location of the northern anchor of the frontier boundary described in Section 1. The mouth of the Cayahoga River on Lake Erie is located in the present day state of Ohio. It will be recalled that in the 1786 Ordinance, the frontier boundary was on the western side of Hudson's river in New York State. By 1796, this line was in Ohio. Thus the area of application of the Trade and Intercourse Act was west of the Cayahoga. Indians residing east of the river on ceded lands surrounded by white settlements were subject to state jurisdiction and were not subject to the Act. The remnants of the Six Nation Iroquois collectively residing in western New York State were in part, still considered subject to treaty rights previously negotiated by the Federal government, even though splinter groups, such as portions of the Oneida, Cayuga and Onondaga, resided in eastern New York under state jurisdiction as tenants upon state-owned lands. The central council fire of the Six Nations, the representative political entity of the Six Nations at Buffalo Creek, with whom the Federal government specifically treated, still maintained a government-to-government treaty relationship with Congress. The Federal government, concerned that these Iroquois would migrate north into Canada and merge with the Six Nations Iroquois at Grand River under English control upon the Ontario Grand River reserve, took care to ensure that this government-to-government relationship did not lapse. Sixteen years later, England and America were again at war.

The 1799 enactment of the Trade and Intercourse Act specifically dealt with the issue of a westward moving frontier line. A proviso was added to Section 1 that covered any further changes in the frontier line during the lifetime (two years) of this legislation. This proviso further clarified the relationship between the applicability of the Act and the location of the frontier boundary. Section 19 still carried the state non-applicability proviso of the earlier Act.

The very title of the 1799 enactment of the Trade and Intercourse Act leaves no doubt as to the jurisdictional relationship between the Act and the western frontier. As Prucha (1984) noted, the Trade and Intercourse Act only indirectly concerned the Indians. It was the continual behavior of individual United States citizens on or beyond the frontier, a problem then faced in 1735 by Edmund Atkin, for whom the act was intended to apply,[77]

> ...The policy of the United States was based on an assumption that white settlement should advance and the Indians withdraw. The federal government was interested primarily in seeing that this process was as free of disorder and injustice as possible. It was meant to restrain and govern the advance of whites, not to prevent it forever... In the early decades of the nineteenth century the federal government was convinced that once the Indians had been permanently settled on lands west of the Mississippi, the problems of encroachment and removing intruders would be unhappy memories of the past...

> *An Act to Regulate Trade and Intercourse with the Indian Tribes, and to Preserve Peace on the Frontier. March 3, 1799.*[78]

> ...*Provided always,* That if the boundary line between the said Indian tribes and the United States shall, at any time hereafter, be varied, by any treaty which shall be made between the said Indian tribes and the United States, *then all the provisions contained in this act shall be construed to apply to the said line so to be varied,* in the same manner as said provisions apply, by force of this act, to the boundary line herein before recited...
> ...Sec. 12. *And be it further enacted,* That no purchase, grant, lease, or other conveyance of lands, or of any title or claim, thereto, from any Indian, or nation, or tribe of Indians, within the bounds of the United states, shall be of any validity, in law or equity, unless the same be made by way of treaty or convention entered into pursuant to the constitution...

---

[77] Prucha, Francis. 1984, The Great Father. Vol. 1:114. University of Nebraska Press
[78] The Debates and Proceedings in the Congress of the United States, 5th Cong., May 1797-March 1799 : 3956-3963.

...Sec.19. *And be it further enacted, That nothing in this act shall be construed to prevent any trade or intercourse with Indians living on lands surrounded by settlements of the citizens of the United States, and being within the ordinary jurisdiction of any of the individual states...*
...Sec. 21. *And be it further enacted,* That this act shall be in force from and after the third day of March, one thousand seven hundred and ninety-nine, and shall continue in force the term of three years... [emphasis added]

The January 1800 "Act for the Preservation of Peace with the Indian Tribes" clearly stated what the Federal government considered to be violations of the Indian Trade and Intercourse Act by non-Indians. This Act was merged with the existing version (1799) of the Trade and Intercourse Act,[79]

Be it enacted, &c. That if any citizen or other person residing within the United States, or the territory thereof, shall send any talk, speech, message, or letter, to any Indian nation, tribe, or chief with the intent to produce a contravention or infraction of any treaty or law of the United States, or to disturb the peace and tranquillity of the United States, he shall forfeit a sum not exceeding two thousand dollars, and be imprisoned not exceeding twelve months...
...Sec. 4. *And it further be enacted,* That the provisions of the act entitled "An Act to regulate trade and Intercourse with the Indian tribes and to Preserve Peace on the Frontiers" passed the third day of March, one thousand and seven hundred and ninety-nine, be, and the same are hereby extended to carry into effect this act, and for the trial and punishment of offenses against it, in the same manner as if they were herein specially recited.
Sec. 5. *And it further be enacted,* That this act shall continue and be in force until the third day of March, in the year one thousand eight hundred and two, and no longer.

---

[79] The Debates and Proceedings in the Congress of the United States, 6th Cong., December 1799-March 1801: 1436-1437.

The 1802 enactment was the culmination of all previous versions of the acts to regulate the trade and intercourse between independent Indian tribes on the frontier and the neighboring Anglo-American population. Gone were the 'sunset provisions' limiting the duration of these individual Acts. The 1802 enactment was to remain in force, with one minor amendment added in 1822 (Senate Bill 79), until it was superseded in 1834. The March 1802 reenactment *("An Act to Regulate Trade and Intercourse with the Indian Tribes and to Preserve Peace on the Frontier")* defined the present frontier boundary. It accounted for future changes in frontier boundaries and defined the perimeters of jurisdictional applications and their limitations,[80]

> *Be it enacted by the Senate and House of Representatives of the United States of America in Congress assembled,* That the following boundary line established by treaty between the United States and various Indian tribes, shall be clearly ascertained, and distinctly marked in all such places as the President of the United States shall deem necessary, and in such manner as he shall direct, to wit: Beginning at the mouth of the Cayahoga river on
> Lake Erie, and running then up the same to the portage between that and the Tuscaroras branch of the Muskingum; thence, down that branch to the crossing place above Fort Laurence; thence westerly to a fork of that branch of the Great Miami river running into the Ohio, at or near which fork stood Laromie's store, and where commences the portage, between the Miami of the Ohio and St. Mary's river, which is a branch of the Miami, which runs into Lake Erie; thence a westerly course to Fort Recovery, which stands on a branch of the Wabash; thence southwesterly, in a direct line to the Ohio, so as to intersect that river, opposite the mouth of Kentucky or Cuttawa river; thence down the said river Ohio to the tract of one hundred and fifty thousand acres, near the rapids of the Ohio…thence around said tract on the line of said tract, till it again intersect the said river Ohio; thence down the same to a point opposite the high lands or ridge between the mouth of the Cumberland and Tennessee rivers…*Provided always,* that *if the boundary line between the said Indian*

---

[80] U.S. Congress. House. Gales & Seaton's Register. U.S. Congressional Documents and Debates, 1774-1873, 21st Cong., 1st sess., 6, pt. 2:1080 and 1118.

> tribes and the United States shall at any time hereafter, be varied, by any treaty which shall be made between the said Indian tribes and the United States, then all the provisions contained in this act shall be construed to apply to the said line so to be varied, in the same manner as said provisions apply, by force of this act, to the boundary line herein before recited...
>
> ...Sec. 12. *And be it further enacted*, That no purchase, grant, lease, or other conveyance of lands, or of any title or claim thereto, from any Indian or nation, or tribe of Indians, within the bounds of the United States, shall have no validity in law or equity, unless the same be made by treaty or convention, entered into pursuant to the constitution...
>
> ...Sec.19. *And be it further enacted*, That nothing in this act shall be construed to prevent any trade or intercourse with Indians living on lands surrounded by settlements of the citizens of the United States, and being within the ordinary jurisdiction of any of the individual states...
>
> ...Sec. 22. *And be it further enacted*, That this act shall be in force from the passage thereof... [emphasis added]

In regard to the jurisdictional limitations implied in Sections 1 and 19, what were the implications for Indians still residing in the "old States" of this Act? Congress was well aware of this situation and acknowledged they were under state jurisdiction,

> Debate on House of Representatives Bill 319.
> (by Representative Wilde)
>
> ...Nearly all the old states, except Georgia, most of them while they were yet colonies, had assumed the guardianship of the Indians within their limits, and legislated for them...

In his January 1831 opinion in *Cherokee Nation v. The State of Georgia*, Chief Justice John Marshall[81] denoted two types of tribes. Justice Marshall found the Cherokee tribe residing within Georgia to have been at one time a "people capable of maintaining the relations of peace and war; of being responsible in

---

[81] 5 Peters 300 (1831)

their political character for any violation of their engagements." At this point in time Justice Marshall noted there was no "common allegiance" to the United States and they were therefore considered a "foreign" nation. What Justice Marshall determined in their present situation was, "It may well be doubted whether those tribes which reside within the acknowledged boundaries of the United States can with strict accuracy be denominated foreign nations. They may more correctly perhaps be denominated domestic dependent nations...They are in a state of pupilage...Their relations to the United States resemble that of a ward to his guardian."

Justice Marshall further affirmed this point in his 1832 *Worcester v. Georgia* opinion, [82]

> The Federal Government has the exclusive regulation of the intercourse with the Indians, and so long as this power shall be exercised it cannot be obstructed by a State. But, if a contingency shall occur, which shall render the Indians who reside in a State incapable of self-government, either by moral denigration or reduction of their numbers, it would undoubtedly be in the power of a State government to extend to them the a*egis* of its laws. Under such circumstances, the agency of the Federal Government, of necessity, must cease

In 1853 the question of constitutional jurisdictional limitations and the intended application of Federal Indian policy, including the Trade and Intercourse Acts were further affirmed by the United States Supreme Court.

"the State of Maine is in accordance with the Constitution" : Veazie v. Moor

---

[82] Worcester v. Georgia, 6 Peters 515 (1831).

In 1850 the Maine Supreme Court made a decision regarding the state's right to regulate a waterway that lay entirely within the State. A portion of such a waterway ran through lands occupied by a Maine Indian tribe, the Penobscot. The Penobscot did not have a treaty-based government to government relationship with the United States

In this instance the plaintiffs' argued the right of the State of Maine to require a commercial license to transit the Penobscot River, which lies completely within the State of Maine. A portion of this transit went through an area occupied by the Penobscot Indians. It was argued by the plaintiffs that,

> The right of Congress to regulate "commerce with the Indian tribes," extends to and embraces the Penobscot tribe of Indians, and the Legislature of Maine has no right to restrict the people to, or deprive them of, any particular mode of intercourse or trade with them…
>
> That any Act of a State Legislature contravening such right of navigation, as does the Act set forth in defendant's bill of complaint is absolutely null and void.

In regard to the plaintiffs' assertions that the Penobscot are covered by the Constitution's "commerce clause", it would if true include the application of the Indian Trade and Intercourse Act. The state's Supreme Court concluded,[83]

> …the Constitution manifestly refers to independent tribes with which the general government may come in conflict; not to those small remnants of tribes scattered over the country, which are under state jurisdiction and guardianship.

---

[83] Samuel Veazie and Levi Young v. Wyman B. S. Moor 32 Main 343

The Court's finding was appealed by the plaintiffs to the United States Supreme Court. During December 1852, the Court issued a decision affirming the state court's findings, [84]

> The Penobscot tribe of Indians own all the islands in the Penobscot River above Old Town Falls, some of which they occupy; and this tribe always have been, and now are, under the jurisdiction and guardianship of the State of Maine...
>
> Upon the whole, we are of the opinion that the decision of the Supreme Judicial Court of the State of Maine is in accordance with the Constitution of the United States, and ought to be, and is hereby affirmed.

Of singular importance was the fact that the United States Supreme Court upheld the state court's opinion that the Penobscot/Passamaquoddy Indians were not a tribe subject to federal jurisdiction on the basis of Justice Marshall's 1831 and 1832 opinions, a point ignored by later Maine (*Passamaquoddy v. Morton, 528 F2 370, (1975)*) and federal jurists (*Oneida Indian Nation v. County of Oneida, 414 US 661, (1974)*). Of even greater significance in this often overlooked decision was the fact that this decision defined the parameters of the application of the federal Trade and Intercourse Acts, "...the Constitution manifestly refers to independent tribes with which the general government may come in conflict...."

As noted earlier, independent tribes were those tribes considered by the Federal government to be politically independent and to possess a non-ceded land base. Thus this decision not only provided the parameters of application for the Indian Trade and Intercourse Acts, but also substantiates the requirements for an Indian group to be federally recognized as an independent Indian tribe.

---

[84] 52 US 568 (1852)

In summary, the focus and intended application of these federal Acts was not upon Indian tribes or communities residing in a state subject to its legal jurisdiction, but only upon those sovereign Indian tribes as defined by the Supreme Court in the *Veazie v. Moor* decision. They were Indian tribes that continued to maintain their political independence from the United States and that continued to reside on lands not ceded to the Federal government "with which the general government may come in conflict."

This intended application was clearly stated in the correspondence of President Washington and Secretary of War Knox, the two persons most responsible for formulating the Indian Trade and Intercourse Act of 1790. They were concerned about maintaining the peace with the sovereign independent tribes that resided along this country's ever changing western frontier.

At the same time, the Indian Trade and Intercourse Acts raised the question of federal recognition of tribes, that is, those Indian tribes that were the focus of Federal Indian law. What constituted federal recognition? As will be seen, the *Cherokee Nation v. Georgia, Worcester v. Georgia*, and the *Veazie v. Moor* decisions provided the basis for our understanding of the Congressional requirements for recognizing a tribe via a treaty as a politically independent sovereign entity. Such recognition was an essential aspect of treaty-making.

We have observed to this point that the Federal government clearly considered sovereignty to be an absolute. We also note that the focus of Federal Indian policy was to maintain peace with these independent tribes in the process acquiring lands from them, as needed without the presence of frontier conflict. Tribal remnants, even those that still maintained some, but not all of the attributes of a sovereign entity, under state jurisdiction were not a consideration of the Federal government.

Chapter 3.

The Process of Federal Recognition of Indian Tribes

The *Veazie v. Moor* affirmation clearly defined the applicability of the federal Indian Trade and Intercourse Acts. These Acts constituted an essential part of Federal Indian Policy. Another critical aspect of Federal Indian policy was the establishment of government-to-government treaty relationships between the United States and particular sovereign Indian tribes. What process and requirements were involved?

What were the essentials for the creation of such a political relationship? We know that such tribes had to be politically independent and have an un-ceded land base. But these factors alone do not explain how, and by what manner, such a relationship was created.

This chapter examines the evolution of Congressional recognition of Indian tribes as political sovereigns from the Revolutionary War to 1871. It also demonstrates that the Federal government prior to 1871 only recognized and entered into government-to-government treaty relationships with those Indian tribes or, more aptly, Indian nations that held a non-ceded land base and maintained an independent tribal political leadership. These tribes were what the Federal government perceived to be sovereign Indian nations.

During this period, Congress, the Executive branch, and the federal courts considered many Indian groups, especially those within the New England states, to be non-independent remnants of once independent tribes. By 1824 the Federal government clearly noted Indian groups such as the St. John, Passamaquoddy and Penobscot of Maine, the Mashpee, Herring Pond, Martha's Vineyard of Massachusetts, the Narragansett of Rhode Island, and the Mohegan and the Pequot groups at Groton and Stonington as being tribal remnants subject to state jurisdiction.[85] An Indian group's relationship with these states was one of dependency, as individual indigent wards.

The requirements for tribal recognition held by the Federal government from 1776 through 1871 differed quite radically from the non-statutory procedures currently being applied by the Bureau of Indian Affairs (under 25 CFR 83.7 (a)-(g)) in considering the applications of Indian groups petitioning for federal recognition or acknowledgement of a tribal neo- or quasi-sovereign status entitling them to federal services and benefits.

The result of this process was, tribal fragments that, 250 years ago were no longer considered sovereign tribes by the Federal government, only remnants under state or territorial jurisdiction. They were being granted federal recognition as neo-sovereign nations by the same government under new historically unjustified revisionist criteria. An associate once noted, "In 1866 John Wilkes Booth was convicted of assassinating President Lincoln. One hundred and forty-three years later the same government decides to retry the case using new revised

---

[85] American State Papers, Documents. Legislative and Executive of the Congress of the United States, Vol. II: 542, Indian Affairs.

evidentiary standards". The result, "Booth was acquitted and his gun was found to be the guilty party."

"...in Congress assembled": The Constitution and the Recognition of Indian Tribes

Following the Revolutionary War and into the period of state confederation, Congress was given the sole right to manage and regulate Indian Affairs. The 1782 enactment of the "Articles of Confederation and Perpetual Union between the States..." noted,

> Art. IX. The United States in Congress assembled, shall have the sole and exclusive right and power of...regulating the trade and managing all affairs with the Indians, not members of any of the states, provided that the legislative right of any state within its own limits be not infringed or violated....

Such regulatory and managerial actions were accomplished by enacting treaties with independent Indian nations. This required both an enactor and executor. Serious debates occurred within the existing confederated government over the nature of, and responsibilities for, these Indian related activities. Was Congress to be both the enactor and executor? The office of the Secretary of War, a component of the Executive branch, was responsible for carrying out federal Indian policy. Was the Secretary answerable to the Congress or the President? Who was responsible for authorizing treaty making?

Alexander Hamilton, in his 1788 essay promoting the new Constitution, "The Treaty Making Power of the Executive" (Federalist Papers, Federalist No.75), effectively addressed the problem.

> The essence of the legislative authority is to enact laws, or in other words, to prescribe rules for the regulation of society; while the execution of the

laws, and the employment of the common strength, either for this purpose or for the common defense, seem to comprise all the functions of the executive magistrate. The power of making treaties is, plainly, neither the one nor the other. It relates neither to the execution of subsisting laws, nor the enaction of new ones; and still less to an exertion of the common strength. Its objects are CONTRACTS with foreign nations, which have the force of law, but derive it from the obligations of good faith. *They are not rules prescribed by the sovereign to the subject, but agreements between sovereign and sovereign.* The power in question seems therefore to form a distinct department, and to belong, properly, neither to the legislative nor to the executive...[emphasis added]

Hamilton described the basic functional dichotomy between the Legislative (prescriber or enactor) and the Executive (executor or administrator) branches as adopted for the new federal Constitution. He envisioned the making of treaties (recognizing the existence of a government-to-government or sovereign-to-sovereign relationship) as a functional dynamic between enactor (law maker) and executor (law executor). A treaty, therefore, is the total sum of both functions, Congress enacts, or grants, recognition to the relationship and the Executive branch executes the relationship via provisions of an enacted treaty.

Hamilton's Federalist arguments are readily perceptible in the new 1789 federal Constitution:

Article 1.

Section 1. All legislative Powers herein granted shall be vested in a Congress of the United States, which shall consist of a Senate and House of Representatives...

Section 8. The Congress shall have Power...To regulate Commerce with foreign Nations, and among the several States, and with the Indian Tribes;....

Article 2.

Section 2. …He [the President] shall have Power, by and with the Advice and Consent of the Senate, to make Treaties, provided two thirds of the Senators present concur….

Thus, Congress enacted the interchange and communicated (recognized the validity of the relationship) with sovereign independent Indian nations. The Executive then executed the interchange and communication (recognition) enacted by Congress, thereby establishing a sovereign-to-sovereign (government-to-government) relationship via treaty. It must also be noted that the term "Commerce", unlike its present day commercial connotation, was within the context of the time (1789) understood to imply "interchange" and "communication." In addition, the term "Treaty" was also understood to mean "A contract between States relating to peace, truce, alliance, commerce or other international relation."[86]

Joseph Blunt, a former congressman and congressional constitutional historian of the period (1825), summed up the totality of this relationship,[87]

> By this instrument [Federal Constitution], *the states were prohibited from entering "into any treaty or alliance;"* but the treaty-making power was confided exclusively to the general government. This grant of power comprehended all agreements with the Indians; and in another part of the Constitution congress was authorized to regulate commerce with the Indian tribes. These two clauses were intended as an equivalent to the provision in the articles of confederation; by which congress was invested with the power "to regulate the trade and manage all affairs with the Indians, not members of any state; provided that the legislative right of any state within its own limits, shall not be infringed or violated." *All our intercourse with the Indians, so long as they continue to be independent,*

---

[86] The Shorter Oxford Dictionary on Historical Principles, Third Edition (1953) Vol. 1: 349. Oxford Claredon Press
[87] Blunt, Joseph. 1825, A Historical Sketch of the Formation of the Confederacy Particularly with Reference to the Provincial Limits and the Jurisdiction of the General Government over Indian Tribes and the Public Territory: 92-93. New York Geo. & Chas. Carville

> *was in the way of trade, or in making treaties, and these were placed under the control of the general government.* **It was not contemplated, under either system, that congress should have any legislative power over the Indians; but it should have the exclusive power to regulate the trade, and to make treaties with them.** *So long, therefore, as they were independent, and proper parties to treat with, congress was invested with the power to manage our relations with them; but when they lost that character, and became members of a state, they fell under the power of the local government, and congress, from that moment, ceased to interfere with them.* [emphasis added]

It is important to note, as Blunt stated, that once a tribe comes under the jurisdiction of a state and ceases to be independent, any existing treaty relationship between the tribe and the Federal government ceases. At this early date, 78 years before the 1903 *Lonewolf v. Hitchcock* Supreme Court decision[88] which affirmed the right of Congress to abrogate Indian treaties, Congress was aware (circa 1820) of its right to do so if the situation, as described by Blunt, warranted such an action. Chief Justice John Marshal in his 1832 *Worcester v. Georgia* opinion[89] also affirmed the right to cease federal agency with tribes.

Initially the responsibility for carrying out treaty requirements devolved upon the Secretary of War. As the number and particular demands of treaties increased, a need for a specialized authority to carry out the requirements set forth was realized. In 1832, Congress enacted a law to create the Executive branch position of Commissioner of Indian Affairs. This act was titled: "An Act to Provide for the Appointment of a Commissioner of Indian Affairs, and for other purposes",[90]

---

[88] 187 US. 553 (1903)
[89] 31 US. (6 Peters) 515 (1832):588-590 Samuel A. Worcester v. The State of Georgia
[90] Congressional Debates, 23rd Cong., 1st sess., 1832, 8, pt. 3:32.

> *Be it enacted, & c.* That the President shall appoint, by and with the consent of the Senate, a Commissioner of Indian Affairs, who shall, under the direction of the Secretary of War, and agreeably to such regulations as the President may, from time to time, prescribe, have *the direction and management* of all Indian *Affairs*, and of all matters *arising out of Indian relations*,… [emphasis added]

It is quite apparent from the wording of this act that this Commissioner was responsible only for the *management* of Indian affairs as directed by Congress. This included ensuring the fulfillment of obligations arising from treaties with recognized tribes. This Commissioner acted as an assistant to the Secretary of War. He clearly did not have the authority to initiate a government-to-government relationship with any Indian tribe, only the "direction and management" (process) of that relationship once it had been established by Congress. Initiating the relationship was the constitutional prerogative of Congress. The Commissioner's position and function was in keeping with the constitutionally derived role of the Executive branch as the executioner of legislative acts. This law is still a federal statute codified under 25 USC 2.

Two years later, in June of 1834, Congress, at the request of the Executive branch, created a new and separate Department of Indian Affairs which was the precursor of the current Bureau of Indian Affairs. This new position was created by an act titled: "An Act to Provide for the Organization of the Department of Indian Affairs",[91]

> Sec.2. *And it be further enacted,* That there shall be a superintendency of Indian Affairs for all the Indian country *not within the bounds of any State or Territory west of the Mississippi river,* the superintendent of which shall reside at St. Louis….

---

[91] Congressional Debates, 23rd Cong., 1st sess., 1834, 10, pt. 4:347.

Sec.17. *And be it further enacted,* That the President of the United States shall be, and he is hereby, authorized to *prescribe* such *rules and regulations* as he may think fit *for carrying into effect the various provisions of any act relating to Indian affairs,* and for the settlement of accounts of the Indian department....

Section 17 is still a federal statute, 25 USC 9. The key understanding of this act was that the Executive branch and this new department were only authorized to *"prescribe such rules and regulations...*for carrying into effect the various provisions of *any act* relating to Indian affairs." They were not the "enactors." Congress still maintained its full legislative powers over all Indian affairs.

Section 4 of this act established specific Indian agencies. The locations of these authorized Indian agencies were listed. However, no individual Indian agents were appointed for any of the New England states or New York. The activities of Department of Indian Affairs was excluded from states having Indians residing within them who were considered to be under the ordinary laws or jurisdiction of the state.

According to the Federal government, a recognized tribe had to maintain itself as an independent political entity in order to continue to qualify for a government-to-government or treaty relationship with the Federal government. If an Indian nation ceased to maintain its independent nature, its treaty relationship with the Federal government would cease. Such a group would not require the services of a federal Indian agent or agency.

Blunt's observations clearly anticipated this eventuality and subsequent Supreme Court decisions, most notably *Cherokee Nation v. Georgia, Worcester v. Georgia,* and *Veazie v. Moor,*

...undoubtedly...to that class of Indians...consisting of mere remnants of tribes, which have become almost extinct; and who have, in a great measure, lost their original character and abandoned their usages and customs, and become subject to the laws of the State, although in many parts of the country living together and surrounded by the whites. They cannot be said to have any distinct government of their own, and are within the ordinary jurisdiction and government of the State where they are located.[92]

...The Federal Government has the exclusive regulation of the intercourse with the Indians, and so long as this power shall be exercised it cannot be obstructed by a State. But, if a contingency shall occur, which shall render the Indians who reside in a State incapable of self-government, either by moral denigration or reduction of their numbers, it would undoubtedly be in the power of a State government to extend to them the a*egis* of its laws. Under such circumstances, the agency of the Federal Government, of necessity, must cease.[93]

...the Constitution manifestly refers only to independent tribes with which the general government may come in conflict; not to those small remnants of tribes scattered over the country, which are under state jurisdiction and guardianship.[94]

A treaty with the Federal government was the most critical component in order for a tribe to be recognized as an Indian nation. Without it, during this pre-1871 era recognition would not be possible. A treaty defines the nature of a relationship and the agreed upon rights and obligations that go with it. In 1830, the Senate Committee on Indian Affairs[95] referred to, "Everything which relates to those Indian tribes or nations with which we have political relations, created by or regulated by treaties..." in describing the totality of federal-tribe relations.

---

[92] Cherokee Nation v. Georgia, 5 Peters 300 (1831)
[93] Worcester v. Georgia, 6 Peters 515 (1831)
[94] Samuel Veazie and Levi Young v. Wyman B. S. Moor, 55 US. 568 (1852)
[95] Report of the Committee on Indian Affairs, 21st Congress., 1st session.

The Senate committee clearly noted that between the Federal government and Indian tribes "political relations are created and regulated by treaties…" Tribes that had a treaty relationship with the Federal government were considered by the Federal government to be sovereign political entities; hence a government-to-government relationship could exist. Congress could not legislate over such tribes. It lacked the plenary authority to do so. A treaty defines status as a sovereign entity. Congress (the Senate), by authorizing the treaty, grants its recognition and approval of the relationship. Without its approval the relationship cannot exist. Such relationships brought upon the Federal government certain obligations mandated by such treaties. It was the duty of the Executive branch to carry out these treaty responsibilities. On the other hand, the Committee implied that those Indian tribes not having a treaty relationship with the Federal government did not have any political or sovereign standing with the United States and so were not recognized and treated as sovereign political entities.

The essential point is that a political relationship between an Indian tribe and the United States came into being via recognition by Congress, meaning that the tribe was 'recognized' as being both independent and sovereign. Sovereignty is to be understood as an absolute. That status was confirmed by the enactment of a treaty between the United States and the tribe. Congress approved the treaty relationship and the Executive branch was responsible for carrying out the obligations and requirements set forth in the treaty. The 1852 Supreme Court affirmation (*Veazie v. Moor*) pointedly affirmed, on the basis of earlier Supreme Court decisions, the types of tribes that would be considered for establishing such a relationship with the United States, "those independent tribes with which the general government may come in conflict."

President Jackson's Removal Policy

In the aftermath of the Revolutionary War, the new national government envisioned a nation extending from the East Coast to the banks of the Mississippi River. One result of the enactments of the 1790 and 1802 Indian Trade and Intercourse Acts was the emergence of a national Indian policy of removal of those remaining sovereign independent tribes west of the Mississippi River. The plan was to establish a permanent region wherein such tribes could remain unhindered by a planned national expansion. The federal policy of treaty-making with such tribes was to become an essential aspect this policy.

As early as 1803, President Thomas Jefferson began to advocate the removal of Indian tribes west of the Mississippi River into the newly acquired lands of the Louisiana Purchase. At that time and through the early 1820's the focus of Federal Indian policy and that of the states was in part, the acculturation and civilization of Indian tribes in-situ. That is civilizing them in place. In contrast, President James Monroe thought the prospect of a westward tribal removal would provide a solution to two pressing issues; (1) the land needs of an expanding population within the states and into newly acquired territories; (2) and the real threat of extinction of Indian tribes. Subsidiary to these two problems were those of displaced tribes pressing into newly settled states and territories which, in turn, did not want them within their borders, thus creating the real possibility of further conflict between these two differing cultural groups. The goal was to lessen the friction between the states, territories, and the tribes. The tool was the Indian Trade and Intercourse Acts.

Compelled by the demands of the State of Georgia which was pressing the Federal government to live up to its obligations derived from the Compact of 1802, wherein the State surrendered its claims to western lands in exchange for the extinguishment of Indian title to lands within her borders, President Monroe proposed the removal of Indian tribes to west of the Mississippi River. As Berkhofer (1979)[96] noted,

> Fearing their "degradation and extermination" if they remained in the East, Monroe proposed that removal might be made honorable to the United States and attractive to the Indians if Congress guaranteed the emigrant Indians a permanent title to their Western lands, organized some kind of government among the removed tribes to protect their territory from intrusion, preserved peace among the tribes native to the West and the emigrant tribes, and continued funding of civilization agents among them to prevent further "degeneracy."

Federal policy for tribes under its jurisdiction was to shift from forced assimilation to paternalistic-based gradual acculturation and eventual assimilation via segregation. This policy, while put into practice by Monroe's successors, did not assume statutory authority until the enactment of the May 28, 1830 "Act to Provide for an exchange of lands with the Indians residing in any of the states or territories and for their removal west of river Mississippi" or more commonly, the "Indian Removal Act". It was signed into law by President Andrew Jackson. With this formal authorization, Jackson,

> ... had authorization to exchange unorganized public domain in the trans-Mississippi West for Indian land in the East. Indian emigrants would receive perpetual title to their new land as well as compensation for improvements in the East and assistance in emigrating"[97]

---

[96] Berkhofer, Robert A., 1979, The White Man's Indian:158, New York, Vantage Books.
[97] Satz, Ronald N., 1974, American Indian Policy in the Jacksonian Era: 51, University of Oklahoma Press, Norman.

It must be clearly understood that it was within this political environment promoting the removal of Indian tribes to west of the Mississippi that many treaties were enacted with sovereign independent tribes. Two such treaties for example, were the July 29, 1829 Treaty at Prairie du Chien. And the September 26, 1833 Treaty at Chicago with the "United Nation of Chippewa, Ottawa and Potawatamie Indians..."[98] At the Chicago treaty proceedings[99] the following was agreed upon,

> ...The Chiefs signified a wish to have the general features of this Treaty explained...[41] By this Treaty my Children, you cede to your great father all your lands between Lake Michigan and the Mississippi River. You have made no reservations, You agree to remove.
> It provides that your great Father set apart for your use and occupancy beyond the Mississippi river as much and as good land as you have here...[42] You are required by this Treaty, my children to remove beyond the Northern boundary of Illinois within one year...[43] September 27th 1833... Gov Porter said-Yesterday- a Treaty was concluded by which the Prairie Indians ceded to their great father all the lands which they owned west of Lake Michigan...[100]

The use of the term "my children" by the Federal agents in addressing the gathered tribes is of critical importance in discerning the basis of the tribe-federal government relationship. It denoted that the gathered tribes acknowledged that the Federal government was their "Father." That is, the tribes present were politically subordinate to the United States. If such were not the case, the gathered chiefs would have protested and insisted upon the use of the term "brother" as a signifier of a relationship as sovereign equals.

---

[98] Kappler, Charles J., 1904, Indian Affairs. Laws and Treaties, Volume II, Treaties:402, Washington, Government Printing Office.
[99] Journal of the Proceedings of a Treaty between the United States and the United Tribes of Pottawatamies, Chippeway & Ottawas. Chicago, Cook County Illinois. September 26, 1833. Treaties Ratified and Unratified NARA Washington D.C., T494, Roll 3:40-43.
[100] Tucker, Sarah J. 1942, Indian Villages of the Illinois Country, Volume II, Scientific Papers, Illinois State Museum, Springfield Plate LII. Map of Lands Ceded by the Potawatamies north of 1829 cession to the Michigan territory.

The underlying goal of this treaty was the removal of the Chippewa, Ottawa, and Potawatomi from northern Illinois and their eventual removal westward out of the state to federal lands west of the Mississippi River. The three were recognized treaty tribes. These newly vacated lands would then be surveyed, new townships established, and the newly surveyed lands would be made available to settlers via sale at public auction by the Federal government's General Land Office.

This national removal policy did not encompass all Indian groups and communities. The Removal Act bought into sharp focus the Federal government's policy distinction between independent tribes and tribal remnants residing within the various states.[101]

>Report of the Committee on Indian Affairs, February 24, 1830; Removal of Indians.
>
>The Committee on Indian Affairs, to whom were referred that part of the first Message of the President which relates to "Indian Affairs;" and also sundry Resolutions and Memorials upon the same subject, make the following report...
>
>...The Governor of the only one of the old States, except Georgia, inhabited by any considerable number of Indians, is, by law, a standing Commissioner to treat with the Indians for any and all their lands...One of the first acts of most of the States, after assuming jurisdiction over the Indians, has been to declare unequivocally, their utter incompetency to make a contract upon equal terms with the whites, or which should, in equity and good conscience, be enforced against them.
>
>Their lands and persons are both taken in wardship; and the members of ancient and independent communities appear no sooner to have yielded up their political privileges, than they have been declared in a state of pupilage and incapable of managing their own affairs. Most of the tribes in the old States have guardians, under some denomination or other,

---

[101] U.S. Congress. House. 21st Cong., 1st sess. 1830. Rep. 227.

appointed by law to take charge of their property... It appears to this committee, that when it is conceded, as it must be, that a State or nation cannot exist, except in connection with territory, the single consideration of the nature of the title under which the Indian tribes occupy their reservations, is decisive of the extent of their separate *political privileges.* [emphasis added]

As noted earlier, in 1832, the United States Supreme Court (*Worcester v. Georgia*) concurred with Congress on the jurisdictional limits of federal law regarding Indians no longer capable of self-government[102] residing within a State,

> The Federal Government has the exclusive regulation of the intercourse with the Indians, and so long as this power shall be exercised it cannot be obstructed by a State. *But, if a contingency shall occur, which shall render the Indians who reside in a state incapable of self-government, either by moral denigration or reduction of their numbers, it would undoubtedly be in the power of a State government to extend to them the aegis of its laws. Under such circumstances, the agency of the Federal Government, of necessity, must cease...*

> ...some of the old states, *Massachusetts, Connecticut, Rhode Island and others*, where small remnants of tribes remain, *surrounded by white population*, and who, by their reduced numbers, *had lost the power of self government*, the laws of the state have been extended over them, for the protection of their persons and property. (emphasis added)

The Court agreed with what had been the yardstick for determining state jurisdiction since the Revolutionary War, the ability to independently self-govern and the holding of non-ceded tribal lands. Indian tribes that maintained the ability to independently govern themselves and continued to hold non-ceded lands came under the aegis of federal jurisdiction, namely, they were protected by the Trade

---

[102] Digest of Decisions Relating to Indian Affairs, HR 538, 56th Cong., 2nd sess., Vol. 1.:545,:580

and Intercourse Acts. As such, they were recognized as sovereign powers via treaty by the Federal government; hence a government-to-government relationship via treaty, as authorized by the U.S. Constitution, existed. State governments could not enter into such a relationship with a sovereign tribe. A state attempting to establish a government-to-government relationship with an independent Indian tribe would be in violation of federal law and the Constitution. Only the President with the advice and consent of the Senate, under the Constitution, was vested with such authority. Non-independent tribal remnants residing within a state were considered wards under the jurisdiction of state law. A government-to-government political relationship was not possible, as the remnant group had previously yielded its political independence and territory to the state,[103]

> On Removal of Indians, Senate, February 22, 1830.
> Report from the Committee on Indian Affairs.
>
> Mr. White made the following report:
>
> > Every thing which relates to those *Indian tribes or nations, with which we have political relations, created or regulated by treaties* is becoming, every year, more and more interesting; especially those relating to such as reside within any of the States of the Union, or of the territories belonging to it…, *that the second section of the second article of the Constitution, which gives to the President, with the advice and consent of two-thirds of the Senate, power to make treaties, has no application to the Indians within the charted limits of any of the States; nor the eighth section of the first article, which gives Congress power to regulate commerce with the Indian tribes.* That if Indians can be treated with, it must be those only who *reside out of the limits of the States*, and those with whom commerce may be regulated, must be similarly situated; otherwise, that part of the second section of the first article, which forbids the enumeration of the Indians residing within the States, and "not taxed" will be without appropriate meaning… [emphasis added]

---

[103] Register of Debates in Congress, 21 Cong., 1st sess., 1830, 1: 92-98.

In 1852, the *Vieaze v. Moor* decision also affirmed that it was only with tribes external to state jurisdiction that a treaty relationship could be created or to whom Congress's authority under the "commerce" clause could be asserted. On the other hand, the nature of the state-Indian relationship was one of dependency,[104]

> May 19, 1830, Debate on House of Representatives Bill 319.
> (by Representative Lamar)
>
> ...What, then, has been the conduct of the States towards the Indians within their limits? *In Connecticut, the State legislature has extended its jurisdiction over them, and exercised all acts of legislation necessary and incident to her sovereign character. She has appointed overseers or supervisors for them, and entertains no more distrust of her authority in legislating for them, than for persons of color, idiots, lunatics, or minors.* If it is yielded that if she can interfere at all in their municipal regulations, either in restraining their privileges, or defining and securing their rights, the principle is admitted, and the manner of enforcing this authority is conferred on the States...*In Massachusetts, the same unlimited acts of sovereignty have been exerted....* [emphasis added]

In fact, when the Federal government raised the question of Indian removal to west of the Mississippi, President Jackson already considered the remnant tribes in states such as those in New England to be under state jurisdiction,[105]

> Just before the Georgia laws establishing jurisdiction [over the Cherokee] were to go into effect, the Congress considered Jackson's proposed Indian Removal Act, and in acrimonious debate, members of both houses made their position clear...The president's and the bill's supporters called the northern and eastern congressmen hypocrites, since *"the Indians in New York, New England and Virginia etc etc"* had already been left *"to the tender mercies of those States,"*.... [emphasis added]

---

[104] U.S. Congressional Documents and Debates, 1774-1873, 7th Cong., 1st sess.: 139-147.
[105] McDonald, Forrest, 1990, States' Rights and the Union: Imperium in Imperio, 1776-1876 :100 Lawrence, University Press of Kansas.

Jackson's predecessor, President James Monroe, concurred. Monroe considered these remnants to be so insignificant as that these groups did not qualify for removal to west of the Mississippi. In an 1824 letter to the Secretary of War, Monroe stated,[106]

> ...The arrangements for removal, it is presumed, is not intended to comprehend the small remnants of tribes in Maine, Massachusetts, Connecticut, Rhode Island, Virginia, and South Carolina...Maine: St John Indians, Passamaquoddies, Penobscots; Massachusetts: Mashpee, Herring Pond, Martha's Vineyard, Troy; Rhode Island: Narragansetts; Connecticut: Mohegan, Stonington, Groton;...

President Monroe also noted that in his opinion, remnant tribes residing in New York in 1819, were in a similar situation. He noted,[107]

> It is believed that those pieces [of Indian reservation lands] at Onondaga, Oneida, Stockbridge and St. Regis are vested in this state, and the others in the United States, all subject to the right of possession by Those Indians during their residence thereon.

In June 1834, the Trade and Intercourse Acts underwent their final metamorphosis. The area of application of this Act was clearly delineated in Sections 1, 2, 12, and 24. Indian country, as defined by this Act, was generally located on territorial lands west of the Mississippi. Section 1, in part, reflected the intent of the Indian Removal Act of February 1830 ("A Bill to provide for the removal of the Indian tribes within any of the States and Territories, and for their permanent settlement West of the river Mississippi.")[108] In 1834, a new version of

---

[106] American State Papers, Documents, Legislative and Executive of the Congress of the United States, Vol. II: 542, Indian Affairs.
[107] Adelaid, R. 1965 "Documents of the States of the USA 1789-1904:*587*, Albany, N.Y.: Krause Reprints.
[108] HR 287, 21st Cong., 1st sess., February 24, 1830.

the Trade and Intercourse Act was enacted. The 1802 Indian Trade and Intercourse Act was specifically repealed in Section 29 except for one very important proviso. This proviso stated that the new sections in the 1834 Act would not; *"impair or effect the intercourse act of eighteen hundred and two, so far as the same relates to, or concerns Indian tribes residing east of the Mississippi..."* This proviso meant that Section 19 of the 1802 Act remained in effect,

> ...Sec.19. *And be it further enacted, That nothing in this act shall be construed to prevent any trade or intercourse with Indians living on lands surrounded by settlements of the citizens of the United States, and being within the ordinary jurisdiction of any of the individual states...*

> An Act to regulate trade and intercourse with the Indian tribes, and to preserve peace on the frontiers, June 30, 1834.

> *Be it enacted by the Senate and House of Representatives of the United States of America in Congress assembled,* That all that part of the United States west of the Mississippi river, and not within the states of Missouri and Louisiana, or the territory of Arkansas, and also, *that part of the United States east of the Mississippi river, and not within any state to which Indian title has not been extinguished, for the purposes of this act, be taken and deemed to be the Indian country.*

> ...Sec. 24. *And be it further enacted,* That for the sole purpose of carrying this act into effect, all that part of the Indian country west of the Mississippi river, that is bounded north by the north line of lands assigned to the Osage tribe of Indians, produced east to the state of Missouri; west by the Mexican possessions; south by Red river; and east, by the west line of the territory of Arkansas and the state of Missouri, shall be, and hereby is, annexed to the territory of Arkansas; and that for the purpose aforesaid, the residue of Indian country west of the said Mississippi river shall be, and hereby is, annexed to the judicial district of Missouri; and for the purpose aforesaid, the several portions of Indian country east of said Mississippi river, shall be, and are hereby, severally annexed to the territory in which they are situate...

> ...Sec.29. An be it further enacted, That the following acts and parts of acts shall be, and the same are hereby repealed, namely:... An act to regulate trade and intercourse with the Indian tribes and to preserve peace on the frontiers, approved March thirty, eighteen hundred and two; an act supplementary to the act passed thirtieth March eighteen hundred and two, to regulate trade and intercourse with the Indian tribes, and to preserve peace on the frontiers, approved April twenty-ninth eighteen hundred and sixteen...
>
> ...*Provided however, That such repeal shall not effect [affect] any rights acquired, or punishments, penalties, or forfeitures incurred, under either of the acts or parts of acts, nor impair or affect the intercourse act of eighteen hundred and two, so far as the same relates to, or concerns Indian tribes residing east of the Mississippi...* [emphasis added][109]

In sum, it is clear that the enacted federal policy of Indian removal to west of the Mississippi was applicable only to federally- recognized treaty tribes. Remnant Indian groups residing within a state were under state jurisdiction upon state-owned lands to be gradually "civilized" and "assimilated." The removal legislation and its enactment remained consistent with the basis premise of colonial and federal Indian policy which was the maintenance of peace with tribes on the borders via legislation and the establishment of treaty relations with these sovereign tribes. The secondary goal was to bring such tribes under the legal jurisdiction of the United States. The recognition of a tribe as an absolute sovereign was fundamental to the policy and process. Congress was to radically alter this fundamental tenet.

---

[109] U.S. Congressional Documents and Debates, 1774-1873, 23rd Cong., 1st sess., Ch. 161.

Chapter 4.

"...mere domestic communities" The March 3, 1871 Congressional Proviso

> "It is undoubtedly a well established principle in the exposition of statutes, that every part is to be considered, and the intention of the legislature to be extracted from the whole"
>
> United States Supreme Court, *United States v. Fisher*, 2 Cranch 358, 385 (1805)

Perhaps one of the most misunderstood and undervalued actions of the United States Congress in regard to Federal Indian policy was a simple sixty-four word "proviso" attached to the 1872 Indian spending bill. This proviso forever altered the nature of Federal Indian policy. Not only did the proviso end the practice of treaty-making with Indian tribes and by extension, the congressional recognition of such tribes as sovereign political entities, but it also radically altered the fundamental basis of Indian policy. Congress was no longer in "commerce" with Indian tribes Congress became the paternalistic plenary authority over them.

In the aftermath of the Civil War, the Federal government's attention again focused upon the western half of the nation and its settlement. At the same time, the government was attempting to pay down the huge debts incurred as a result of the war and the following reconstruction of the South. As a result, Congress, especially the House of Representatives, was concerned with growing expenditures as well as opening up the western territories for settlement and eventual statehood.

Traditionally within Congress, the House of Representatives held the monetary purse strings, while the Senate initiated legislative actions such as treaty affirmations. Committees from the two bodies reconciled the tensions between what was desired and what was fiscally permissible.

Indian affairs, namely the yearly cost of fulfilling the obligations agreed to in treaties with recognized Indian tribes, was a concern to the House. At this time a growing number of Senators were coming to a common realization—the granting of recognition status to those remaining reservation-bound and non-sovereign Indian tribes was compounding a political fallacy and placing an unwarranted burden on the national treasury.

"…generally it is the power of the Senate to decide"

The House of Representatives, alarmed over the growing obligatory expenditures for the supported treaty tribes, wanted a greater say in the matter of tribal recognition and treaties. During this time period treaties with Indian tribes took three forms. These types were spelled out by Commissioner of Indian Affairs George Manypenny in his 1856 annual report,[110]

> These treaties with but a few exceptions of a specific character, be separated into three classes: first treaties of peace and friendship; second, treaties of acquisition, with a view of colonizing the Indians on the reservations; third, treaties of acquisition, and providing for the permanent settlement of the individuals of the tribes, at once or in the future, on separate tracts of land or homesteads, and for the gradual abolition of the tribal character.....

---

[110] Senate Executive Document no. 5, 34th Congress, 3rd session, serial 875:571-575

In his December 1869 "Annual Report of the Commissioner of Indian Affairs"[111], Commissioner Ely Parker, a Seneca Indian, expressed his misgivings over the continuation of treaty-making with Indian tribes,

> Arrangements now, as heretofore, will doubtless be required with tribes desiring to be settled upon reservations for the relinquishment of their rights to the lands claimed by them and for assistance in sustaining themselves in a new position, but I am of the opinion that they should not be of a treaty nature. It has become a matter of serious import whether the treaty system in use ought longer to be continued. In my judgment it should not. *A treaty involves the idea of a compact between two or more sovereign powers, each possessing sufficient authority and force to compel a compliance with the obligations incurred.* The Indian tribes of the United States are not sovereign nations, capable of making treaties, as none of them have an organized government of such inherent strength as would secure a faithful obedience of its people in the observance of compacts of this character. They are held to be wards of the government, and the only title the law concedes to them to the lands they occupy or claim is a mere possessory one. But, because treaties have been made with them, generally for the extinguishment of their supposed absolute title to land inhabited by them, or over which they roam, they have become falsely impressed of the notion of national independence. It is time that this notion be dispelled, and the government cease the cruel farce of thus dealing with its helpless and ignorant wards....[emphasis added]

The result of these two factors, the maintenance costs of tribes and their changed political status, a number of debates ensued as yearly Indian appropriation budgets were produced. The 1871 debate on the 1872 appropriation is quite insightful,[112]

> Debate on the Lawrence Amendment to the 1871 Indian Appropriation Act, January 26, 1871.
>
> **Mr. Maynard:** I will ask the gentleman whether the regulation of diplomatic intercourse and the deciding with what people we shall hold

---

[111] House Executive Document No. 1, 41st Congress, 2nd session, serial 1414:448
[112] The Congressional Globe, 41st Congress. 3rd session, 1871: 767.

such intercourse is the work of congress or of the treaty making power?

> **Mr. Potter:** Mr. Chairman, I answer to both gentlemen *that generally it is the power of the Senate to decide with whom treaties shall be made*; but I am not willing for myself to say that the discretion of the Senate is so absolute, and can extend to such extreme cases, as the *Congress may not say that this is not a proper body or person with whom to treat; and therefore this is not a treaty.* (emphasis added)

Representative Armstrong, a Republican from the State of Pennsylvania, introduced a resolution to the House of Representatives on February 11, 1871. This resolution, in the form of House Bill 502, was titled, "To Restrain the Making of Treaties with Indian Tribes." The Bill's intent was clearly stated in Representative Armstrong's own testimony,[113]

> Debate on House of Representatives Resolution 502: To Restrain the making of Treaties with Indian Tribes, March 1, 1871.
>
> **Mr. Armstrong:** Mr. Speaker, the resolution which I had the honor to introduce early in February, and to which the honorable chairman of the committee has referred as having been embodied in the report under consideration, I am happy to believe, settles definitively the vexed and troublesome question of Indian treaties.
> The right to make treaties is vested by the Constitution in the "President, by and with the consent of the Senate." As a power vested by the direct provision of the Constitution, it is lifted beyond the control of Congress; for it is plain that it is not competent by force of mere law to withdraw a power conferred by the Constitution. But the right to determine who are nations or Powers with whom the United States will contract by treaty belongs to the political power of the Government, or in other words, the law-making power… I believe it to be fully competent for Congress to declare that this Government will not in the future recognize any foreign State or Power whom they may choose to designate, and where further recognition is in their judgment inimical to the national

---

[113] The Congressional Globe, 41st Congress, 3rd sess.pt.3:1812.

interests. *Much more may they withdraw our recognition of the national character of a people in the anomalous condition of an Indian tribe.* The recognition of one government by another is a matter of political expediency as to all future contacts and treaties. We may lawfully refuse and by law we will withdraw our recognition and will not hereafter recognize as a Power with whom we will contract by treaty, even England and France, or any other nation whatever; and such nation would have no right to interfere with such action of our sovereign discretion.

She could rightfully insist upon the fulfillment of our covenant obligations already contracted, but she could not force herself upon our continued recognition beyond the limit of our own discretion. It is a question of comity and not of absolute right.

The remedy therefore, in my judgment, consists not in the denial of the right of the President, by and with the advice and consent of the Senate, to make treaties with Indian tribes, for they stand at present recognized by all departments of the Government as competent Powers, and so long as they continue to be so recognized the Constitutional right to make treaties with them is beyond legislative control, but to withdraw our recognition of them, one and all, and the assertion by law that they shall cease hereafter to be recognized as Powers with whom we shall contract by treaty. <u>The result will be that in the future our dealings with them will be as mere domestic communities</u>, with whom we may contract, but only with the approval of Congress. They will be contracts, not treaties. Of course, such withdrawal of our recognition would not affect the validity of any treaties already lawfully made, but there is propriety in the distinct reaffirmance of our adherence to all our treaty obligations….(emphasis added)

"that no tribe of Indians shall hereafter be acknowledged…"

Armstrong's resolution was carried by the House of Representatives and was forwarded to the Senate for further debate,[114]

Senate Debate, Indian Appropriation Bill, Armstrong Amendment, March 1, 1871.

Mr. Stockton: *This provision is simply that no tribe of Indians shall hereafter be acknowledged as an independent tribe, and treated with as*

---

[114] The Congressional Globe, 41st Congress, 3rd sess., pt. 3:1823-1824.

such... we never have acknowledged their independence in any other way than by making treaties with them.

Mr. Davis: The Supreme Court have put the matter of treaties between the government of the United States and foreign nations and between the United States and the Indian tribes on precisely the same basis.

Mr. Stockton: ...*The question is, are they foreign nations? I insist that Congress has a perfect right to declare whether these tribes are independent nations in its view, for the purpose of making treaties with them or not.*

Mr. Harlan: ...But he will agree with me *that the relation of the Indian tribes to the United States and their condition is continuously changing, and nations of Indians might have been so recognized years ago may now be well regarded as having deteriorated to such an extent as to justify the adoption of this declaration on the part of Congress.*

Mr. Harlan: ...the effect of this proposition of the conference committee is to declare on the part of Congress that *hereafter we will not recognize Indian tribes residing within the limits of the United States as nations in that sense which will justify the negotiation of treaties with them hereafter.* (emphasis added)

Senator Harlan's comments echoed the opinion of Supreme Court Justice Marshal in *Worcester v. Georgia* who argued that if there was no recognition by Congress, there could be no treaty. The Resolution was passed by the Senate and was added as an amendment, or in the language of the time, a proviso, to the 1872 Indian Appropriation Act,[115]

> No Indian nation or tribe within the territory of the United States shall be acknowledged or recognized as an independent nation, tribe, or power with whom the United States may contract by treaty; but no obligation of any treaty lawfully made and ratified with any such Indian nation or tribe

---

[115] Chap. CXX.- An Act making appropriations for the current and contingent Expenses of the Indian Department, and for fulfilling Treaty Stipulations with various Indian Tribes, for the year ending June thirty, eighteen hundred and seventy-two, and for other Purposes:..., March 3, 1871.

prior to March third, eighteen hundred and seventy-one, shall be hereby invalidated or impaired.

With President Grant's signature to the legislation, the era of tribal sovereignty had ended.

Intent

Recognition as a sovereign tribe by Congress was, as we have seen in earlier chapters, a prerequisite for the establishment of a treaty relationship by the Executive branch. Thus this proviso, passed by Congress and signed into law by President Grant was a permanent prohibition against federal recognition of Indian tribes by the Federal government as sovereign political entities. Tribes were now wards of the government, "mere domestic communities". This resolution remains currently codified under 25 USC 71, sec. 2079.

Subsequent legal construction based upon of this proviso is appalling to say the least due to the lack of understanding of the original intent of Congress and a lack of comprehension of Indian policy up to 1871 by numerous jurists.

According to both the resolution's sponsor and later governmental documents, one intention of this proviso was, as Congressman Armstrong stated, "to withdraw our recognition of them…" or in other words, to simply cease recognizing Indian tribes as sovereign political entities. That is, withdrawing something that had previously been given, recognition as sovereign independent tribes and to end future treaty-making with Indian tribes. Those obligations made to tribes under cover of existing treaties would still be respected, However, the tribe itself would no longer be considered as sovereign.

Congress realized that it could not simply ban treaties, a constitutional power given to the President of the United States, with the advice and consent of the Senate. In order to prevent future Indian treaties, Congress's recognition of Indian tribes as independent political powers and sovereign tribal entities had to be legislatively prohibited. This was a power constitutionally granted to Congress to decide.

The result was a major transformation of Federal Indian policy. Indian tribes had, by virtue of this proviso, transitioned from sovereign to ward, from recognized tribe to dependent community. Commerce was no longer carried on with them as co-equals to the Federal government. They were of domestic dependent communities subject to the all-encompassing plenary powers of Congress, that is, the actions of both the House of Representatives and the Senate. So many acts of litigation were to follow to the present day due to the lack of both judicial and legislative understanding of the intentions and implications of those sixty-four words. The 1871 proviso banned the word sovereign from the lexicon of Federal Indian policy.

Chapter 5.

Under the Plenary Control of Congress

"The Indians hold the relation of wards..."

In its immediate aftermath, the 1871 proviso placed Indian tribes on a level parallel to that of a community within a state. However, instead of being communities subordinate to a state's jurisdiction, they became dependent communities subordinate to the plenary powers of Congress. The political status of Washington D.C. as a federal enclave is an analogous example to this new tribal standing. As with a state community and the District of Columbia, they had the political right to self-govern. Beyond that, they exercised no other powers. The 1886 *US v. Kagama* decision[116] gave a context to the status of such "domestic communities",

> But these Indians are within the geographical limits of the United States. The soil and the people within these limits are under the political control of the government of the United States, or of the states of the Union. There exists within the broad domain of sovereignty but these two. There may be cities, counties, and other organized bodies, with limited legislative functions, but they are all derived from, or exist in, subordination to one or the other of these.

Additionally the Department of the Interior noted,

---

[116] United States v. Kagama 118 US. 375 (1886)

> ...that hereafter no recognition by treaty or otherwise should be made by the United States of the claim of any Indian tribe as being an independent nation, tribe, or power[117]

That this proviso to the 1872 Indian Appropriation Act prohibited future recognition of any Indian tribe as a politically independent, sovereign entity is attested to in the following in the following federal documents,[118]

Report on Indians Taxed and Indians Not Taxed in the United States (except Alaska) at the Eleventh Census: 1890:663-664.

> After the government of the United States was organized the Indian was looked upon as a subject, still not a citizen. When the superintendency and agency system combined was in operation the Indians were still considered independent nations until the adoption of the reservation system, and until 1871, when President Grant ceased to treat with them as nations...the Indian tribes residing within the United States were recognized in some sense as political bodies, not as foreign nations, nor as domestic nations, but still possessing and exercising some of the functions of nationality; but by act of Congress of March 3, 1871, it was provided that hereafter no recognition by treaty or otherwise should be made by the United States of the claim of any Indian tribe as being an independent nation, tribe, or power. The Indians hold the relation of wards to the general government and are subject to its control. A state legislature has no jurisdiction over Indian territory contained within the territorial limits of the state....

The U.S. Supreme Court also noted in its 1886 *United States v. Kagama* decision that,[119]

> ...By the act of March 3, 1871, the legal fiction of recognizing the tribes as independent nations within which the United States could enter into

---

[117] Department of the Interior, Census Office, Census Reports, V.17 1894. Report on Indians Taxed and Indians Not Taxed in the United States (except Alaska) at the Eleventh Census: 1890:663-664
[118] Department of the Interior, Census Office, Census Reports, v. 17, 1894.
[119] Royce, Charles C. 1896-97, "Indian Land Cessions in the United States" : 641. in, Eighteenth Annual Report of the Bureau of American Ethnology to the Secretary of the Smithsonian Institution Washington D.C. Smithsonian Institute.

solemn treaty was, after it had continued nearly a hundred years, finally done away with. The effect of this act was to bring under the immediate control of the Congress the transactions with the Indians and to reduce to simple agreements what had before been accomplished by solemn treaties....

"The plan is obviously a wise and humane one"

Now that a new dimension to Indian policy had been enacted by the Federal government, what were its implications for Indian tribes or communities not under state jurisdiction? The Grant administration instituted a new policy that was commonly referred to as the "Peace Policy." This is a misnomer in that the maintenance of peace with Indian tribes residing on the peripheries of colonial, national, and state boundaries had been at the heart of Indian policy since its inception back in 1735. The post-Civil War difficulties with the western Indian tribes, especially the Sioux and the horrendous 1865 "Sand Creek" massacre were not the result of a flawed federal Indian policy, but, as a congressional committee concluded, of the actions of abuse by individuals.[120]

In 1867, Congress created a "Peace Commission' that was tasked to identify the causes of the growing conflict with Indian tribes and to recommend remedies. In its report[121] the Commission identified the unfettered quest for land as the root cause of the conflicts with the western tribes. At the same time, the Commission's report chided the various "missionary societies and benevolent societies" who "have annually collected thousands of dollars from the charitable, to be sent to Asia and Africa for purposes of civilization, scarcely a dollar is expended or a thought bestowed on the civilization of the Indians at our very doors. Is it because

---

[120] Report of the Doolittle Commission, "Condition of the Indian Tribes", Report of the Joint Special Committee. Senate Report 156, 39th Congress 2nd session, serial 1279:3-10
[121] House Executive Document No. 1, 40th Congress, 2nd session, serial 1366:486-510

the Indians are not worth the effort at civilization?" The Commission's paternalistic conclusion was to civilize these Indian tribes,

> Through sameness of language is produced sameness of sentiment and thought, customs and habits are moulded and assimilated in the same way, and thus in process of time the differences producing trouble would have been gradually obliterated...

The Commission concluded that,

> The object of the greatest solitude should be to break down the prejudices of tribe among the Indians; to blot out the boundary lines which divide them into distinct nations, and fuse them into one homogeneous mass. Uniformity of language will do this-nothing else will. As this work advances each head of a family should be encouraged to select and improve a homestead. Let the women be taught to weave, to sew and to knit. Let polygamy be punished. Encourage the building of dwellings, and the gathering there of those comforts which endear the home.

Stepping back, the former Jacksonian-era policy of removal in conjunction with the Louisiana Purchase, had been a success from the Government's perspective. The goals were removal of tribes to west of the Mississippi settling them on federal territorial lands as a means of maintaining peace and bringing the tribes under Federal jurisdiction. In their isolation a policy of promoting the gradual assimilation of Indians into the general population and facilitating national expansion was envisioned. That goal was almost totally achieved. As long as the national goal was to have the Mississippi River as the nation's western states' boundaries, this accomplishment was sufficient. What had not been anticipated was the rapid growth of the nations population. With the predominate social practice of male primogeniture, immigration, and the presence of lands acquired in the aftermath of the Mexican War, as well as the discovery of gold in California and later in Montana, the Mississippi River no longer proved a viable boundary. As George W. Manypenny, a Commissioner of Indian Affairs, noted in his November 1856 Annual Report,[122]

> The wonderful emigration to our newly acquired States and Territories, and its effect upon the wild tribes inhabiting them and the plains and the prairies, is well calculated at the present period to attract special attention. Not only are our settlements rapidly advancing westward from the Mississippi river towards the Pacific ocean, and from the shores of the Pacific eastward towards the Mississippi river, but large settlements have been made in Utah and New Mexico between the two…

The end of the Civil War further accelerated the need for more land. The establishment of new federal territories and states ushered in a new, yet old problem, re-emerging tensions with the Indian tribes settled within these western federal territories. How then was peace to be maintained and armed conflicts with tribes avoided? Within the vastness of these new territories, the application of the Indian Trade and Intercourse Acts were ineffective. Federal control and authority, apart from widely separated military posts and the occasional, and oftentimes corrupt, federal Indian agent, was weak. This led to a renewed emphasis upon "civilizing" the reservation-bound tribes. This policy was not new. It was common for Indian tribal remnants residing within a state under its jurisdiction to be the subject of such efforts with the ultimate goal that these wards would shed their tribal identity and become full citizens of their respective states. One such example was to be found in Connecticut wherein the Mohegan tribal remnants, residing on a state-established reservation did, en mass, in 1872,[123] vote to detribalize and assume full state citizenship including the assumption of voting

---

[122] Report of the Commissioner of Indian Affairs for the Year 1856, Senate Executive Document no. 5, 34th Congress, 3rd session, serial 875:571-575

[123] An Act conferring upon the Mohegan Indians the Privileges of Citizenship, and Regulating the Ownership, Sale, Distribution and Use of the Property sequestered for their Benefit, and also providing for the Taxation of their Polls and Ratable Estates

rights and the right to sell property as full fee-holders, and also become subject to taxation.

As early as 1869 progressive religious organizations, perhaps as a result of the 1867 Peace Commission's ringing criticism in particular, as well as concerns that management of Indians affairs might be placed under the army's jurisdiction, became the government's primary agents of change amongst the Indian tribes. A Quaker delegation convinced President Grant to appoint selected Quakers to posts as Indian Agents within the western territories.[124] President Grant's aide-de-camp, the Seneca-Iroquois union general, Ely S. Parker wrote to the Quaker Society of Friends Secretary Benjamin Hallowell[125], "any attempt which may or can be made by your Society, for the improvement, education, and Christianization of the Indians, under such Agencies, will receive…all the encouragement and protection which the laws of the United States will warrant…." As then Secretary of the Interior Knox noted, [126]

> The Friends were appointed not because they were believed to have any monopoly of honesty or good will toward the Indians, but because their selection would of itself be understood by the country to indicate the policy adopted, namely the sincere cultivation of peaceful relations with the tribes…

One year later Eli Parker, who was appointed Commissioner of Indian Affairs, commented, [127]

> The plan is obviously a wise and humane one…Under a political management for a long series of years, and the expenditure of large sums

---

[124] Tatum, Lawrie, 1899, Our Red brothers and the Peace Policy of President Ulysses S. Grant:17-19, Philadelphia, John C. Winton & Co.
[125] Kelsy, Raynor, 1917, Friends and the Indians:1655-1917:168, Philadelphia, Executive Committee of Friends on Indian Affairs.
[126] 1869, House Executive Document 1,41-42. 41st Congress, sess. 1, Report of the Secretary of the Interior.
[127] Report of the Commissioner of Indian Affairs to the Secretary of the Interior for the year 1870:474

of money annually, the Indians made but little progress toward that healthy Christian civilization in which are embraced the elements of material wealth and intellectual and moral development…the president wisely determined to invoke the cooperation of the entire religious element of the country to help, by their labors and counsels, to bring about and produce the greatest amount of good from the expenditure of the munificent annual appropriations of money by Congress for the civilization and Christianization of the Indian race.

President Grant, echoing the 1867 Peace Commission's proposals, addressed the goals of this plan in his December 1870 "Annual Message to Congress"[128] wherein he stated,

…I entertain the confident hope that the policy now pursued will in a few years bring all the Indians upon reservations, where they will live in houses, and have schoolhouses and churches, and will be pursuing peaceful and self-sustaining associations….

The isolation of Indian tribes on federally-established reservations was the cornerstone of the Presidents approach to reform the Indian and maintain peace in the West. There, apart from large-scale white contact, the process of civilization and assimilation could proceed.

In conjunction with the appointment of Quakers and representatives of other religious groups as agents to the Indian tribes, a Board of Indian Commissioners was created by legislative fiat via the 1869 Indian Appropriation Act. This Commission, not to exceed ten members selected by the president, was,[129]

"to be selected by him from men eminent for their intelligence and philanthropy, to serve without pecuniary compensation, who may under

---

[128] Richardson, James D. ed. "Messages and Papers of the Presidents", vol. 7:109-10, in Prucha, Francis, 2000, <u>Documents of United States Indian Policy</u>:134, University of Nebraska Press, Lincoln
[129] U.S. Statutes at Large, 16:40

his direction, exercise joint control with the Secretary of the Interior over appropriations made by this act or an part thereof..."

Among the powers granted to this Board by President Grant were, "make its own organization and employ its own clerical staff...shall be furnished with full opportunity to inspect the records of the Indian Office...to be present, in person of by sub-committee, at purchases of goods for Indian purposes...full power to inspect, in person or by sub-committee the various Indian superintendencies and agencies in Indian country...to be present at the payment of annuities...."[130] Ominously, President Grant clarified the principal goals of his Indian policy[131] during his first meeting with the Board on May 27, 1869. The first goal was an end to the long-established treaty system, securing, protecting, and educating the Indians who settled upon the federally-established reservations and ultimately securing title to lands that individual Indians received via allotment. The Board in turn advocated small reservations, the destruction of tribal relations, an end to treaty-making and annual annuities, the division of lands into severalty and ultimately, formal citizenship.[132]

According to the Board's report, the government's role toward the Indians as "wards of the government" was "to protect them, to educate them in industry, the arts of civilization, and the principals of Christianity" and ultimately "elevate them to the rights of citizenship, and to sustain and clothe them until they can support themselves."

---

[130] Annual Report of the Board of Indian Commissioners, 1869:3-5
[131] National Archives and Records Administration (NARA), Washington D.C., Record Group (RG) 75, Records of the Board of Indian Commissioners, Minutes of Board Meetings, Vol.1:6-7, May 27, 1869
[132] NARA. Washington D.C. RG 75, Report of the Board of Indian Commissioners for the year 1869:9-11

These actions by the Federal government, the policy of reservation settlement, Christianization and civilization of the Indian tribes and their management by the Board were propelled in part by a then prevalent post-Civil War national reformist sentiment that emerged from the Civil War era anti-slavery movement. The desire to address the costs associated with the maintenance of recognized tribes by the national treasury and the political actions associated with the 1871 Proviso (tribes now being dependent wards of the Federal government under congressional plenary authority), became the "Perfect Storm" that propelled this new federal civilization policy. This phenomena not only created a favorable political environment that facilitated the addition and passage of the 1871 proviso that ended the fiction of tribal sovereignty, but it also promoted the onset of a formal paternalistic-orientated Federal Indian policy. The impact of the 1871 proviso still is present within Federal Indian policy. This wardship-based paternalism, although not referred to as such, is still the cornerstone of the Bureau of Indian Affairs management policy for Indian affairs.

It was not long before other civic and religious-orientated groups, in addition to the Quakers were vying for the opportunity to Christianize and civilize the western tribes and to politically influence federal Indian policy. By 1872 ten different religious-affiliated philanthropic organizations and organized churches were in charge of seventy-three different Indian agencies[133]. The following denotes the various organizations and the number of Indians who were their governmentally-assigned wards,

American Board of Commissioners for Foreign Missions...41,800
Roman Catholic Church..17,856
Christian Church..8,287
Congregational Church...14,476

---

[133] U.S. Department of the Interior, A Report of the Commissioner of Indian Affairs for the year 1872:461-462. House Executive Document no. 1, 42nd Congress, 3rd session, serial1560:460-462

Friends (Hicksite faction)	6,598
Friends	17,724
Lutheran Church	273
Methodist	54,473
Presbyterian	38,069
Episcopal	26,929
Reformed Dutch	8,300
Unitarian	3,800

These seventy-three agencies were in essence missions whose goal was the religious conversion and civilization of the Indian tribes. As Commissioner of Indian Affairs Francis Walker noted, [134]

> The importance of securing harmony of feeling and concert of action between agents of the Government and the missionaries at the several agencies, in the matter of moral and religious advancement of the Indians, was the single reason formally given for placing the nominations to Indian agencies in the hands of denominational societies.

Civilizing the tribes was not a new or novel idea. As early as 1816, the continued policy of civilization was being promoted by Secretary of War William Crawford. He wrote in a May 13, 1816 letter to the US. Senate, [135]

> The amelioration in their condition desired by the Government has continued to advance, but in so slight a degree as to be perceptible only after a lapse of years. If the civilization of the Indian tribes is considered an object of primary importance, and superior to that of rapidly extinguishing their titles and settling their lands by the whites, the expediency of continuing the system now in operation, under such modifications as have been suggested by the experience already acquired, appears to be manifest.

In this situation, Secretary Crawford was arguing for the continuation of government trading posts as the means of inducing such civilizing behaviors.

---

[134] ibid.:461
[135] American State Papers: Indian Affairs Vol.2:26-28

In his 1838 annual report,[136] Commissioner of Indian Affairs T. Hartley Crawford promoted ideas presented to him by the Missionary Society of the Methodist Episcopal Church concerning the civilization of the Indian tribes. Commissioner Crawford promoted their ideas,

> The principal lever by which the Indians are to be lifted out of the mire of folly and vice is education…based upon the idea suggested for establishing a large central school for the education of the Western Indians…that separate schools for the respective tribes…are not so useful as one common school for the benefit of all…knowledge of the English language is necessary…the government of the western tribes of Indians contemplates an interior police of their own…there shall be a separate allotment of land to each individual….Common property and civilization cannot co-exist…They are governed, and their legislation by each community for itself…supervised and controlled by the parent country [tribe]

Elements within this proposal clearly anticipated those contained in the future Dawes Allotment Act and the 1934 Indian Reorganization Act.

In his November 1851 "Annual report of the Commissioner of Indian Affairs", the Commissioner stated, "The civilization of the Indians within the territory of the United States is a cherished object of the government…any plan for the civilization of our Indians will, in my judgment be fatally defective, if it do not provide, in the most efficient manner, their ultimate incorporation into the great body of our citizen population."[137]

Also of interest is the lack of a religious conversion aspect. This was to change. In 1869 the civilizing agent was to be the government-appointed missionary. As President Grant noted in 1870,[138]

---

[136] Senate Document No. 1, 25th Congress, 3rd Session, serial 338:450-451,:454-456
[137] House Executive Document no. 2, 32nd Congress, 1st session, serial 636:273-274
[138] Richardson, James D. ed. "Messages and Papers of the Presidents", vol. 7:109-10, in Prucha, Francis,

Reform in the management of Indian Affairs has received the special attention of the Administration from its inauguration to the present day. The experiment of making it a missionary work was tried in a few agencies given to the denomination of Friends, and has been found to work most advantageously....

In theory, this plan appeared logically consistent. In practical application, it was fatally flawed. It assumed that the reservation-bound Indian population wanted to change *en mass* ideologically, culturally, and economically. Some desired to, but many did not. Tradition and change were at loggerheads.

Missionary agents from many denominations, of varying competency and theological persuasions, especially in terms of their respective theological positions in understanding human nature, vied to save the souls of their Indian brethren. These numerous organizations lacked a coherent and consistent policy as to how to Christianize their wards and how to alter their cultural norms and social behaviors. Inter-denominational bickering further affected the effectiveness of their activities. Perhaps the greatest impediment to their efforts was the continued political effectiveness of those who profited from the corruption within the Interior Department, especially after the appointment of Christopher Delano as Secretary of the Interior in 1870. These missionary/agents were also ignorant of the dire psychological consequences of attempting to induce rapid and disorientating change within a population. One need only look back to the eighteenth century missionary efforts of John Mayhew and the Gay Head Indians residing upon Martha's Vineyard and those of the Moravian Missionaries of western Connecticut and Eastern New York. Both were relatively successful in that they allowed ideological and social change to gradually occur within the individual whilst allowing the Indians to continue normative economic and social

---

2000, <u>Documents of United States Indian Policy</u>:134, University of Nebraska Press, Lincoln

patterns. Forcing both internal and external change simultaneously on large populations was pre-ordained to failure. The body of these appointed missionary agents contained saints, and sinners, as well as politically-connected rouges and idealist reformers who oftentimes were ill-prepared to carry out such a complex task amongst peoples they knew so little of.

Within a broader context, with the ending of treaty-making with Indian tribes in 1871 by Congress and the Grant administration, all tribes subject to federal jurisdiction were now treated as dependant wards. The fiction of tribal sovereignty had been eliminated. This new perspective of Indian tribes allowed for the appearance of an Indian policy based upon a paternalistic perspective by the public and federal authorities that in turn led to the development of a national Indian policy of conversion and civilization. The eventual goal of this policy was the destruction of tribal organization and the assumption by individual Indians of their rightful place as full-fledged citizens of the Republic. In doing so, this policy advocated the settlement of all Indian tribes upon federal reservations wherein the dual process of conversion and civilization of the Indians could occur, in the process, freeing the Indian from tribalism and perceived primitive beliefs. This policy envisioned that each adult Indian would eventually receive an allotment of federal reservation lands upon which to establish a homestead and to practice the art of industry and the eventual attainment of citizenship. What remained to be established was a formal institutionalized process to achieve these ends.

Chapter 6.

Working Towards the "Dawes Act."

Official governmental paternalism and evolving dependency derived from the 1871 proviso coupled with socio-religious activism and excessive governmental expenditures led to the ultimate manifestation of these impulses into what was to become known as the "Dawes" Allotment Act. It will be recalled that in 1838 Indian Commissioner T. Hartley Crawford first advocated, as part of his policy, how the Indians "are to be lifted out of the mire of folly..." by "a separate allotment of land to each individual." Allotment itself was not a new idea. Several treaties, especially those with treaty tribes within the Illinois- Wisconsin- Michigan region such as the Stockbridge-Munsee and the Saganaw Chippewa had allotment language in them. Many others did not. Allotment's time had come.

"No general law exists..."

In his October 30, 1876 "Annual Report"[139] to Congress, Commissioner John Q. Smith advanced three principles of Indian policy to modify the existing under-performing policy then in place. Commissioner Smith advocated,

> First. Concentration of all Indians on a few reservations
> Second. Allotment to them of lands in severalty.
> Third. Extension over them of United States law and the jurisdiction of United States Courts.

---

[139] House Executive Document No.1, 44th Congress, 2nd session, Serial 1749:vii-xi

Regarding his allotment proposal, Commissioner Smith went on to say,

> It is doubtful whether any high degree of civilization is possible without individual ownership of land…No general law exists which provides that Indians shall select allotments in severalty, and it seems to me a matter of great moment that provision should be made not only permitting, but requiring, the head of each Indian family, to accept the allotment of a reasonable amount of land, to be the property of himself and his lawful heirs, in lieu of any interest in any common tribal possession. Such allotments should be inalienable for at least twenty, perhaps fifty years, and if situated in a permanent Indian reservation, should be transferable only among Indians.

In November of 1880, Secretary of the Interior Carl Schurtz noted to Congress[140] that,

> Bills have been submitted to Congress for two sessions providing for the division of farm tracts among the Indians in severalty on their respective reservations; the issuance of patents to them individually and their investment in fee-simple title to their farms inalienable for a certain number of years until they have presumed to overcome the improvident habits in which a large part of the present generation have grown up; and this being accomplished, for the disposition of the residue of the reservations not occupied and used by the Indians, with their consent and for their benefit, to white settlers….

The idea of allotting land to Indians was one of long standing. As early as 1665, we find the General Court of Plymouth Colony establishing an English-style plantation wherein Indian Christian converts of Cape Cod could settle as in an English plantation. Lands were allotted to members, community common lands were designated and Indian constables appointed. These "South Sea Indians" later became known as the Mashpee, an Indian community that is still in existence. As we shall see, this Mashpee model was to bear a strong resemblance to what became known as the Dawes Act; lands were divided in severalty, alienation of

---

[140] House Executive Document No. 1, 46th Congress, 3rd session, serial 19593-4

lands was restricted, educational services were provided by the Colony, there was a strong church presence, and the presence of a community constabulary.

It was a fundamental tenant of Indian policy that the Indians' relationship to the land had to be altered as to negate the influence of tribalism and to develop a vested interest in private land ownership as a means towards civilization and citizenship. Yet in the early days of the Republic, there was another aspect to the notion of allotting lands to Indians. It was altruistic in nature. The historical record depicts President Jefferson attempting to put a halt to the practice of unscrupulous tribal chiefs selling tribal lands from under their feet.[141] As an example, in 1833 a treaty was made with the gathered chiefs of the "Chippewa, Ottawa and Potawatamie Indians" at Chicago.[142] In this treaty the "Potawatomis" ceded their remaining lands in northern Illinois and agreed to move west of the Mississippi River within one year. One Pottawatomie village chief, Shabenay, agreed to sell his band's lands in return for a yearly two hundred dollar stipend. In addition, unbeknownst to his band members, he was to receive fee simple ownership to his village tract (1,280 acres) at Shabbona in Dekalb County, Illinois. These were the very lands he ceded to the federal agents in the treaty. After his band removed west to Council Bluffs, Missouri, Shabenay later returned to Illinois believing that he had a fee-parcel of land of his own. Little did he know that in 1833, prior to ratification of the treaty, the Senate removed his special land provision.[143] To this day, descendants of his band still revile his name. To Jefferson's way of thinking, if Shabenay's band had individual land allotments, their chief could not have sold their lands at Shabbona and then surreptitiously regained sole possession of it

---

[141] Lipscomb, Andrew A. ed., Writings of Thomas Jefferson, Vol.XVI:452-453. December 21, 1808 Address to Indian chiefs.
[142] Kappler, Charles J., 1904, Indian Affairs Laws and Treaties, Vol.II:402. Government Printing Office Washington.
[143] Illinois State Archives, Springfield, RG 592.363 Records, Dixon Land Office, Indian Files.

"in atonement for what we have inflicted"

However, Jefferson's opinion concerning Indian land allotment was in a minority. Allotment as a civilizing tool was the primary rationale used in the argument for allotment. We find two strains of thought regarding allotment of lands to Indians. It centered upon the question of reservation consolidation as first advocated by Commissioner John Q. Smith in 1876, noted earlier. In September 1884, the Indian Rights Association, a leading reformist organization, resolved at their second annual meeting,[144]

> That careful observation has conclusively proved that the removal of Indians from reservations which they have long occupied, to other reservations far distant from the former and possessing different soil and climate, is attended by great suffering and loss of life. Such removals destroy the fruits of past industry and discourage the Indians from further efforts in the habits of civilized life…When the removal of an Indian tribe becomes a necessity, individual Indians belonging to the tribe who have formed settled homes should have the privilege of taking homesteads upon the lands they occupy prior to the opening of the reservation….

The following year, Secretary of the Interior Lucius Lamar also considered the concept of reservation consolidation as ill-considered. He noted,[145]

> The policy of change and unsettlement should give way to that of fixed homes with security of title and possession, and hereafter the civilizing influences and forces already at work among the Indians should be pushed forward upon the lands which they now occupy.

---

[144] Second Annual Address to the Public of The Lake Mohonk Conference Held at Lake Mohonk, N.Y., September1884:15-16 Philadelphia Executive Committee of the Indian Rights Association.
[145] Annual Report of the Secretary of the Interior for the Year 1885, House Executive Document no.1, part 5, vol.I:49 serial 2378,

Earlier in 1880, Commissioner Carl Schurz declared his support for the concept of allotment. Allotment, he noted, [146]

> ...is a measure correspondent with the progressive age in which we live, and is indorsed by all true friends of the Indian, as evidenced by the numerous petitions to this effect presented to Congress from citizens of various states.

That same year, Commissioner Schurz originated the first substantial piece of allotment legislation, a bill that was to become known as the "Coke Bill".[147] This bill addressed all Indian tribes under federal jurisdiction. Although it did not become a law, this bill contained the key elements that were contained in the 1887 Dawes Allotment legislation as to acreage allotments, patents, and a twenty-five year trust period. These very elements were contained in allotment legislation aimed at specific Indian tribes, such as the Crow in April 1882[148], the Omahas in August 1882[149], and the Umatillas in March 1885[150].

Senator Henry Dawes of Massachusetts, whose name is forever linked to the forthcoming 1887 Act unofficially bearing his name, viewed allotment as a form of restitution for the perceived injustices inflicted upon the American Indian. In 1885, Senator Dawes spoke before the Friends of the Indian Association conference at Lake Mohonk, New York. The Senator stated,[151]

---

[146] Report of the Commissioner of Indian Affairs for the year 1880: xvii
[147] The Congressional Record, Vol. X:3507, May 19, 1880
[148] 22 Stat. 42 (April 11, 1882, Kappler, Charles J., 1904, Indian Affairs: Laws and Treaties vol.I:195-196, Washington D.C. Government Printing Office
[149] 22 Stat. 341 (April 7, 1882), Kappler, Charles J., 1904, Indian Affairs: Laws and Treaties vol.I:212-215, Washington D.C. Government Printing Office
[150] 23 Stat. 340 (March 3, 1885) Kappler, Charles J., 1904, Indian Affairs: Laws and Treaties vol.I:224-228, Washington D.C. Government Printing Office
[151] Proceedings of the Third Annual Meeting of the Lake Mohonk Conference of the Friends of the Indian

Those who controlled the Government tried every method to get rid of the burden of the Indian. We broke our treaties with him and drove him out of his reservations; we hunted him with our arms; we spent millions of dollars in endeavoring to slay him; but all in vain...

I feel just this; that every dollar of money, and every hour of effort that can be applied to each individual Indian, day and night, in season and out of season, with patience and perseverance, with kindness and with charity, is not only due him in atonement for what we have inflicted upon him in the past, but is our own obligation towards him in order that we may not have him as a vagabond and a pauper, without home or occupation among us in this land....

By 1886 as a matter of policy, the Bureau of Indian Affairs began, as a matter of policy, to instruct its field agents to begin promoting the idea of reservation-based land allotment to their Indian wards.[152] This policy was publicly supported by President Cleveland in his 1886 annual message to Congress [153].

"There is nothing more dangerous to an Indian reservation than a rich mine...."

Underlying the general reformist drive for allotment and the civilization and assimilation of the Indian was an undercurrent of economic expediency that provided additional impetus for the wholesale adoption of land allotment. In addition to being a means for reducing government support costs by promoting assimilation, the allotment concept also stood for Indian land preservation via the fee allotment of sections to individual Indians. We touched lightly on this issue earlier noting the practice of some tribal chiefs to convey collectively-shared tribal lands out from under the feet of their tribal constituents. Additional

---

[152] Report of the Commissioner of Indian Affairs for the Year 1886, October 7-9, 1885:35,:37, Philadelphia Sherman & Company Printers
[153] Otis, Delos S., 1934 (1973 ed.) The Dawes Act and the Allotment of Indian Land:6, Norman University of Oklahoma Press.

protection of the land was afforded by the allotment of lands to the individual in fee patent. In theory this would curtail encroachment-related abuses that had occurred earlier. On the other hand, when the Dawes Act was finally enacted in February 1887[154] the excess lands on the expansive western reservations, that is, those lands not actually needed for allotment purposes, became surplus and available for sale to non-Indians. In his 1880 Annual Report, Secretary of the Interior Carl Schurz provided his thoughts on the relationship between allotment and the opening of reservation lands to non-Indians in regard to the pending "Coke" allotment bill, a bill that Senator Harry M. Teller of Colorado declared was "a bill to despoil the Indians of their lands and to make them vagabonds on the face of the earth."[155] The House Indian Affairs Committee concurred with Senator Teller's understanding of the implications of, and the motives behind, the Coke legislation,[156]

> The real aim of this bill is to get at the Indian lands and open them up to settlement. The provisions for the apparent benefit of the Indian are but the pretext to get at his lands and occupy them....

Secretary Schurz, on the other hand believed that by enacting allotment, surplus reservation lands,[157]

> ...will eventually open up to settlement by white men the large tracts of land now belonging to the reservations, but not used by the Indians. It will thus put the relations between the Indians and their white neighbors in the western country upon a new basis, by gradually doing away with the system of large reservations....

---

[154] 24 Stat. 388. Chap 119 49th Congress, 2nd sess.
[155] The Congressional Record vol. XI:934 (January 26, 1881)
[156] House report No. 1576:10, 46th Congress, 2nd session, serial 1938 (1880)
[157] Report of the Secretary of the Interior for the year 1880, House Executive Document No. 1, pt. 5:12, 46th Congress, 3rd session serial 1959.

Dawes' enactment also opened up great opportunities for land and mineral speculation. As Commissioner of Indian Affairs Carl Schurz noted in 1881,[158]

> There is nothing more dangerous to an Indian reservation than a rich mine. But the repeated invasions of the Indian Territory, as well as many similar occurrences have shown clearly enough that the attraction of good agricultural lands is apt to have the same effect, especially great railroads enterprises are pushing in the same direction.

Dawes, which was intended to protect Indian lands, instead provided a stimulus and means for its loss. The reformist agenda that promoted detribalization and the end to the collective reservation, became allied with those economic interests seeking to profit from allotment. Senator Dawes, speaking at the 1887 "Friends of the Indian" Conference at Lake Mohonk, New York addressed the phenomena when he stated,[159]

> The Indian of the past has no has no place to live in this country. You talk about the necessity of doing away with the reservation system; a power that you can never resist has broken it up into homesteads, has taken possession of it, has driven the game from out of it…The railroad has gone through there, and it is black with emigrants ready to take advantage of it…The greed of these people for the land has made it utterly impossible to preserve it for the Indian.

What of the railroads? Beginning in 1888, the Federal government granted 106 railroad "rights of ways" through Indian reservations and territories.[160] These grants oftentimes created twenty mile wide swaths through Indian lands.[161] The

---

[158] Quoted in, Otis, Delos S., 1934 (1973 ed.) The Dawes Act and the Allotment of Indian Land:13, Norman University of Oklahoma Press.
[159] Fifth Annual Address to the Public of The Lake Mohonk Conference Held at Lake Mohonk, N.Y., September1887:68 Philadelphia Executive Committee of the Indian Rights Association.
[160] Kappler, Charles J., 1904, Indian Affairs: Laws and Treaties vol.I:1136-1139- Washington D.C. Government Printing Office
[161] 1886, Proceedings of the Third Annual Meeting of the Lake Mohonk Conference, October 7-9, 1885:44, Philadelphia, Sherman & Company.

effect of the railroads upon the reservation-bound Indians was noted by the Indian Rights Association in its 1887 Annual Report,[162]

> If any person accustomed to weight evidence could still think it possible to maintain the old system of the isolation of the Indians, and to perpetuate the common ownership of their lands, a little reflection upon the relations of the railroads of the country to the Indian reservations would be sufficient to expel this delusion from his mind finally and forever…This process of opening up the reservations to railroads is certain to continue. In most cases the Indians themselves are in favor of it, thus showing they have a truer conception of the meaning of civilization than is exhibited by the opponents of the severalty law….

"the road our fathers walked is gone."

Together, political, economic, and philanthropic impulses propelled the concept of allotment towards its 1887 enactment as a federal statute. They were the cost to the national treasury of maintaining Indian tribes on their reservations the need to bring peace to the western half of the country, the needs of a migrating population for land, the growing economic demand for natural resources, and the liberal progressive paternalistic -assimilative ideology prevalent, especially in the northeastern portion of the country.

But such a change in national policy could not occur until the legal roadblock of tribal sovereignty was removed. That was accomplished by Congress in March of 1871. In affirmation, the 1886 United States Supreme Court decision in *US. v. Kagama*[163] reaffirmed that there were only two sovereigns, the national government and those of the states. From 1871 onwards all Indian tribes residing on federal lands were legally considered dependent wards of the Federal government. Tribes on federal lands under its jurisdiction were now considered

---

[162] Quoted in, Otis, Delos S., 1934 (1973 ed.) The Dawes Act and the Allotment of Indian Land:30, Norman University of Oklahoma Press
[163] 118 US 375

"domestic communities." Those Indian communities within state boundaries, on state land were subject to the states jurisdiction. The application of land allotments to individual tribes already subject to federal jurisdiction was commonplace as in the February 8, 1871 "Act for the relief of the Stockbridge and Munsee tribe of Indians in the State of Wisconsin"[164] wherein inalienable allotments to individual heads of Indian families were carried out. The surplus land was to be made available to the State of Wisconsin.

The belief during this era was that the Indian had no choice but to conform to the national ethos of liberal progressive change. Allotment and detribalization formed the millstone of assimilation. As one elderly Omaha Indian remarked, "the road our fathers walked is gone."[165] The new road to be tread was fraught with dangers.

---

[164] 16 Stat. 404 in Kappler, Charles J., 1904, Indian Affairs: Laws and Treaties vol.I:128-131 Washington D.C. Government Printing Office

[165] Fletcher, Alice C., LaFlesche, Francis, 1911 "The Omaha Tribe" in Twenty-seventh Annual Report of the Bureau of American Ethnology :637, Washington, Smithsonian Institute

Chapter 7.

Dawes

What followed these debates was the 1887 enactment of the Dawes Act[166], wherein Federal Indian policy formally and statutorily became the assimilation of Indians into the mainstream of American society via the civilization of, and allotment of lands to, individual Indians. Released from the political and legal restraints posed by the presence of tribal sovereignty, federal paternalism had now reached a new zenith.

"most everyone seems to have been enthusiastic about allotment-except the Indians"

Within all the political and philanthropic debates concerning allotment of Indian lands and the Indians' civilization and assimilation, the Indian himself and his opinions seem to have been overlooked. Some felt as did one Omaha Indian whose lands were subject to allotment under legislation enacted in1882, that "We want titles to our lands that the land may be secured to our children" [167] The Creeks, Choctaws, and Cherokee of Oklahoma in a joint petition to Congress

---

[166] "An act to provide for the allotment of lands in severalty to Indians on the various reservations, and to extend the protection of the laws of the United States and the Territories over the Indians, and for other purposes,"

[167] Fletcher, Alice C., LaFlesche, Francis, 1911 "The Omaha Tribe" in <u>Twenty-seventh Annual Report of the Bureau of American Ethnology :637</u>, Washington, Smithsonian Institute

noted[168] "The change to individual title would throw the whole of our domain in a few years into the hands of a few persons." The Iowa expressed concerns about allotting lands to "half-breeds" on the basis of previous problems with this segment of their tribal population.[169] Another point of resistance to allotment came from tribal leadership. The superintendent of the Rosebud Indian Agency wrote,[170]

> The old fogies or chiefs, who look to their supremacy and control over the people, fearful of losing it, discourage and advise the people to continue in the old rut. It is a contest between the young and progressive, with the prospect of disregarding the chiefs, and the young men assuming the responsibility of their own acts.

Here we find that even the impending prospect of allotment was already undermining existing tribal political leadership and producing factionalism within the social group. In reviewing the data, one certainly gets the impression that there was not significant support amongst the western Indians for such a radical change. Some Indian agents even argued against the imposition of allotment and the resistance to white settlement upon and amongst their wards. For instance, the Agent for the Coeur d' Alene argued that the tribe was "not willing or capable of mixing with them."[171]

One significant piece of information came from an 1883 Creek tribal petition to the House Indian Affairs Committee[172] that addressed the tribe's experience with allotment and its consequences. The Creek presented statistical documentation that showed a decline in tribal population after the application of

---

[168] The Congressional Record, vol.XI:781. January 20,1881.
[169] Annual Report of the Commissioner of Indian Affairs for the year 1884:94
[170] Annual Report of the Commissioner of Indian Affairs for the year 1885:44
[171] Annual Report of the Commissioner of Indian Affairs for the Year 1887: 205
[172] House Miscellaneous Document no. 18, 47th Congress, 2nd session, serial 1938:58

allotment. When allotment was rescinded upon their reservation, the tribe's population increased.

"No measure could be devised more efficient..."

Resistance to the enactment of the Dawes legislation came not only from some of Indian country, but also from academia. In 1885, a group of such academics, principally ethnologists and anthropologists, was formed. It became known as the "Indian Defence Association." The rationale for its founding was premised upon, "the fact that powerful organizations are already advocates of the policy [allotment] to be opposed renders it necessary that the effort to counteract their influences should be an organized effort also."[173] This group was opposed to the division of lands on Indian reservations, claiming that doing so would not provide sufficient motivation and preparation to survive in Anglo-American society. The Association was in agreement with the ultimate goals posited by the philanthropists, but its members were very wary of the rapidity of the application of the proposed changes. Time was to prove the validity of their concerns. Not all ethnologists were supportive of the positions assumed by the Indian Defense Association. Alice Fletcher, a strong advocate of the Omaha Allotment Act of 1882,[174] was a strong supporter of a rapid application of allotment and civilization. John Wesley Powell of the Bureau of American Ethnology also wrote,[175]

"...No measure could be devised more efficient for the ultimate civilization of the Indians of this country than one by which they could successfully and rapidly

---

[173] Preamble, Platform, and Constitution of the National Indian Defence Association :5. Washington D.C. Library of Congress.
[174] 22 Stat. 341, August 7,1882, An Act to provide for the sale of a part of the reservation of the Omaha tribe of Indians in the State of Nebraska, and for other purposes.
[175] The Congressional Record, vol. XI :911. January 25, 1881

obtain lands in severalty." The Indian Rights Association in their 1887 Annual Report referred to the Indian Defense Association as "obstructionists."

"The passage of the Dawes bill closes the century of dishonor."

An allotment bill was introduced to the Senate on April 25, 1885, by Senator Dawes who, at this time was Chairman of the Senate Indian Affairs Committee. Dawes' bill was passed in the Senate on February 25, 1886, during the first session of the forty-ninth Congress. This bill was considered in conjunction with the Mission Indian Relief Act.[176] Dawes was not taken up by the House until the forty-ninth Congress' second session during December 1886. It was voted on and passed on December 15 and signed into law by President Cleveland on February 8, 1887.[177] Pertinent portions of the Act were,

> An act to provide for the allotment of lands in severalty to Indians on the various reservations, and to extend the protection of the laws of the United States and the Territories over the Indians, and for other purposes.
>
> Be it enacted &c., That in all cases where any tribe or band of Indians has been, or shall hereafter be, located upon any reservation created for their use, either by treaty stipulation or by virtue of an act of Congress or executive order setting apart the same for their use, the President of the United States be, and he hereby is, authorized, whenever in his opinion any reservation or any part thereof of such Indians is advantageous for agricultural and grazing purposes to cause said reservation, or any part thereof, to be surveyed, or resurveyed if necessary, and to allot the lands in said reservations in severalty to any Indian located

---

[176] House report no.1835, 49th Congress, 1st session, serial 2440:49
[177] 24 Stat. 388 Chap. 119. Kappler, Charles J., 1904 , Indian Affairs: Laws and Treaties vol.I:33-36. Washington D.C. Government Printing Office

The President of the United States could at his discretion, impose the Act upon any federal Indian reservation via the resurveying and subsequent allotting of its lands in severalty.

> SEC.2. That all allotments set apart under the provisions of this act shall be selected by the Indians, heads of families selecting for their minor children, and the agents shall select for each orphan child, and in such a manner as to embrace the improvements of the Indians making the selection. ...
>
> *Provided*, That if anyone entitled to an allotment shall fail to make a selection within four years after the president shall direct that allotments be made on a particular reservation, the Secretary of the Interior may direct the agent of such tribe or band, if such there be, and if there be no agent, then a special agent appointed for that purpose, to make a selection for such Indian, which section shall be allotted as in cases where selections are made by the Indians, and patents shall issue in like manner.

The Indian occupants of an allotted reservation would have the right to choose their allotment section, subject to the Indian agent's approval (see Section Three). Any Indian not doing so within four years after the President designated a particular reservation for allotment would have an allotment assigned to him by an agent.

> SEC. 3. That the allotments provided for in this act shall be made by special agents appointed by the President for such purpose, and the agents in charge of the respective reservations on which the allotments are directed to be made, under such rules and regulations as the Secretary of the Interior may from time to time prescribe, and shall be certified by such agents to the Commissioner of Indian Affairs,

Allotments will be made by the agent were subject to any rules and regulations that may be instituted by the Secretary of the Interior.

> SEC.4. That where any Indian not residing upon a reservation, or for whose tribe no reservation has been provided by treaty, act of Congress, or executive order, shall make settlement upon any surveyed or unsurveyed

lands of the United States not otherwise appropriated, he or she shall be entitled upon application to the local land office for the district in which the lands are located, to have the same allotted to him or her, and to his or her children, in quantities and manner as provide in the act for Indians residing upon reservations; and when such settlement is made upon unsurveyed lands, the grant to such Indian shall be adjusted upon the survey of the land so as to conform thereto; and patents shall be issued to them for such lands in the manner and with the restrictions as herein provided.

Allotments to individual Indians were not restricted to existing Indian reservations, but federal fee lands could also be utilized. The allotment to Indians of such federal lands did not constitute the creation of a tribal reservation, only a fee-right to an individual under the same stipulations as an allotment established on an existing federal Indian reservation.

SEC. 5. That upon the approval of the allotments provided for in this act by the Secretary of the Interior, he shall cause patents to issue therefore in the name of the allottees, which patents shall be of the legal effect, and declare that the United States does and will hold the land thus allotted, for the period of twenty-five years, in trust for the sole use and benefit of the Indian to whom such allotment shall have been made, or in the case of his decease, of his heirs according to the laws of the State or territory where such land is located, and that at the expiration of said period the United States will convey the same by patent to said Indian, or his heirs as aforesaid, in fee, discharged of such trust and free of all charge or encumbrance whatsoever: *Provided,* That the President of the United States may in any case at his discretion extend the period..., That anytime after the lands have been allotted to all Indian of any tribe as herein provided, or sooner if in the opinion of the president it shall be for the best interest of the said tribe, it shall be lawful for the Secretary of the Interior to negotiate with said Indian tribe for the purchase and release by said tribe, in conformity with the treaty or statute under which such reservation is held, of such portions of its reservation not allotted as such tribe shall, from time to time, consent to sell, on such terms and conditions as shall be considered just and equitable between the United States and said tribe of Indians, which purchase shall not be complete until ratified by Congress, and the form and manner of executing such release shall also be prescribed by Congress..

Lands allotted to an Indian would be held in trust by the federal government for a period of twenty-five years, after which a patent in the name of the fee-holder would be issued. At that time all restrictions on alienation would be lifted. The President had the authority to arbitrarily extend the period of trust. If the Federal government desired to purchase any lands belonging to a tribe, it could only do so at the direction of the President, and only in accordance with the terms of an existing treaty stipulation or enacted legislative statutes, and with the approval of Congress.

> SEC. 6. That upon the completion of said allotments and the patenting of the lands to said allottees, each and every member of the respective bands or tribes of Indians to whom allotments have been made shall have the benefit of and be subject to the laws, both civil and criminal, of the State or Territory in which they may reside; ; and no Territory shall pass or enforce any law denying any such Indian within its jurisdiction the equal protection of the law.
> .And every Indian born within the territorial limits of the United States to whom allotments shall have been made under the provisions of this act, or under any law or treaty, and every Indian born within the territorial limits of the United States who has voluntarily taken up, within said limits, his residence separate and apart from any tribe of Indians therein, and has adopted the habits of civilized life, is hereby declared to be a citizen of the United States, and is entitled to all the rights, privileges, and immunities of such citizens, whether said Indian has been or not, by birth or otherwise, a member of any tribe of Indians within the territorial limits of the United States without in any manner impairing or otherwise affecting the right of any such Indian to tribal or other property.

Upon the issuance of a patent to an Indian allottee, all federal agency and jurisdiction would cease. The Patentee would become subject to either territorial or state jurisdiction. No state or territorial government could deny such Indians their right under existing state or territorial law. Such an Indian upon becoming an allottee was considered to be no longer living in tribal relations, and thus became a full citizen of the United States.

SEC. 7. That in cases where the use of water for irrigation is necessary to render the lands within any Indian reservation available for agricultural purposes, the Secretary of the Interior be, and is hereby authorized to prescribe such rules and regulations as he shall deem necessary to secure a just and equal distribution thereof among the Indians residing upon any such reservations; and no other appropriation or grant of water by any riparian proprietor shall be authorized or permitted to the damage of any other riparian proprietor.

All riparian land-owners were to have equal access to water for irrigation purposes. No action could be taken to impair the equal water rights of Indian allottees upon a reservation or federal fee lands.

SEC. 8. That the provision of this act shall not extend to the territory occupied by the Cherokees, Creeks, Choctows, Chickasaws, Seminoles, Osage, Miamies and Periorias, and Sacs and Foxes, in the Indian Territory, nor to any of the reservations of the Seneca Nation of New York Indians in the State of New York, nor to that strip of territory in the State of Nebraska adjoining the Sioux Nation on the south added by executive order.

SEC.10. That nothing in this act contained shall be construed to affect the right and power of Congress to grant the right of way through any lands to an Indian, or to a tribe of Indians, for railroads or other highways, or telegraph lines, for the public use, or to condemn such lands to public uses, upon making just compensation.

Public rights of way under eminent domain would not be affected by this enactment.

Dawes contained two primary goals: the allotment in severalty of Indian lands and Indian citizenship upon the severing of tribal relations via the acceptance of an allotment. The ultimate purpose of Dawes was, as President Theodore Roosevelt stated in his December 3, 1901 address to Congress, " The general

Allotment Act is a mighty pulverizing engine for breaking up the tribal mass." Out of this process it was envisioned that agricultural-based communities would emerge. Intermingling with these former reservation Indians would be non-Indian settlers to whom excess reservation lands could only be sold. Their presence would further facilitate civilization and assimilation of these former tribal Indians.

"The child must become a man"

At the 1887 "Friends of the Indian" conference held at Lake Mohonk, New York, the paternalistic mentality driving Dawes to enactment was fully articulated by the organization's newly appointed chairman, Clinton B. Fiske,[178]

> We congratulate the country on the notable progress towards a final solution of the Indian problem which has been made during the past year. The passage of the Dawes Bill closes the "century of dishonor", it makes it possible for the people of America to initiate a chapter of honor in the century to come…While the Dawes Bill will change the Indian's legal and political status; it will not change his character. The child must become a man, the Indian must become an American, the pagan must be new created a Christian….

President Cleveland wasted no time in putting Dawes into action. By the time the conference convened in September 1887, six reservations had, by his direction, been put under an allotment executive order. By year's end that number had increased to twenty-seven.[179] From the onset, neither the Federal government nor the supporting philanthropic organizations took heed of the warning made by

---

[178] 1887, Proceedings of the Fifth Annual Meeting of the Lake Mohonk Conference, September 28-30, 1887:104, Philadelphia, Sherman & Company.
[179] NARA. Washington D.C. RG 75,Records of the Board of Indian Commissioners, Report of the Board of Indian Commissioners for the year 1887:7

Senator Dawes at the 1885 Lake Mohonk conference in reference to the similar Coke legislation,[180]

> Again, under this bill, it must be the Indian's choice. It is now supposed that you can take an Indian against his will-by the nape of his neck, if I may say so-tell him to be a farmer and then go off and leave him, but you can't make anything of him under that process. An Indian will not make much of a farmer unless he can be inspired with the desire to be one, and unless you show him how. It is a work of time....

The concerns of experienced field agents were likewise ignored. In 1889, the Agent for Ponca and the Pawnee wrote,

> I find from four years of experience, not lightly taken, that to substitute the ways of the white man for the ways of the Indian can not be achieved short of prolonged, very painstaking, and very patient work. Small faith in the advice or counsel of the white man remains with the Indian character to-day.[181]

One year later the Commissioner of Indian Affairs, Thomas J. Morgan wrote,[182]

> This might seem like a somewhat rapid reduction of the landed estate of the Indians, but when it is considered that for the most part the land relinquished was not being used for any purpose whatever, that scarcely any of it was in cultivation, that the Indians did not need it and would not be likely to need it at any future time, and that they were, as believed, reasonably well paid for it, the matter assumes quite a different aspect. The sooner the tribal relations are broken up and the reservation system done away with the better it will be for all concerned....

"breaking up the tribal mass"

---

[180] 1885, Proceedings of the Third Annual Meeting of the Lake Mohonk Conference, October 7-9, 1885:39, Philadelphia, Sherman & Company.
[181] Report of the Commissioner of Indian Affairs for the year1889:195
[182] Report of the Commissioner of Indian Affairs for the year 1890:xxxix

The eminent historian, Francis Prucha[183] noted that beginning with the 1871 Proviso, it was, "the conscious intention thereby to denigrate the power of the chiefs that resulted in a loss of old systems of internal order without the substitution of new ones in their place." In his place the federal Indian agent reigned supreme, his empowering credentials post 1887, the Dawes Act.

In that regard the enactment of the 1887 "Dawes Act"[184], that "mighty pulverizing engine", made it explicitly clear that tribal political leadership had no significant part to play in the application of this legislation. Federal paternalism and ward-ship did,

> Be it enacted, That in all cases where any tribe or band of Indians has been, or shall hereafter be, located upon any reservation created for their use, either by treaty stipulation or by virtue of an act of Congress or executive order setting apart the same for their use, the President of the United States be, and he hereby is, authorized, whenever in his opinion any reservation or any part thereof of such Indians is advantageous for agricultural and grazing purposes to cause said reservation, or any part thereof, to be surveyed, or resurveyed if necessary, and to allot the lands in said reservations in severalty to any Indian located thereon in quantities as follows....

The President imposed allotment on a reservation when he deemed it "advantageous" to do so. The leadership of any tribal political entity residing on such a federal reservation had no say in this decision. In fact, Dawes focused upon individual civilization and land, not tribal organizations. As President Theodore Roosevelt remarked in 1901, " In my judgment the time has arrived when we should make up our minds to recognize the Indian as an individual and not as a

---

[183] Prucha, Francis. 1984, The Great Father: The United States Government and the American Indians. Vol. 2. : 676, University of Nebraska Press.
[184] An act to provide for the allotment of lands in severalty to Indians on the various reservations, and to extend the protection of the laws of the United States and the Territories over the Indians, and for other purposes,

member of a tribe."[185] Tribal organization was considered deleterious to the civil and moral advancement of the individual Indian. This detribalization policy was described in 1910 by the constitutional scholar W.W. Willoughby as,[186]

> A policy decided upon to abolish, as rapidly as possible, the tribal relations and governments, to extinguish the Indian titles to lands, and to incorporate the individual Indians in the general citizenship bodies of the states and territories in which they live.

Another dimension of allotment was the inclusion of those landless Indians. How did the federal authorities address these people?

That where any Indian not residing upon a reservation…

A frequently overlooked dimension of the Dawes Act was the role of Indians not residing upon a reservation who wished to participate in allotment and to gain eventual citizenship. No aspect of Dawes has caused so much misunderstanding and later contention than the intent and application of Section 4 of the Dawes Act, especially involving Indian bands residing in Southern California. Section 4 of Dawes read,

> SEC.4. That where any Indian not residing upon a reservation, or for whose tribe no reservation has been provided by treaty, act of Congress, or executive order, shall make settlement upon any surveyed or unsurveyed lands of the United States not otherwise appropriated, he or she shall be entitled upon application to the local land office for the district in which the lands are located, to have the same allotted to him or her, and to his or her children, in quantities and manner as provide in the act for Indians residing upon reservations; and when such settlement is made upon unsurveyed lands, the grant to such Indian shall be adjusted upon the survey of the land so as to conform thereto; and patents shall be issued to

---

[185] Messages and Papers of the Presidents and the Supreme Court, vol. XV:6672, Government Printing Office, Washington D.C.
[186] 1910, The Constitutional law of the United States. Cited in Goodrich, Chauncy S., 1926, The Legal Status of the California Indians, pt.1, California Law Review, Vol.14, No.2:84, fn #6.

them for such lands in the manner and with the restrictions as herein provided.

This Act was further amended in March 1891[187] in a revised Section 1 that expanded upon Indian allotment rights, including those Indians residing upon federal-fee lands depicted in Section 4 of Dawes. That same year, Congress enacted legislation, the Mission Indian Relief Act, [188]that specifically addressed the situation of former Mission Indians in Southern California. This Act has to be understood within the context of Section 4 of the Dawes Act. The Relief Act in part read,

> Section 2. That it shall be the duty of said Commissioners to select a reservation for each band or village of the Mission Indians residing within said State, which reservation shall include, as far as practicable, the lands and villages which have been in actual occupation and possession of said Indians, which shall be sufficient in extent to meet their requirements, which selection shall be valid when approved by the President and Secretary of the Interior. They shall also appraise the value of the improvements belonging to any person to whom valid existing rights have attached under the public- land laws of the United States, or to the assignee of such person, where such improvements are situated within the limits of any reservation selected and defined by said Commissioners subject in each case to the approval of the Secretary of the Interior. In cases where the Indians are in occupation of lands within the limits of confirmed private grants, the Commissioners shall determine and define the boundaries of such lands, and shall ascertain whether there are vacant public lands in the vicinity to which they may be removed. And the said Commission is hereby authorized to employ a competent surveyor and the necessary assistants.

Section 2 provided the authority for the Indian Commissioners to purchase land which would become "public land" upon which each landless band was to settle. Section 3 noted that such lands would be held in trust by the Federal

---

[187] 26 Stat., 794 February 28, 1891. See Kappler Charles,1904, Indian Affairs. Laws and treaties vol.I:56 Washington, Government Printing Office.
[188] An Act for the relief of the Mission Indians in the State of California, January 12, 1891, 26 Stat. 712.

government for a twenty-five years at which time the trust would cease and the land remaining would be patented to the band, excepting those lands allotted in severalty to Indian individuals, free of all encumbrances,

> Section 3. That the Commissioners upon the completion of their duties, shall report the result to the Secretary of the Interior, who, if no valid objection exists, shall cause a patent to issue for each of the reservations selected by the Commission and approved by him in favor of each band or village of Indians occupying any such reservation, which patents shall be of the legal effect, and declare that the United States does and will hold the land thus patented, subject to the provisions of Section four of this Act, for the period of twenty-five years, in trust, for the sole use and benefit of the band or village to which it is issued, and that at the expiration of said period the United States will convey the same or the remaining portion not previously patented in severalty by patent to said band or village, discharged of said trust and free of all charge and incumbrance whatsoever: Provided, that no patent shall embrace any tract or tracts to which existing valid rights have attached in favor of any person under any of the United States laws providing for the disposition of the public domain…And provided further, That said patents declaring such lands to be held in trust as aforesaid shall be kept in the Interior Department, and certified copies of the same shall be forwarded to, and be kept at the Agency by the agent having charge of the Indians for whom such lands are to held in trust, and said copies shall be open to inspection at such agency.

Section 4 depicted the primary purpose of the Relief Act, the allotment of reservation lands by the Secretary of the Interior to individual former Mission Indians and their transition to civilization

> Section 4. That whenever any of the Indians residing upon any reservation patented under the provisions of this act, shall in the opinion of the Secretary of the Interior, be so advanced in civilization as to be capable of owning and managing land in severalty, the Secretary of the Interior may cause allotments to be made to such Indians, out of the land of such reservation, in quantity as follows…

Lands allotted to individuals were to be separate from any band interests or patented lands. After the standard twenty-five year in-trust period, the individual allottees' land would be patented to the allottee free of all encumbrances. At that point in time the lands in question would become subject to state and local jurisdiction.

> Section 5. That upon the approval of the allotments provided for in the preceding section by the Secretary of the Interior he shall cause patents to issue therefore in the name of the allottees, which shall be of the legal effect and declare that the United States will hold the land thus allotted for the period of twenty-five years, in trust for the sole use and benefit of the Indian to whom such allotment shall have been made, or, in the case of his decease, of his heirs according to the laws of the State of California, and that at the expiration of said period, the United States will convey the same by patent to the said Indian, or his heirs as aforesaid, in fee, discharged of said trust and free of all charge or incumbrance whatsoever…Provided, These patents, when issued to the band or village as aforesaid, and shall separate the individual allotment from the lands held in common, which proviso shall be incorporated in each of the village patents.

Such reservations created by Presidential proclamation or executive order did not constitute a federal recognition of a government to government relationship. Federal Indian policy under the Dawes Act discouraged such relationships as an impediment to advancement. The institution of such relationships ended with the enactment of the 1871 proviso ending treaty-making and heralded the advent of Congressional plenary authority over Indians living in tribal relations. Instead, in December 1875, President Grant began ordering the establishment of reservations, "for the permanent use and occupancy of the Mission Indian in Lower California."[189]

---

[189] Executive Orders Relating to Reserves, December 27, 1875, in Kappler, Charles, 1904, Indian Affairs: Laws and treaties, vol.I:520-521, Washington, Government Printing Office.

In the aftermath of the July 13, 1883 Report "On the Condition and Needs of the Mission Indians of California..."[190] the three appointed agents who comprised the investigating committee reported to the Commissioner of Indian Affairs that one of the Commission's main concerns should be the vulnerability of those Mission Indian reservations that were established by Presidential executive proclamation or order to repeal or alteration at will. One such action occurred in February 1871,[191]

> Commissioner transmits papers in reference to San Pasqual and Pala Valley Reservations in Southern California, and recommends that the order of the President setting apart the same be revoked and the lands restored to Public domain.

The Commission recommended that such reservations be placed under a twenty-five year trust period at the end of which the lands would be patented to the band, excepting those that had been allotted to individuals. This would prevent future acts of revocation. The Commission further advocated that,

> The best way and time of allotting these Indian's lands to them in severalty must be left to the decision of the Government, a provision being incorporated in their patent to provide for such allotments from time to time as may seem desirable...

Section 3 of the 1891 Mission Indian Relief Act incorporated these concerns and recommendations.

Within the context of both the 1887 and 1891 Dawes Acts and the 1891 Mission Indian Relief Act, these federally-established Mission Indian reservations

---

[190] In, Jackson, Helen, 1880 (1994 edition), A Century of Dishonor: A sketch of the United States Government's Dealings With Some Of The Indian Tribes:458, New York Indian Head Books
[191] Kappler, Charles, 1904, Indian Affairs: Laws and Treaties, vol.I:820, Government Printing Office Washington D.C.

served as platforms upon which to carry out the provisions and intent of the Dawes Act: detribalization, allotment, civilization, and citizenship.

To ensure that lands were so-provided, the Mission Indian Relief Act was amended in the 1907 Indian Department Appropriation Act.[192] In this amendment the Secretary of the Interior was authorized, "to select, set apart, and cause to be patented to the Mission Indians..." such public lands found "to have been in the occupation and possession of the several bands or villages of Mission Indians, and are now needed and required by them."

In the 1917 Bureau of Indians Affairs Appropriation Act[193] the Mission Indian Relief Act was again amended in two areas. These amendments further proved the point that the intent of the Mission Indian Relief Act was allotment and not tribal creation or continuation. The first stipulation was,

> ...to authorize the President, in his discretion and whenever he shall deem it for the interests of the Indians affected thereby to extend the trust period for such time as may be advisable on the lands held for the use and benefit of the Mission Bands or villages of Indians in California

Secondly,

> That the Secretary of the Interior be, and is hereby, authorized and directed to cause allotments to be made to the Indians belonging to and having tribal rights on the Mission Indian reservations in the State of California...Provided, That this act shall not affect any allotments heretofore patented to these Indians.

We can conclude from the preceding that the Mission Indian Relief Act was in reality a subset of the 1887 Dawes Act. Their goals were identical. In the case of

---

[192] 34 Stat. 1015, March 1, 1907. See Kappler, Charles, 1917, Indian Affairs: Laws and Treaties, vol.III:274, Washington Government printing Office.
[193] An Act Making appropriations for the current and contingent expenses of the Bureau of Indian Affairs, for fulfilling treaty stipulations with various Indian tribes, and for other purposes...(39 Stat. 969) March 2, 1917, see Kappler, Charles, 1929, Indian Affairs: Laws and Treaties, vol. IV:107 (:114).

the Southern California Mission Indians and also those landless northern Californian Indians, a land base was needed for these people to participate in the Dawes assimilative process. Lands had to be acquired and turned into federal fee lands. These lands had to be proclaimed as Indian reservations or rancheria's, upon which these landless people could be settled. In the case of the Mission Indians, these communities received a twenty-five year in-trust period during which time lands could be allotted to individuals. At the expiration of the in-trust period, those remaining unallotted lands would be patented to the community free of alienation restrictions and subject to local and state jurisdiction unless the trust period was extended by a specific Presidential order. Those lands held by allottees would also be relieved of trust restrictions and receive similar unrestricted patents and also come under local and state jurisdiction. The aim was not tribal creation or recognition but assimilation.

...discontinuing guardianship of all competent Indians

To speed up the assimilative process of Dawes, on May 8, 1906, the "Burke Act"[194] was enacted by Congress. This Act amended the 1887 Indian Allotment Act by allowing the Secretary of the Interior, at his discretion, to release individual Indian allottees from their twenty-five year in-trust obligation at an earlier date, if the Secretary felt that such individuals were ready to assume full fee ownership and citizenship. The appropriate text is as follows,

> Provided, That the Secretary of the Interior may, in his discretion, and he is hereby authorized, whenever he shall be satisfied that any Indian allottee is competent and capable of managing his or her own affairs, at any time cause to be issued to such allottee a patent in fee simple, and thereafter all restrictions as to sale, incumbramce, or taxation of said land

---

[194] An Act to amend section six of an act approved February eighth, eighteen hundred and eighty-seven...34 Stat. 182. See Kappler, Charles 1924, Indian Affairs: Laws and Treaties, vol. III: 179.

shall be removed and said land shall not be liable to the satisfaction of any debt contracted prior to the issuing of such patent

This enactment was followed in 1917 with a declaration by Commissioner of Indian Affairs Cato Sells for the separation of full blooded and mixed blood Indians into competent and incompetent categories, with those Indians having ½ blood quantum or less being considered the more competent for an early release.[195]

> The time has come for discontinuing guardianship of all competent Indians and giving even closer attention to the incompetent that they may more speedily achieve competency…

Such "competent" Indians who were allottees should, according to the Commissioner, be given full fee patent rights to their respective allotments. Such decisions were adjudicated by Department-established "Competency Commissions" that issued 9,894 fee simple patents to such individuals between 1917 and 1920, when this process ended. Many of these "competent" individuals, upon their release from federal supervision and jurisdiction, quickly sold their allotments to non-Indians. At the same time another Federal action set the stage for an even larger failure of these revised allotment actions, by allowing leasing of allotted lands to non-Indians.

"That whenever it shall be made to appear…" Allotment leasing.

Not long after the 1887 enactment of the Dawes Act, the same activist groups that promoted paternalism over the American Indian began to advocate for its

---

[195] "Declaration of Polict in the Administration of Indian Affairs", April 17, 1917, Report of the Commissioner of Indian Affairs for the Year 1917, serial 7358:3

removal. During the proceedings of the 1889 Lake Mohonk conference,[196] Professor Charles C. Painter, an idealistic advocate of equality of allotments irregardless of age or sex, speaking of Indian land rights, decried the fact that,

> "…his condition under the severalty law is no better than under the old reservation system, unless it go so far as to destroy utterly the old conditions imposed by that system. A step is taken, it is true, in the right direction, but not long enough to take him out of his difficulties.

Dr. Painter went on to note that the Indians could not progress towards civilization and citizenship under the governmental economic constraints imposed by Dawes. Painter argued that the Indian alone should be able to decide how to best use the lands allotted to him or her.

At the same conference, former U.S. Supreme Court Justice William Strong argued,[197]

> But on one subject I am perfectly convinced,-namely, that the government has not the shadow of a right to interfere with an Indian having an allotment, either in the use of his property…

Justice Strong went on to advocate for a diversity in land usage. One such usage he spoke of was the partial leasing of allotted land. It would stimulate the allottee to productive endeavors and at the same time provide income to assist in his or her transition.

The following year, at the 1890 Lake Mohonk conference,[198] Senator Dawes prophetically cautioned against the leasing of allotment lands. He warned the gathered activists,

---

[196] 1889, Proceedings of the Seventh Annual Meeting of the Lake Mohonk Conference of the Friends of the Indian:84-89
[197] ibid:94

> A bill has already passed the House, and is now pending in the Senate, authorizing the leasing of allotted lands whenever the agent shall deem it best for the Indian. Such a law, in my opinion, would speedily overthrow the whole allotment system. The Indian would at once seek to let his land, and relieve himself from work; and there would be whites so ready to take possession that all barriers would be broken down. Thus the allotment law would gradually be undermined and destroyed, and the Indian would abandon his own work, his own land, and his own home...

Senator Dawes was not alone in cautioning against allotment leasing. The Agent administering the Sac and Fox reservation in Oklahoma issued a similar warning,[199]

> Should authority be given for the Indians to lease their lands, nearly all would avail themselves of the privilege and their land would immediately be taken up by whites at ridiculously low compensation and the Indian would squander the proceeds and still live an idle, vagabond life. The average Indian is not competent to make leases...

On the other hand there were agents who saw a positive aspect to allotment leasing. In the same Commissioner's report quoted above the Agent responsible for the Santee reservation noted,[200]

> It would seem probable to me that it might give the Indian more idea as to the value of the land to see others making use of it, and be also a source of income for himself...

Surprisingly, the Indian Office in 1890 showed no interest either way concerning allotment leasing. The Office's attention was diverted towards getting Congress to approve legislation that provided for equal acreage allotments for all Indians, regardless of their sex or age. Such lease-related legislation was introduced by Senator Dawes on March 10, 1890 in Section 2, in spite of his

---

[198] 1890, Proceedings of the Eight Annual Meeting of the Lake Mohonk Conference of the Friends of the Indian:82-83
[199] Report of the Commissioner of Indian Affairs for the Year 1892:404
[200] Annual Report of the Commissioner of Indian Affairs for the Year 1892:188

warnings made to the attendees at the 1890 Lake Mohonk conference. The Senator's bill provided for the limited leasing of allotment lands.

Additionally, a general sense was emerging amongst the Lake Mohonk group that while the President was quick to impose allotment upon existing reservations, the Federal government was faltering in providing the funds and training to enabled the transition from a communal tribal society to one of independent farmers and to a lesser degree ranchers. Indeed, during 1888, 3,568 allotments were made to individual Indians, but only $30,000.00 was allocated by Congress "…for the commencement of farming."[201]. That amounts to roughly $10.00 per allottee. Yet the Federal government was not entirely at fault. The numerous philanthropic organizations that aggressively promoted Indian civilization and individual land allotment to Congress and its eventual successful legislative enactment, were themselves too blinded by the idealistic theoretical aspects of their proposals to concern themselves with the realities involved in such a massive cultural and socio-economic transition. Essentially, once they achieved their legislative goal, many lost interest in the task at hand. As the daughter of Senator Dawes remarked at the 1890 Lake Mohonk conference, [202]

> I am quite sure that, while it is true that the interest of the country in the Indian and the sense of justice among the people at large is greatly increased and the whole situation is better understood, it is also true that particular concrete interest is declining. At first it was glorious work…That time has passed by. With few exceptions the work is no longer interesting. ..The public cares little about details in the matter of help for the individual…No one is willing to keep up the constant effort which is necessary to carry out such work.

---

[201] Annual Report of the Commissioner of Indian Affairs for the Year 1888:444
[202] 1890, Proceedings of the Eight Annual Meeting of the Lake Mohonk Conference of the Friends of the Indian:113

These two impulses, the activist pressure for leasing and a need for funding the civilization of the Indian allottee created a positive political environment within which allotment leasing legislation could be enacted.

"by reason of age, disability or inability."

On February 28, 1891, Congress enacted Dawes' Indian Leasing Amendment to the 1887 Allotment Act.[203] Within this enactment was language permitting allotment leasing under restricted circumstances,

> Sec.3. That whenever it shall be made to appear to the Secretary of the Interior that, by reason of age or other disability, any allotment under the provisions of the said act, or any other act or treaty can not personally and with benefit to himself occupy or improve his allotment or any part thereof the same may be leased upon such terms, regulations and conditions as shall be prescribed by such Secretary, for a term not exceeding three years for farming or grazing, or ten years for mining purposes.
>
> That whenever it shall be made to appear to the Secretary of the interior that by reason of age, disability, or inability, any allottee of under this or former Acts of Congress can not personally and with benefit to himself occupy or improve his allotment or any part thereof the same may be leased in the discretion of the Secretary upon such terms, regulations, and

---

[203] 26 Stat. 794, February 28, 1891, An act to amend and further extend the benefits of the act approved February eight, eighteen hundred and eighty-seven..., in Kappler, Charles,1904, Indian Affairs: Laws and Treaties, vol.I:56

conditions as shall be prescribed by him, for a term not exceeding five years for grazing or farming purposes...[204]

...the same may be leased upon such terms, regulations, and conditions as shall be prescribed by the Secretary for the term not exceeding five years, for farming purposes only...[205]

Section 3 of this legislation permitted the Secretary of the Interior to make determinations as to "age or other disability" in regard to permitting leasing. In the 1893 report of the Commissioner of Indian Affairs[206] "age and other disability" were defined as, "age" being applicable to any Indian allottee under the age of eighteen or those allottees who suffered from mental incapacities such as senility. For "other disability", mental impairment was also a factor as well as the situation of unmarried women allottees, and married women whose spouse or offspring were unable to work the land allotted, as well as to widows. That same year the Commissioner of Indian Affairs wrote,[207] "The matter of leasing allottee has been placed largely in the hands of the agencies were allotments have been made" subject to the ultimate approval by the Secretary of the Interior.

The stipulations present in Section 3 of the Indian Leasing Amendment were broadened by an amendment to the 1894 Indian Department Appropriation Act. This amendment expanded "age or other disability" to read "by reason of age, disability or inability."[208] Another amendment was the extension of agricultural and grazing leases from three years to five. Most importantly, the term "inability"

---

[204] 29 Stat. 321, June 10, 1896, An act making appropriations for current and contingent expenses of the Indian department..., in Kappler, Charle3s, 1904, Indian Affairs: Laws and Treaties, vol.I:79
[205] 31 Stat. 170, May 7, 1900, An act for the appointment of an additional United States commissioner in the northern judicial district of the Indian territory, in, Kappler, Charles, Indian Affairs: Laws and Treaties, vol.1:105
[206] Report of the Commissioner of Indian Affairs for the year 1893:476
[207] ibid:27
[208] 28 Stat. 206, August 15. 1894, An act making appropriations for current and contingent expenses of the Indian department..., in Kappler, Charle3s, 1904, Indian Affairs: Laws and Treaties, vol.I:520

that appeared in 1894 was not defined by the Interior Department. As a result, two distinct factors came into play that seriously undermined the objectives of the Dawes Act. The first was the ability of the Secretary of the Interior to bestow an unrestricted patent on allottees prior to the expiration of their twenty-five year trust period as set forth in the original 1887 Dawes Act. The second was the 1894 amendment and its inclusion of the word "inability." An immediate result, according to the Board of Indian Commissioners, [209] was that in 1892 only two Indian allotment leases were approved. In 1893, there were four. In 1894, the number of such leases rose to 295. Despite the assertions by the Indian Department that no leases were granted by the Interior Secretary to Allotment Indians who had the ability to either farm or herd, the number of leases grew from 295 in 1894[210] to 330 in 1895[211] and to 933 in 1896[212] and an astounding 1,287 in 1897.[213] By 1900, the number of annual leases made by Indian allottees to non-Indians approved by the Secretary of the Interior on the recommendation of the field agents was 2,500.[214] That same year, 55,996 allotments of land were made to individual Indians. Twenty years later (1920), the number of reservation allotments had grown to only 217,572.[215] The rate of demand for land allotments was declining, but the race to become landlords wasn't. By 1913, the Indian Office had a backlog of 40,000 lease applications. That same year, Congress authorized a leasing fee of $15.00 for each application to defray administrative costs.[216] The Indian agent became in essence, a real estate broker. The issuing of early patents ending trust alienation restrictions led to actual loss of Indian-owned

---

[209] Report of the Board of Indian Commissioner to the Secretary of the Interior for the year 1894:7, Report of the Commissioner of Indian Affairs for the Year 1894:33
[210] ibid:33
[211] ibid 1895:34
[212] ibid 1896:39
[213] ibid 1897:41
[214] Report of the Commissioner of Indian Affairs for the Year 1900:76
[215] Report of the Commissioner of Indian Affairs for the year 1920:82
[216] Report of the Commissioner of Indian Affairs for the Year 1913:4

land. The prospect of the Indian learning to make a living off the fruits of his or her allotted lands was disappearing. The 1900 Report of the Commissioner of Indian Affairs[217] spoke despairingly of this situation,

> The better to assist them the allottees should be divided into small groups, each to be put in the charge of persons who by precept and example would teach them how to work and how to live. This is the theory. The practice is very different. The Indian is allotted land and then is allowed to turn over his land to whites and go on his aimless way. This pernicious practice is the direct growth of vicious legislation.

The Commissioner of Indian Affairs placed the blame squarely in the hands of Congress, although one might quickly add a number of local Indian agents, as well as the Secretary of the Interior, as willing accomplices to these actions by Congress. Without the defenses that sovereignty once afforded many Indian tribes, the onset of Indian paternalism, an off-shoot from the Civil War era emancipation movement, led to the political and social domination of the non-citizen Indian. In turn, when these Indians were at their most vulnerable, corruptions within the national political processes began to wreak havoc amongst these peoples. The result, federal paternalistic political control created Indian dependency, which in turn created Indian political vulnerability and land exploitation. Federal Indian policy, though for the most part well intended by both the philanthropist and politician, led to consequences that could not be foreseen by its enactors.

"Experience has demonstrated...": The "Heff" Fix

Another issue relating to Dawes was that of citizenship. Section 6 of the 1887 Act provided that when an Indian took up an allotment he or she was no longer

---
[217] ibid 1900:13

considered to be living in tribal relations. Thus at the end of the trust period, the individual became a citizen of the United States. It will be recalled that in 1906, Congress enacted the "Burke Act"[218] that allowed competent Indian allottees to receive land patents prior to the expiration of the twenty-five year trust period. The Burke Act also amended Article 6 of Dawes by declaring that citizenship would no longer be given upon the assumption of an allotment, but only upon the issuance of a federal patent to the allottee for the land so held. The trust period thus represented a liminal status wherein the allottee was betwixt and between, neither living in tribal relations, nor an individual entitled to the rights and protections afforded to a citizen. This action was taken in part at the request of Commissioner of Indian Affairs Francis Leupp, who in his annual Report to the Secretary of the Interior[219] declared,

> Experience has demonstrated that citizenship has been a disadvantage to many Indians. They are not fitted for the duties or able to take advantage of its benefits…

The compelling factor was a 1905 decision by the US Supreme Court in[220] "*Matter of Heff*" as to whether Indians who were no longer under federal jurisdiction were subject to restrictions of Indian liquor laws. The Court concluded that any Indian who was a citizen was no longer considered to be a ward of the United States,

> Under the act of February 8, 1887, 24 Stat. 24, an Indian who has received an allotment and patent for land is no longer a ward of the government, but a citizen of the United States and of the state in which he resides, and as such, is not within the reach of Indian police regulations on the part of Congress, and this emancipation from federal control cannot be set aside without the consent of the Indian or the state, nor is it affected by the provisions in the act subjecting the land allotted to conditions against

---

[218] US. Statutes at Large, v.34:182-183
[219] February 8, 1906, House Report 1558 59-1, serial 4906
[220] Matter of Heff, 197 US. 488 (1905)

alienation and encumbrance, and guaranteeing him an interest in tribal or other property,

Thus, the Burke Act was legislatively enacted. That such an Indian who was an allottee and who was now a citizen was no longer subject to the paternalistic constraints and control of the Indian Office created problems, both for the Indian and the federal authorities. For the Indian, the protections afforded by federal supervision were no longer in place for the allottee. For the government, this decision had the potential to nullify the Dawes Act at the inception of the process, that is, at the land allotment stage. The Burke Act surmounted this issue by moving citizenship back in the process to the time when a federal land patent was issued to the allottee despite. This act was passed despite the objections of the Board of Indian Commissioners. The Board argued that citizenship should be bestowed at the time of allotment. On one hand, the Burke Act prevented the premature alienation of allotments, whilst at the same time promoted it by permitting the Secretary of the Interior to grant early releases from the alienation restrictions of the Dawes Act's twenty-five year trust period. In 1907 alone, 753 such applications were approved by the Secretary.[221] By 1909, that number had increased to 1,116.[222]

Yet further legislation was enacted that was to effect Indian land allotment. It will be recalled that on February 28, 1891, Congress enacted an amendment to the 1887 Dawes Act that addressed the issue of land leases for Indians incapable of tending their allotments.[223] Specifically, the Act stated

---

[221] Report of the Commissioner of Indian Affairs for the year 1907:63-64
[222] ibid 1909:65
[223] 26 Stat. 794, February 28, 1891, An act to amend and further extend the benefits of the act approved February eight, eighteen hundred and eighty-seven…, in Kappler, Charles,1904, Indian Affairs: Laws and Treaties, vol.I:56

> Sec.3. That whenever it shall be made to appear to the Secretary of the Interior that, by reason of age or other disability, any allotment under the provisions of the said act , or any other act or treaty can not personally and with benefit to himself occupy or improve his allotment or any part thereof the same may be leased upon such terms, regulations and conditions as shall be prescribed by such Secretary, for a term not exceeding three years for farming or grazing, or ten years for mining purposes.

Yet, by 1900, the question of leasing was still a major issue for the Indian Office. William Jones, then the Commissioner of Indian Affairs, wrote in his 1900 report,[224]

> The dangers and the bad effects of leasing Indian lands grow more evident with every year. The department does not and can not make careful investigation of the circumstances in each application for permission to lease individual holdings of land, but is compelled to depend upon recommendations which are too often colored by interest or influenced by local pressure to get the best Indian lands at the lowest prices, and by the desire of lazy Indians to escape work. Since this is so, and since the bad effects of payment of lease money to Indians who do not work are most evident, we urge the refusal of applications for such leases unless convincing reasons are shown why the leasing should be permitted…No able-bodied Indians who can work their own lands should be allowed to lease them.

Additionally, both Congress and the Interior Department were concerned about the efficient use of allotted lands by the Indians. One concern involved lands allotted but not utilized, due to the fact that the allottee was incapable utilizing the lands parcel allotted to him. In 1907, Congress took a further step against land under-utilization by so-called incompetent Indians. On March 2, 1907, Congress enacted, "An act providing for the allotment and distribution of Indian tribal funds"[225] or more commonly referred to as the "Lacey Act". The bill

---

[224] Annual Report of the Commissioner of Indian Affairs for the year 1900:648
[225] 34 Stat. 1241, Fifty-ninth Congress, second session, in Kappler, Charles, 1913, Indian Affairs: Laws and Treaties, vol.III:306, Washington, Government Printing Office.

was first introduced in 1905 by Representative John F. Lacey of Iowa. Despite its title, the bill authorized the Secretary of the Interior to sell the allotment lands of Indian allottees who were"…blind, crippled, decrepit, or helpless from old age, disease, or accident" and to deposit the proceeds into that particular tribe's trust fund to be used for the support of such individuals. The following year, Indian Commissioner Francis Leupp defined what persons would be considered incompetent to tend to land allotment,[226]

> That general class of Indians, who through mental or physical infirmities incident to accident, disease, or old age, are unable to avail themselves of the benefits arising from the development of their allotments, and whose best interests require that their lands be converted into money, so that funds may be available for medical attendance, and for their support….

The selling of such lands, in combination with allotment leasing, led to the further erosion of lands upon which the goals of the original Dawes enactment could be carried out. At the same time, these losses produced a growing body of landless Indians. The process was further propelled by an efficiency mindset expressed by Secretary of the Interior Franklin Lane in 1914, "I am of the opinion that it would be better, far better, to sever all ties between the Indians and the government…give every man his own and let him go, rather than keep alive in the Indian the belief that he is to remain a ward of the government."[227] Franklin's goal was to rid the Department of wards who were deemed competent, free them from federal jurisdiction in order to direct more resources to those wards still in need of assistance. Again the Burke Act provided the means of doing so by providing the Secretary with the authority to grant early releases from Dawes-mandated trust terms. In 1916, with the recommendation of compliant

---

[226] NARA, Washington D.C. RG 75, Records of the Commissioner of Indian Affairs (Microfilm) M1121, Reel 9 Office of Indian Affairs Circular # 181, January 9, 1908
[227] Annual Report of the Secretary of the Interior to the Congress for the year 1914, House Document 1475, 63-3 serial 6814:3-12

competency commissions, 1,525 fee patents were approved by the Secretary totaling 220,490 acres of land.[228] Many of these patentees quickly sold their lands to non-Indians.

Secretary Lane's Indian Commissioner, Cato Sells, utilizing the blood quantum guidance he established for the use by competency commissions, mandated the separation of full blooded Indians and mixed blood Indians into competent and incompetent categories. He did so in his October 17, 1917 "A Declaration of Policy. Those Indian allottees having a demonstrable Indian blood quotient of one half or more were considered incompetent to receive early fee patents, unless such competency could be clearly demonstrated. Generally half bloods and above were to remain under federal jurisdiction whilst those below one half were considered competent to receive early release and citizenship.[229] Sells stated,

> The time has come for discontinuing guardianship of all competent Indians and giving even closer attention to the incompetent that they may more speedily achieve competency...

Such "competent" Indians who were allottees should, according to the Commissioner, be given full fee patent rights to their respective allotments, as well as citizenship. Sells noted,

> To all able-bodied adult Indians of less than one half Indian blood, there will be given as far as may be under the law full and complete control of all their property. Patents in fee shall be issued to all adult Indians of one half or more Indian blood who may, after careful investigation, be found competent, provided where deemed advisable patents in fee shall be withheld for not to exceed 40 acres as a home...

---

[228] Report of the Commissioner of Indian Affairs for the year 1916:49
[229] "Declaration of Policy in the Administration of Indian Affairs", April 17, 1917, Report of the Commissioner of Indian Affairs for the Year 1917, serial 7358:3

This blood quantum distinction was to continue into the era of the Indian Reorganization Act, manifesting itself in Section 19 of that legislation.[230] Sell's "Competency Policy" was well received as a means of reducing costs to the government which was contending with massive war expenditures. Sells further stated that this policy heralded "the beginning of the end of the Indian problem."

Citizenship

Congress amended the 1887 Dawes Act in March of 1901[231] granting U.S. citizenship to all Indians residing in "Indian Territory" upon taking up an allotment. As noted earlier, there was a growing sentiment amongst various philanthropic groups and organizations for the granting of complete citizenship to all Indians. Yet in 1906, as a result of the enactment of the "Burke Act" that amended Article 6 of Dawes, citizenship would no longer be given upon the assumption of an allotment, but only upon the issuance of a federal patent to the allottee for the land so held. Additionally, in that same year, on November 19 the US Supreme Court ruled,[232] that the lands of such an allottee could be either voluntarily or involuntarily alienated and also subject to taxation, when a patent for the land was issued by the Federal government. Citizenship and full fee-

---

[230] Commissioner Sells blood quantum threshold was to have a lasting effect in Federal Indian policy. Section 19 of the 1934 Indian reorganization Act contained what then Commissioner John Collier called a "Class III" qualification for participating in the Reorganization Act, wherein an Indian, not a member of a recognized tribe or residing upon a reservation, or a descendant of such a tribe but having 50% or more Indian blood would qualify to participate in IRA.
[231] 31 Stat. 1447, Citizenship accorded Indian in Indian Territory: An Act to Amend section six, chapter 119, (An Act to provide for the Allotment of lands in severalty to the Indians on the various reservations....) United States Statutes at Large, numbered twenty-four. Kappler 1904, vol.1:114.
[232] Goudy v. Meath 203 US. 146 (1906)

simple land ownership was the golden ring to be obtained by the Indian upon completion of the Dawes program of assimilation.

Exceptions to Burke occurred. On March 1, 1901 the Cherokee were given full citizenship[233], yet as Section 36 of this legislation noted, "but the same shall in no wise effect his rights as a member of said tribe." Oddly, this section appeared only to bestow citizenship upon Cherokee males despite the fact that Dawes called for female allottees as well as males. Three years earlier, on June 28, 1898, Congress enacted legislation[234] that granted citizenship to the Choctaws and Chickasaws. Citizenship was to be granted under the proviso, "...when their tribal government cease." In the same act, the Creeks were accorded citizenship[235] with the same proviso that was accorded to Choctaw and Chickasaw. Furthermore, in the aftermath of World War I, honorably discharged Indian veterans were also accorded citizenship by an act of Congress.[236] This Act also stipulated that such Indians should be granted citizenship, "without any manner impairing or otherwise affecting the property rights, individual or tribal, of any such Indian or his interest in tribal or other Indian property."

In such cases, a duality of citizenship and rights was established, both tribal and federal. In others, one right had to be surrendered to achieve another. With significant numbers of male Indians receiving citizenship a momentum was created to grant citizenship to all Indians not holding this status. In 1924 the first moves towards that end occurred in Congress wherein New York Representative

---

[233] 21 Stat. 848, An Act to ratify and confirm an agreement with the Cherokee tribe of Indians, and for other purposes. Kappler, 1904, vol.I:715;726.
[234] 30 Stat. 495, An Act for the protection of the people of the Indian Territory, and for other purposes. Kappler 1904, vol. I:646;655.
[235] ibid 1904, vol. I:661
[236] 41 Stat. 350, November 6, 1919, An Act Granting citizenship to certain Indians. Kappler, 1929,vol. IV:232

Homer Synder introduced legislation[237] calling for the bestowal of citizenship upon all Indians whom the Secretary of the Interior deemed, at his discretion, to receive such a standing. Obviously, such legislation if enacted would have coupled the bestowal of such citizenship with political expediency. While passing unopposed in the House of Representatives, the Senate modified the bill[238], removing the necessity of the Secretary of the Interior's approval and blanket asserted that, "… all non-citizen Indians born within the territorial limits of the United States be, and they are hereby, declared to be citizens of the United States." Oddly, the Senate kept the original title of the Synder bill that included the authorization of the Secretary of the Interior language. The legislation became law on June 2, 1924.[239]

This law did contain one proviso that was a carry-over from earlier tribal-based and veteran-based citizenship enactments, "That the granting of such citizenship shall not in any manner impair or otherwise impair or otherwise affect the right of any Indians to tribal or other property. Thus, the duality of citizenship concept remained, but the paternalistic aspect, "at the discretion of the Secretary of the Interior" first introduced by Representative Synder, was removed.

What was the impact on the process of the assimilation propounded by the Dawes Act? The Indian citizenship legislation provided the golden ring without the need to complete the process. Tribal rights were continued, including the tax exempt status of reservation lands and the exemption from state jurisdiction for those federally-established reservations located within the boundary of a state. Why then bother to assimilate? An Indian who owned an allotment remained a

---

[237] HR. 6355, "An act To authorize the Secretary of the Interior to issue certificates of citizenship to Indians" House Report, Sixty-eighth Congress, Session 1, Number 222:68-1, Serial 2977
[238] Senate Report, Sixty-eighth Cong4ress, Session 1 number 441, 68-1, serial 8221.
[239] 43 Stat. 253 Chap. 233.

tribal member due to the stipulations present in the Burke Act. Why then petition the Secretary of the Interior for a patent of fee ownership when one has the best of both worlds? The Indian citizenship act of 1924 virtually dismantled the Dawes Allotment Act. An Indian could still obtain an allotment of land that could not be taken from him or her that was inheritable by ones descendants and was tax-free with no state jurisdictional oversight. Additionally, with no requirement for the termination of tribal government, tribal relations could indefinitely remain and the boundaries of a reservation could remain intact even in the presence of Indian held allotments. What incentive was there to complete the Dawes process that offered possible dispossession and taxation and state governance? The law of unintended consequences seemingly had reared its head, a political and social stasis had, at first glance emerged. But within this environment of political smoke and mirrors, the Federal government, via the Department of the Interior's Indian office and its gatekeepers, the onsite Indian agents still asserted its paternalistic patronage over the occupants of federal Indian reservations.

Was this situation of paternal dominance to continue in the post-citizenship era of Federal Indian policy? The evidence tells us yes.

Chapter 8.

The Advent of Red Atlantis: The Era of the Indian Reorganization Act of 1934

In 1917, Indian Commissioner Cato Sells believed that by his newly announced Indian policy for the early release of Indians from the strictures of federal trust over Indians holding land allotments, he was leading the Federal government towards the elimination of the Indian as a ward of the nation. Yet, the Federal government devised other means of maintaining paternal control over reservation-bound Indians. During November of 1921, Congress enacted what has become known as the Snyder Act.[240] It read in part:

> Be it enacted by the Senate and House of Representatives of the United States of America in Congress Assembled, That the Bureau of Indian Affairs, under the supervision of the Secretary of the Interior, shall direct, supervise and expend such money's as Congress may from time to time appropriate, for the benefit, care and assistance of the Indians throughout the United States for the following purposes:
> General support and civilization, including education.
> For relief of distress and conservation of health.
> For industrial assistance and advancement and general administration of Indian property.
> For extension, improvement, operation. and maintenance of existing Indian irrigation systems and for development of water supplies....

---

[240] 42 Stat. 208, An Act Authorizing appropriations and expenditures for the administration of Indian Affairs. Kappler 1914, vol. IV:330

What is important to note was that these appropriations were not being made to support or benefit Indian tribes, but instead were directed towards individual "Indians" in general. Detribalization as well as continued paternalism, remained important parts of Federal Indian policy.

As an example, in 1921, the Rappahannock Indian Association petitioned the Administration to recognize tribal and intertribal councils. Secretary of the Interior Albert Fall disapproved and responded to the petitioners by stating,[241]

> It has long been the policy of the Indian Bureau to eliminate tribal government and much of the old tribal customs and social conditions, and to fit the Indians as rapidly as possible by education and industrial direction for self support simply as American citizens

It was this denigration of tribal leadership in conjunction with extensive reservation land loses to non-Indians that created a political vacuum and set the stage for the Indian Reorganization Act.

The implications of the Synder Act were noted in a 1972 Department of the Interior publication:[242]

> The Indian Agent, and his staff, replaced the tribal government in large measure. Substantive legislation reflecting this transition was adopted by the Congress in 1921.
> Often referred to as the Synder Act, it indicated that the objective of the Bureau of Indian Affairs was to provide for the general support and civilization of the Indians...
> Indians not on Federal reservations became subject to State law.

---

[241] NARA Washington D.C. RG 75, Records of the Bureau of Indian Affairs, Central Classified Files 1907-1936, File 41164-1921-054.

[242] Taylor, Theodore W., 1972, The United States and Their Indian Citizens:18-19, US. Department of the Interior, Washington D.C.

Replacing the tribal form of leadership and the point of contact between the Indian community and the reservation agent was the business council, the federally-preferred form of community representation. Interestingly as we shall see, John Collier, an idealistic strident supporter of Indian rights in implementing the Indian Reorganization Act, was an advocate for such a form of community leadership. In 1932, Collier proposed specific congressional legislation (S. 3668, The Tribal Council Bill) that advocated the creation and recognition of such tribal councils.[243] The councils would organize around an organizational charter such as a constitution. They would also have limited powers of self government, such as the authority over tribal lands. Here we find the foundations to Sections 15, 16 and 17 of Collier's later 1934 Indian Reorganization Act. S. 3668 was opposed by both Indian Commissioner Charles Rhodes and his Assistant Commissioner Henry Scattergood, principally on the basis that the legislation would impose a boiler plate form of tribal organization, not taking into account the differences existing amongst Indian tribes. The bill failed to get to a floor vote. Needless to say, Rhodes and Scattergood endured Collier's vengeful wrath and political muckraking for their opposition to his proposal.

In contrast, the Snyder Act, as applied by the Department of the Interior, held that the Federal government considered any Indian not residing upon a federally established or recognized reservation as no longer in tribal relations and was thus under state jurisdiction.

Thus, by 1925 we find the Assistant Secretary of the Interior John F. Edwards noting:[244]

---

[243] Rusco, Elmer R., 2002, A Fateful Time: The Background and Legislative History of the Indian Reorganization Act:163,:168, Reno, University of Nevada Press.
[244] Letter, March 21, 1925, John F. Edwards, Assistant Secretary of the Interior, cited in: Goodrich, Chauncy S., 1926, The Legal Status of the California Indians, pt.1, California Law Review, Vol.14, No.

...The scattering of bands of Indians in the State of California have for some time been considered as citizens and the responsibility for their care when indigent, devolves upon local or state officials rather than upon this Service, just the same as if they were white persons in similar circumstances.

During this period, especially prior to 1930, additional lands were acquired by the Interior Department for landless Indian individuals or groups. The purpose was not to give a "tribe" or "band" a politically-recognized land base, rather these lands were acquired to provide individual Indians with lands that could be divided in severalty and allotted to individual Indians as a vehicle towards achieving assimilation.

The era of the Dawes Act represented two streams of policy. First and foremost was the emphasis of federal Indian policy upon the assimilation of the Indian into the American societal and economic mainstream along with the commeasuring abolishment of tribal and band government. Secondly, was the assumption of legal jurisdiction by the states over these assimilated Indians. The foundation of this entire enterprise was the provision of a protected allotted land base upon which these individual Indians could proceed with this transformation.

The California "rancherias" were an example of this policy. Such lands for landless Indians were acquired by Indian agents via a provision for funds made in the annual Indian appropriation bill by Congress. Yet, within this enterprise there continued the pattern of paternalism fostered not only by the plenary powers of Congress over Indian tribes, but also the administrative philosophy and processes created and instituted by the Department of the Interior that governed the individual Indian ward. The 1930 US Supreme Court decision, *US v. Sandoval* further affirmed this policy,[245]

> ...Taking these decisions together it may be taken as the settled doctrine of this court that Congress, in pursuance of the long-established policy of the government has a right to determine for itself when the guardianship which has been maintained over the Indian shall cease. It is for that body, and not the courts, to determine when the true interests of the Indian require his release from such condition of tutelage.
> Of course, if it is not meant by this that Congress may bring a community or body of people within the range of this power by arbitrarily calling them an Indian tribe, *but only in respect to distinctly Indian communities the questions whether, to what extent, and for what time they shall be recognized and dealt with as dependent tribes requiring the guardianship and protection of the United States are to be determined by Congress and not by the courts...*
> ...Considering the reasons which underlie the authority of Congress to prohibit the introduction of liquor into the Indian country at all, it seems plain that this authority is sufficiently comprehensive to enable Congress to apply the prohibition to the lands of the Pueblos... [emphasis added]

"They must be aided for the preservation of themselves."

This approach and mindset received an additional impetus in 1928 with the publication of the "Meriam Report."[246] This report emphasized, as did the Snyder Act, a broad education of the individual Indian as the primary goal of the Indian Service. The report noted,

> The fundamental requirement is that the task of the Indian Service be recognized as primarily educational, in the broadest sense of that word, and that it be made an efficient educational agency, devoting its main energies to the social and economic advancement of the Indians, so that

---

[245] United States v. Sandoval, 321 US 28 (1913)
[246] Meriam, Lewis et al., 1928, The Problem of Indian Administration, Baltimore, John Hopkins Press

they may be absorbed into the prevailing civilization at least in accordance with a minimum standard of health and decency...

Since the great majority of the Indians are ultimately to merge into the general population, it should cover the transitional period and should endeavor to instruct Indians in the utilization of the services provided by public and quasi public agencies for the people at large in exercising the privileges of citizenship and making their contribution in service and in taxes for the maintenance of the government.

The Report took several new directions in its recommendations to the Indian Service and by extension Indian policy. First,

In the execution of this program scrupulous care must be exercised to respect the rights of the Indian. This phrase "rights of the Indian" is often used solely to apply to his property rights. Here it is used in a much broader sense to cover his rights as a human being living in a free country. Indians are entitled to unfailing courtesy and consideration from all government employees. They should not be subject to arbitrary action

Dawes, it seems, always addressed the Indian in an abstract sense, a monolithic block to be assimilated *en mass* into the main stream. In Dawes, the President, via an executive order, "ordered" that a reservation participate in allotment. Here the emphasis is given to human rights and dignity of the individual. Within this context Meriam goes on to advocate a duality of outcome,

The object of work with or for the Indians is to fit them either to merge into the social and economic life of the prevailing civilization as developed by the whites or to live in the presence of that civilization at least in accordance with a minimum stand of health and decency...Some Indians proud of their race and devoted to their culture and their mode of life have no desire to be as the white men is. They wish to remain as Indians to preserve the what they have inherited from their fathers...It would not recommend the disastrous attempt to force individual Indians or groups of Indians to be what they don't want to be, to break the pride in themselves and their Indian race. Such efforts may break down the good in the old without replacing it with compensating good from the new...

> The position taken, therefore, is that the work with and for the Indian must give consideration to the desires of the Individual Indians. He who wishes to merge into the social and economic of the prevailing civilization of this country should be given all practicable aid and advice in making the necessary adjustments. He who wants to remain an Indian and live according to his old culture should be aided in doing so…
>
> They must be aided in the preservation of themselves….

While Dawes and its assimilative/detribalization processes were still operating, Meriam advocated that legislatively mandated Indian assimilation should not be the ultimate goal as advocated by the nineteenth century philanthropists and Federal government via Dawes. Education was. A variant of this duality of individual choice on a community level was to become a part of the later 1934 Indian Reorganization Act. At the same time, the Meriam Reports emphasis on Indian health set in motion a process that culminated with the 1934 "Johnson-O'Malley Act"[247] whereby the states or territories would be subsidized by the Federal government for costs associated with health, relief, and education services provided to Indians residing within them.

With the 1928 election of Hubert Hoover, the leadership in the Department of the Interior and the Indian Bureau came under the sway of the assimilation-oriented Philadelphia-based Indian Rights Association. President Hoover appointed Ray L. Wilbur as Secretary of the Interior, Charles J. Rhodes as Indian Commissioner, and J. Henry Scattergood as Assistant Commissioner. All three were associated with the Indian Rights Association. Rhodes and Scattergood were also Quakers.[248] The Department's emphasis seemingly would shift back to

---

[247] US. Statutes at Large, vol. 48:596. "An Act Authorizing the Secretary of the Interior to arrange with States or Territories for the education, medical attention, relief of distress, and social welfare of Indians and for other purposes"
[248] Phillip, Keneth R., 1977, <u>John Collier's Crusade for Indian Reform, 1920-1954</u>:92-93, Tucson, University of Arizona Press.

assimilation as its primary policy goal. This was not to be the case. Indian land and natural resource protection, especially water rights, as well as education reform topped the Department's new agenda.

Commissioner Rhodes, with the permission of Secretary Wilbur, proposed to Congress[249] that "the allotment act in its entirety, along with the system of reimbursable loans in its entirety, need legislative reconsideration." Rhodes was especially concerned about former allotment lands that were lost via the sale of inherited estates. His second major concern was the loss of "indivisible tribal estates of the Indians", that is, reservation common lands and natural resource rights held collectively by the reservation population. Rhodes concluded his concerns by stating that,

> ...the Government through the Interior Department, is charged with the direct and highly paternalistic administration of these properties, and unless existing law be changed it may well be that the Government 100 years from now will find itself still charged with this responsibility and still maintaining the paternalistic administration....

Rhodes' prophecy has been proven correct.

Rhodes went on to propose to Congress that the remaining Indian tribes be incorporated in such a manner that would enable them, without Interior Department oversight and regulation, to manage their own reservation common lands. Here we find Rhodes anticipating one of the key proposals to be advanced in the 1934 Indian Reorganization legislation. Rhodes concluded, "Hence any plan contemplating the gradual diminishment and the ultimate and final termination of Indian tutelage must concern itself with this aspect of the situation." We also find an echo of the duality concept advanced in the 1928

---

[249] Congressional Record, vol. 72:1051-1053.

Miriam Report. On the one hand Rhodes advocated for the protection of individual fee-held former allotment lands, whilst at the same time arguing for the protection of reservation common lands and resources.

Meaningful Indian education, particularly of Indian children, and educational activities that would enable an Indian individual to function in a non-Indian social and cultural environment were to be at the policy's forefront. This intent was clearly articulated in the Commissioner's report of 1931[250]

> The purpose of education for any indigenous peoples at the present day is to help these peoples, both as groups and individuals, to adjust themselves to modern life, protecting and preserving as much of their own ways of living as possible, and capitalizing their economic and cultural resources to their own benefit and their contribution to modern civilization....

Gone were the Dawes Act notions of Indians having to shed their cultural beliefs. The new proposed goal was to assist the Indian in functioning in a social, ideological, and economic environment different from his or her own. In this notion we find another conceptual cornel that was to be fully articulated in the later 1934 Indian Reorganization legislation. An Indian or Indians could still live within a separate community whilst learning and adopting usable elements from an outside cultural environment.

"...illy digested emotional attacks"

Most of Rhode's policy plans came to naught. During the course of the Hoover administration, no such actions were legislatively undertaken. Instead, both Commissioner Rhodes and Assistant Commissioner Scattergood found themselves and their policies under intense criticism by the American Indian

---

[250] Annual Report of the Commissioner of Indian Affairs for the year 1931:4-5.

Defense Association. The Indian Defense Association was led by a fiery, opinionated young activist by the name of John Collier, who, in conjunction with the New Mexico Association on Indian Affairs and several other Indian activist associations, was pushing Congress towards enacting legislation promoting Indian arts and crafts as a way to preserve Indian culture and to promote economic development amongst Indian communities.

In Colliers eyes, the Indian, was no longer to be merely a farmer or a rancher subjected to forced assimilation as promoted by the Dawes Act. He or she was to become a economically viable artisan and craftsman as well. Rhodes and Scattergood were not in favor of such legislation. Such legislation was subsequently introduced in both the House and Senate in 1930 (Swing-Johnson bill). Rhodes and Scattergood's primary objection to this legislation was based primarily upon depression-era budgetary constraints. Such a bill had to wait until the advent of the Roosevelt Administrations "New Deal" program. They both suffered Collier's wrath for not doing so. Collier accused them through his American Indian Defense Association of having "not rectified the extreme abuses in the treatment of Indians, nor have they put into effect a single constructive plan"[251] whilst in general accusing the Hoover administration of incompetence. Collier threatened to inundate Congress with "critical and muckraking publicity" against the two, stressing that "the injurious effects of such a method would be incalculable."[252] Secretary of the Interior Wilbur, defending his two subordinates, responded to the Indian Defense Association's accusations by stating, "I hope there can be more sober acceptance of legitimate responsibility on the part of

---

[251] American Indian Life, July 30, 1930:20-23. Letter of Haven Emerson of the American Indian Defense Association to Secretary of the Interior Wilbur, May 9, 1930
[252] John Collier Papers, Benecke Library, Yale University. Letter John Collier to Haven Emerson, February 4, 1930.

officials of your organization rather than a continuation of widespread intemperate and illy digested emotional attacks."

Nonetheless, despite Collier's continual rantings, the Interior Department succeeded in instituting many of the reforms advocated in the Meriam Report, especially in reorganizing the Indian Office, Indian health care and especially education. Yet, when Franklin Roosevelt was elected President in 1934, neither Rhoads nor Scattergood were reappointed to their respective positions. Instead, we find Collier self-promoting himself along with two associates, Lewis Meriam and Nathan Margold. Also vying for Secretary of the Interior was Harold Ickes, co-founder of the Chicago-based Indian Rights Association.

"The Whites can take care of themselves, but the Indians need someone to protect them."

The new Roosevelt administration offered Ickes the secretaryship he sought. Ickes, in turn, backed John Collier for the position of Indian Commissioner. Ickes writing of Collier stated,[253]

> ...that no one exceeds him in knowledge of Indian matters or his sympathy with the point of view of the Indians themselves. I want someone in that office who is an advocate of the Indians. The whites can take care of themselves but the Indians need some one to protect them from exploitation...I want the Indians to be helped to help themselves. John Collier, with whatever his faults of temperament he may have, has to a higher degree than any one available for that office, the point of view towards the Indians that I want in the Commissioner of Indian Affairs.

---

[253] Letter Secretary Harold Ickes to Attorney Francis C. Wilson, April 18, 1933, quoted in Prucha 1984, vol.II:941.

Despite the ideal qualities and empathy Secretary Ickes sought in his Indian Commissioner, the paternalistic notions expressed in Federal Indian policy since the mid nineteenth century still remained.

Collier was appointed Commissioner on April 21, 1933. His assistant commissioner was William Zimmerman, who was to remain in that position until 1950. Collier now had his chance to change the direction of Indian policy. Collier's view of the current state of Indian policy affairs was,[254]

> The Commissioner was confronted, so he said, by a situation which was one of continuing drift of Indian physical assets and Indian life. This was do to no malice on the part of the government, but to a policy which took for granted the extinction of the Indian. Policies of a rigid institutionalized Bureau resulted in the alienation of Indian land, disintegration of Indian tribal and cultural life, and the economic decline of Indians as groups and as individuals.

With the aid of Secretary Ickes, Collier sought an end to the policy that emanated from the 1887 Dawes Act and to create a policy that has become known as the "Indian New Deal." At the request of Secretary Ickes and Collier, President Roosevelt, on May 25, 1933, issued an executive order abolishing the Board of Indian Commissioners "to reduce expenditures" and "to increase efficiency" of government operations.[255] In reality, Ickes and Collier did not want any interference from such a committee whilst implementing their new progressive policies. As Philip[256] noted, "Collier and Ickes wanted to end the board's existence for political reasons, because it was controlled by Republicans and

---

[254] Zimmerman, William Jr., 1957, "The Role of the Bureau of Indian Affairs Since 1933" in <u>American Indians and American Life</u>:31-40, The Annals of the American Academy of Political and Social Science, vol. 311, May 1957, Philadelphia.
[255] Philip, Kenneth, 1977, <u>John Colliers Crusade for Indian Reform 1920-1954</u>: 118-120, University of Arizona Press, Tucson.
[256] ibid. 1977:118-119

conservatives who favored the assimilation policies associated with the Dawes General Allotment Act." What began as a liberal progressive inspired program now became draped in a shawl of conservatism being attacked by the same ideological group that created it. Additionally, Collier was also facing pressures from both Secretary Ickes and the White House to implement spending cuts in the Department's budget. Ickes was pushing him for a 25% budget reduction, especially proposing the use of Indian trust funds to cover departmental administrative costs.

One of the first acts of Ickes and Collier was the cessation of allotted land sales. On August 12, 1933[257], Secretary Ickes ordered that " no more trust or restricted Indian lands, allotted or inherited, shall be offered for sale, nor certificates of competency, patents in fee, or removal of restrictions be submitted to the Indian office for approval." The actual cessation of land allotments, being legislatively enacted, had to await the enactment of the Indian Reorganization Act (Section 1). Ickes' and Collier's actions in this regard might very well have been illegal until the enactment of IRA. Certainly the rights of individual Indians to acquire allotments or to rightly inherit land and to receive a patent for their allotments were trampled upon by the two.

A second significant act, this time by Collier, was his issuing of a departmental circular[258] addressing religious freedom. Collier wrote, "No interference with Indian religious life or ceremonial expression will hereafter be tolerated....", thus curtailing on-reservation missionary activities and *defacto* stopping assimilative activities on many Indian reservations. Collier, at this time

---

[257] Annual Report of the Secretary of the Interior for the Fiscal Year Ended June 30, 1933
[258] Circular # 2970, January 3, 1934, John Collier to Field Personnel. "Indian Religious Freedom and Indian Culture", NARA Laguna Niguel, RG 75, Records of the Mission Indian Agency, Correspondence, Box 15, File 9.

was working to stop the loss of Indian lands to non-Indians and to preserve Indian culture.

Collier also issued a pointed criticism detailing Dawes' failures. In his January 20, 1934 memorandum distributed by the Office of Indian Affairs to all reservation agencies[259], the perceived shortcomings of the Dawes Act were discussed and a new course in Indian Affairs suggested,

> ...In considering law enforcement regulation particular study should be made of the extent to which state laws, both civil and criminal, should be made applicable on Indian reservations...
> Experience under the allotment system reveals two major evils:
>
> 1. The loss of local self-government and the breakdown of the Indian community.
> 2. The loss of Indian lands and the uneconomic and unequal distribution of lands remaining in Indian ownership.
>
> 1. The aim of the allotment system was the ultimate absorption of the Indian population in the surrounding white community. It looked forward to the day when the Indian would become absolute owner of his property and manager of his own affairs.
>
> The immediate objective of the Indian Administration during the period of guardianship was to develop the competence of individual Indians in economic affairs...During this process of so-called education of the Indian, the community life and political responsibility of the Indian have largely been destroyed.
>
> 2. The Federal Government has failed to substitute any satisfactory alternative for the Indian community which it attempted to destroy...
>
> It is the belief of the administration that these evils can be remedied by a program directed toward two fundamental principles:

---

[259] 1934, January 20, Office of Indian Affairs Memorandum #80426, Indian Self-government. Effects of the Dawes Allotment Act and the goals of IRA.

1. To establish Indian self-government and to promote a healthy and satisfactory community life.
2. To preserve and develop Indian lands in Indian ownership and to provide the opportunity of economic livelihood for all who choose to remain within Indian Community.

The last two items became the foundational arguments of the Administration's New Deal for Indians. What is especially interesting was Collier's use of the terms "community life" and "Indian community" instead of tribal community and Indian tribe as the focus of his efforts. Collier, writing in his 1933 "Annual Report of the Commissioner of Indian Affairs", stated his plan to Congress,

> If we can relieve the Indian of the unrealistic and fatal allotment system, if we can provide him with land and the means to work the land; if through group organization and tribal incorporation, we can give him a real share in the management of his own affairs, he can develop normally in his own environment. The Indian problem as it exists today, including the heaviest and most unproductive administration costs of public service, has largely grown out of the allotment system which has destroyed the economic integrity of the Indian estate and deprived the Indians of normal economic activity.

We are seeing early hints that Collier, wanting to preserve Indian culture, was not interested in preserving tribalism as the organization focus of Indian society. As Collier noted above, he wanted tribes to "incorporate" and to engage in group, not tribal, organization. We also find in his 1934 critique of the Dawes Act, an advocacy for Indian self-government, economic development, and lastly, continued efforts towards Indian land ownership. Was Collier's vision of federal Indian policy one of simply taking Dawes' notion of gradual assimilation and detribalization in a different direction by shifting the focus from the individual to that of the collective group community? The ultimate goal of Dawes was the assimilation of the individual into the mainstream of American society. Collier's goal, as we shall see, was the political and economic development and transformation of Indian communities to the point where termination of federal jurisdiction could occur. This was the same goal stated in the 1928 Meriam Report. Forced assimilation of the individual would, in theory, be supplanted by gradual voluntary community amalgamation.

Collier's ideal community type was that of the Pueblo Indian communities, like the Taos, with whom he spent a significant amount of time during the 1920's. Collier wrote extensively of his pueblo experiences, especially on religious dances. He was captivated by, "its complex and childlike beauty."[260] One of his major published works in this area was titled, "On the Gleaming Way." Of the Pueblos he wrote in 1922,[261]

> The pueblo is not primitive in the sense of being primordial. Vast spaces of evolution and of compounding of cultures lie behind it. But it is primitive in that it has conserved the earliest statesmanship, the earliest pedagogy of the human race, carrying them forward under geographical conditions which have helped to a result possibly unique, for its complex yet childlike beauty, in the world's history. From this statesmanship and pedagogy our present world needs to learn, and tomorrow's world will learn if given the chance."

As will be seen, Collier, the romanticist and idealist, believed that industrialized capitalist *Gesellschaft* societies had to rediscover their *Gemeinschaft* natural primitiveness. The Indian policies he advocated and later had enacted, were based upon this personal idealistic Gemeinschaft belief.

In 1933, Collier advocated that the new Roosevelt administration end the process of Indian land allotment and focus instead upon the Indian community

---

[260] Collier, "Red Atlantis"18 quoted in: Rusco, Elmer R., 2000, <u>A Fateful Time: The Background and Legislative History of the Indian Reorganization Act</u> :143, Reno, University of Nevada Press.
[261] Ibid."Red Atlantis":18

and its corporative and collective utilization of land assets.[262] Collier envisioned Indian communities governed upon the principles and insights of the social sciences out of which would emerge a "scientific government" facilitated with the help of a cadre of anthropologists, whose primary task was to assist in the creation of such communities in a way that did not disrupt critical Indian cultural patterns, especially cross-cutting community and societal bonds and relationships.

In 1934, Collier wrote[263] to these anthropologists assisting him that,

> we are anxious to build upon the potentialities of cooperative economic activity that exist today with the social organization of various Indian tribes and communities with a view of enlarging the tribal ownership of land in lieu of the present system of Indian dual allotments.

Collier also sought the input and support from many individuals and Indian advocacy groups such as the American Civil Liberties Union, National Council of American Indians, the General Federation of Women's Clubs, the Indian Defense Association, and Indian Rights Association, to end the Indian land allotment system and to carry through on many of the programs advocated in the 1928 Miriam Report.

Out of this emerged Collier's plan for a new progressive socialist-influenced Indian policy whose foundation was to be based upon the Indian's natural tendency towards cooperative use of lands and resources and the replacement of individually-held land ownership with that of the community collective.[264] Colliers "boiler plate" vision of Indian culture and government, based on of his limited experience with Southwest Indian groups was challenged by two

---

[262] American Indian Life, January 1933:1-5
[263] NARA Washington D.C., RG 75, Records Concerning the Wheeler-Howard Act, Correspondence File 48994-1934-066 part 9.
[264] Letter, Commissioner of Indian Affairs John Collier to Professor Forrest Clements, November 20, 1933, NARA Washington D.C., RG 75 Records Concerning the Wheeler-Howard Act Part 10A.

prominent anthropologists, Professor Ralph Linton[265] and Professor Oliver LaFarge[266]. They called his plan unworkable due to the diverse views and cultural concepts of land use and ownership and tribal leadership held amongst the different Indian groups within the United States. In fact, in 1936, when James C. Curry, an Interior Department lawyer visited the Pueblo villages that Collier used as the model for his Red Atlantis vision, he found not the utopian socialist community claimed by Collier, but communities where the majority of livestock and agricultural lands were owned in fee-simple held by a minority of Indians.[267] Collier did not take into consideration the cultural ethos of wealth and status amongst the Indians of the Northwest, or the highly individualistic cultural traits of the Plains Indian tribes. Collier ignored Linton's and LaFarge's warnings in opposition. As Rhodes and Scattergood found out, Collier was quite intolerant of opposition to his idealistic visions.

This situation also exposed a major shortcoming in the development of the IRA legislation. Collier never thought of asking the tribes what they thought of this proposed legislation or even of asking their assistance and input in the creation of the bill. Instead, he had the agencies inform the tribes via *a priori* "Questions and Answers" memorandums what the legislation would or would not do. Most tribes were not aware that the Act had been passed until informed in a manner similar to those Mission Indian Bands in Southern California who received a letter from the Riverside Indian Agency, dated July 3, 1934.[268] It was addressed to, "Spokesmen, Committee Members and Indian People on the

---

[265] Letter, Professor Ralph Linton to Commissioner of Indian Affairs John Collier, (nd.) NARA Washington D.C. RG 75, Records Concerning the Wheeler-Howard Act, Part 10A.
[266] Letter, Professor Oliver LaFarge to Commissioner of Indian Affairs John Collier, December 5, 1933, NARA Washington D. C., RG 75, Records Concerning the Wheeler Howard Act Part 10A.
[267] Letter James E. Curry to Felix S. Cohen, January 27, 1936, Cohen Papers Box 43, Benecke Library, Yale University.
[268] NARA Laguna Niguel, RG 75, Riverside Indian Agency IRA Correspondence File. Box 3, file 15.

Reservations within the Mission Agency Jurisdiction," announcing that IRA was now a law and proceeded to explain the impact of the Act.

Collier's response to such criticism was the January 20, 1934 Departmental memorandum cited above that was to establish the basis for his proposed progressive Indian policy to end the land allotment and individual assimilative policies of Dawes. For Collier, social-cultural change and gradual assimilation within these Indian communities was to occur via existing Indian social institutions. At the same time, they were to provide a model for the transformation of American society. Collier referred to this process of change as "democratic communal organization."[269] From it would emerge his utopian Red Atlantis.

"commanding the imagination of Indians and Congressman alike."

Collier's new tract towards achieving a new progressive, yet paternalistic, Indian policy was instituted with the 1934 enactment of the "Wheeler-Howard" Act and as amended the "*Indian* Reorganization Act" (IRA.). Wheeler–Howard represented the advent of a new federal Indian policy, the termination of federal wardship over Indians. This was the goal envisioned by the architects of Wheeler-Howard. Self-governance and economic self-sufficiency of Indian socialist-based communities was to lead to the end of the Indians federal relationship, excepting that of an ordinary citizen. The proposed legislation was created by Collier with the assistance of the Interior Departments Solicitor Nathan Margold and his two assistants, Felix Cohen, and Charles Fahy. Collier hoped that this legislation "would have a massive and dramatic nature, commanding the imagination of Indians and Congressman alike."[270]

---

[269] American Indian Life, January 1933:1-5
[270] Library of Congress, Bronson Cutting Papers, Box 30. The Purposes and Operations of the Wheeler-Howard Indian Rights Bill.

Collier's plan was introduced to Congress by Congressman Edgar Howard and Senator Burton K. Wheeler. The original bill faced significant opposition from both the Senate Indian Affairs Committee and many Indians. It also faced an uphill battle in Congress. Collier was forced to travel to numerous reservations, holding "congress's" with tribal leaders whom he previously ignored, in his efforts to gain their support for IRA. Many tribal leaders and some religious groups, after hearing, Collier came out in opposition to his proposals. Even more ominous was the fact that many members of both the House and Senate Indian Affairs Committees had difficulty understanding the poorly-written, torturously complex draft of the original fifty-two page bill submitted by Collier. Others were ideologically opposed to what Collier was attempting, wanting assurance that the ultimate goal of IRA was still the assimilation of the Indian into the mainstream of American society. One Congressman, Thomas O'Malley of Wisconsin "doubted whether this experiment in Soviet Style "collectivism"[271] would prove successful." Senator Burton Wheeler, an assimilationist, who was to later become one of the bill's sponsors, upon reading the draft was led to remark,[272] "I have read the bill and I will swear that it is impossible for me to understand some of the provisions of the bill, so as to give an intelligent answer to an Indian who writes to me and tell him just exactly what you are seeking to do." Wheeler continued to chide Collier and his draft stating, "If members of the committee who are lawyers...cannot themselves tell exactly what you are going to do, how do you expect these uneducated Indians...to be able to pass intelligently upon the provisions of the bill."

---

[271] Philip, Kenneth, 1977, <u>John Collier's Crusade for Indian Reform 1920-1954</u>: 157, University of Arizona Press, Tucson.
[272] Rusco, Elmer R., 2000, <u>A Fateful Time: The Background and Legislative History of the Indian Reorganization Act</u> :234, Reno, University of Nevada Press.

Commissioner Collier, realizing that the bill's passage was in doubt, sought political support from President Roosevelt. Collier, true to form, lashed out at the bill's distracters. Secretary Ickes also sought to quell resistance within the Interior Department to the legislation, threatening in a memo[273] addressed to all Interior Department employees that any employee caught speaking out against the bill, "to defeat our program, would face the penalty of dismissal." Collier also realized that the bill would have to be significantly re-written and amended if it was to have a chance for enactment. A heavily revised draft was produced by the joint efforts of Senator Wheeler and Colliers Assistant Commissioner William Zimmerman. The two men reduced the bill from its original sixty sections down to its final nineteen. Most notable in this revision was the removal of original text that established a separate Indian judiciary and court system for Indian communities and the granting of municipal powers to Indian communities established under this bill. With the political support of President Roosevelt, Collier's heavily revised bill was passed by Congress. The final approved legislation read,[274]

> BE IT ENACTED by the Senate and House of Representatives of the United States of America in Congress assembled, That hereafter no land of any Indian reservation, created or set apart by treaty or agreement with the Indians, Act of Congress, Executive order, purchase, or otherwise, shall be allotted in severalty to any Indian.
>
> Sec. 2.The existing periods of trust placed upon any Indian lands and any restriction on alienation thereof are hereby extended and continued until otherwise directed by Congress.
>
> Sec. 3.The Secretary of the Interior, if he shall find it to be in the public interest, is hereby authorized to restore to tribal ownership the remaining

---

[273] NARA Washington D.C. RG 75, Records concerning the Wheeler –Howard Act, 48994-1934-066, Part 7, May 4, 1934
Memorandun, Harold Ickes: "To all Employees of the Indian Service"
[274] U.S. Congress. Wheeler-Howard Act (Indian Reorganization Act). 74th Cong., 2nd sess., June 18, 1934.

surplus lands of any Indian reservation heretofore opened, or authorized to be opened, to sale, or any other form of
disposal by Presidential proclamation, or by any of the public land laws of the United States; Provided, however, That valid rights or claims of any persons to any lands so withdrawn existing on the date of the withdrawal shall not be affected by this Act: Provided further, That this section shall not apply to lands within any reclamation project heretofore authorized in any Indian reservation: Provided further, That this section shall not apply to lands within any reclamation project heretofore authorized in any Indian
reservation: Provided further, that the order of the Department of the interior signed, dated, and approved by Honorable Ray Lyman Wilbur, as Secretary of the Interior, on October 28, 1932, temporarily withdrawing lands of the Papago Indian Reservation
in Arizona from all forms of mineral entry or claim under the public land mining laws is hereby revoked and rescinded, and the lands of the said Papago Indian Reservation are hereby restored to exploration and location, under the existing mining laws of the United
States, in accordance with the express terms and provisions declared and set forth in the Executive orders establishing said Papago Indian Reservation: Provided further, That the damages shall be paid to the Papago Tribe for loss of any improvements of any land
located for mining in such a sum as may be determined by the Secretary of the Interior but not exceed the cost of said improvements: Provided further, that a yearly rental not to exceed five cents per acre shall be paid to the Papago Indian Tribe: Provided further, that in the event that any person or persons, partnership, corporation, or association, desires a mineral patent, according to the mining laws of the United States, he or they shall first deposit in the treasury of the United States to the credit of the Papago Tribe the sum of $1.00 per acre in lieu of annual rental, as hereinbefore provided, to compensate for the loss or occupancy of the lands withdrawn by the requirements of mining operations: Provided further, That patentee shall also pay into the Treasury of the United States to the credit of the Papago Tribe damages for the loss of improvements not heretofore said
in such a sum as may be determined by the Secretary of the Interior, but not to exceed the cost thereof; the payment of $1.00 per acre for surface use to be refunded to patentee in the event that the patent is not required Nothing herein contained shall restrict the granting or use of permits for easements or rights-of-way; or ingress or egress over the lands for all proper and lawful purposes; and nothing contained therein, except as expressly provided, shall be construed as authority by the Secretary of the Interior, or any other person, to issue or promulgate a rule or regulation in

conflict with the Executive order of February1, 1917, creating the Papago Indian Reservation in Arizona or the Act of February 21, 1931 (46 Stat.1202)

Sec. 4.Except as herein provided, no sale, devise, gift, exchange or other transfer of restricted Indian lands or of shares in the assets of any Indian tribe or corporation organized hereunder, shall be made or approved: Provided, however, That such
lands or interests may, with the approval of the Secretary of the Interior, be sold, devised, or otherwise transferred to the Indian tribe in which the lands or shares are located or from which the shares were derived or to a successor corporation; and in all instances such lands or interests shall descend or be devised, in accordance with the then existing laws of the State, or Federal laws where applicable, in which said lands are located or in which the subject matter of the corporation is located, to any member of such tribe or of such corporation or any heirs of such member: provided further, That the Secretary
of the Interior may authorize voluntary exchanges of lands of equal value and the voluntary exchange of shares of equal value whenever such exchange, in his judgment, is expedient and beneficial for or compatible with the proper consolidation of Indian lands and for the benefit of cooperative organizations

Sec. 5.The Secretary of the Interior is hereby authorized, in his discretion, to acquire through purchase, relinquishment, gift, exchange, or assignment, any interest in lands, water rights or surface rights to lands, within or without existing reservations, including trust or otherwise restricted allotments whether the allottee be living or deceased, for the purpose of providing lands for Indians. For the acquisition of such lands, interests in lands, water rights, and surface rights, and for expenses incident to such acquisition, there is hereby authorized to be appropriated, out of any funds in the Treasury not otherwise appropriated, a sum not to exceed $2,000,000 in any one fiscal year: Provided, that no part of such funds shall be used to acquire
additional land outside of the exterior boundaries of Navajo Indian Reservation for the Navajo Indians in Arizona and New Mexico, in the event that the proposed Navajo boundary extension measures how pending in congress and embodied in the
bills (S. 2531 and H.R. 8927) to define the exterior boundaries of the Navajo Indian Reservation in Arizona, and for other purposes, and the bills (S. 2531 and H.R. 8982) to define the exterior boundaries of the Navajo Indian Reservation in New

Mexico and for other purposes, or similar legislation, become law. The unexpended balances of any appropriations made pursuant to this section shall remain available until expended. Title to any lands or rights acquired pursuant to this Act shall be taken in the name of the United States in trust for the Indian tribe or individual Indian for which the land is acquired, and such lands or rights shall be exempt from State and local taxation.

Sec. 6. The Secretary of the Interior is directed to make rules and regulations for the operation and management of Indian forestry units on the principle of sustained-yield management, to restrict the number of livestock grazed on Indian range units to the
estimated carrying capacity of such ranges, and to promulgate such other rules and regulations as may be necessary to protect the range from deterioration, to prevent soil erosion, to assure full utilization of the range, and like purposes.

Sec. 7. The Secretary of the Interior *is hereby authorized to proclaim new Indian reservations on lands* acquired pursuant to any authority conferred by this Act, or to add such lands to existing reservations: Provided, that lands added to existing reservations shall be designated for the exclusive use of Indians entitled by enrollment or by tribal membership to residence at such reservations.

Sec. 8. Nothing contained in this Act shall be construed to relate to Indian holdings of allotments or homesteads upon the public domain outside of the geographic boundaries of any Indian reservation now existing or established hereafter

Sec. 9. There is hereby authorized to be appropriated, out of any funds in the Treasury not otherwise appropriated, such sums as may be necessary, but not to exceed $250,000 in any fiscal year, to be expended at the order of the Secretary of the Interior,
in defraying the expenses of organizing Indian chartered corporations or other organizations created under this Act.

Sec. 10. There is hereby authorized to be appropriated, out of any funds in the Treasury not otherwise appropriated, the sum of $10,000,000 to be established as a revolving fund from which the Secretary of the Interior, under such rules and regulations as
he may prescribe, may make loans to Indian chartered corporations for the purpose of promoting the economic development of such tribes and of their members, and may defray the expenses of administering such loans.

Repayment of amounts loaned under this authorization shall be credited to the revolving fund and shall be available for the purposes for which the fund is established. A report shall be made annually to Congress of transactions under this authorization.

Sec. 11. There is hereby authorized to be appropriated, out of any funds in the United States Treasury not otherwise appropriated, a sum not to exceed $250,000 annually, together with any unexpended balances of previous appropriations
made pursuant to this section, for loans to Indians for the payment of tuition and other expenses in recognized vocational and trade schools: Provided, That not more than$50,000 of such sum shall be available for loans to Indian students in high schools and colleges. Such loans shall be reimbursable under rules established by the Commissioner of Indian Affairs.

Sec. 12. The Secretary of the Interior is directed to establish standards of health, age, character, experience, knowledge, and ability for Indians who maybe appointed, without regard to civil-service laws, to the various positions maintained, now or hereafter, by the Indian office, in the administrations functions or services affecting any Indian tribe. Such qualified Indians shall hereafter have the preference to appointment to vacancies in any
such positions.

Sec. 13. The provisions of this Act shall not apply to any of the Territories, colonies, or insular possessions of the United States, except that sections 9, 10, 11, 12, and 16 shall apply to the Territory of Alaska: Provided, that Sections 2, 4, 7, 16, 17, and 18 of this Act shall not apply to the following named Indian tribes, together with members of other tribes affiliated with such named located in the State of Oklahoma, as follows: Cheyenne, Arapaho, Apache, Comanche, Kiowa, Caddo, Delaware, Wichita, Osage, Kaw, Otoe, Tonkawa, Pawnee, Ponca, Shawnee, Ottawa, Quapaw, Seneca, Wyandotte, Iowa, Sac and Fox, Kickapoo, Pottawatomi, Cherokee, Chickasaw, Choctaw, Creek,and Seminole. Section 4 of this Act shall not apply to the Indians of the Klamath Reservation in Oregon.

Sec. 14. The Secretary of the Interior is hereby directed to continue the allowance of the articles enumerated in section 17 of the Act of March 2, 1889 (25 Stat. L. 891), or their commuted cash value under the Act of June 10, 1886 (29 Stat. L. 334), to all Sioux Indians who would be eligible, but for the provisions of this Act, to receive allotments

of lands in severalty under section 19 of the Act of May 29,1908 (25 (35) Stat. L. 451), or under any prior Act, and who have the prescribed status of the head of a family or single person over the age of eighteen years, and his approval shall be final and conclusive, claims therefore to be paid as formerly from the permanent appropriation made by
said section 17 and carried on the books of the Treasury for this purpose. No person shall receive in his own right more than one allowance of the benefits, and application must be made and approved during the lifetime of the allottee or the right shall lapse. Such benefits shall continue to be paid upon such reservation until such time as the lands available therein for allotment at the time of the passage of this Act would have been exhausted by the award to each person receiving such benefits of an allotment of eighty acres of such land.

Sec. 15. Nothing in this Act shall be construed to impair or prejudice any claim or suit of any Indian tribe against the United States. It is hereby declared to be the intent of Congress that no expenditures for the benefit of Indians made out of appropriations authorized by this Act shall be considered as offsets in any suit brought to recover upon any claim of such Indians against the United States.

Sec. 16. Any Indian tribe, or tribes, residing on the same reservation, shall have the right to organize for its common welfare, and may adopt an appropriate constitution and bylaws, which shall become effective when ratified by a majority vote of the adult members of the tribe, or of the adult Indians residing on such reservation, as the case may be, at a special election authorized by the Secretary of the Interior under such rules and regulations as he may prescribe. Such constitution and bylaws when ratified as aforesaid and approved by the Secretary of the Interior shall be revocable by an election open to the same voters and conducted in the same manner as hereinabove provided. Amendments to the constitution and bylaws may be ratified and approved by the Secretary in the same manner as the original constitution and by-laws. In addition to all powers vested in any Indian tribe or tribal council by existing law, the constitution adopted by said tribe shall also vest in such tribe or its tribal council the following rights and powers: To employ legal counsel, the choice of counsel and fixing of fees to be subject to the approval of the Secretary of the Interior; to prevent the sale, disposition, lease, or encumbrance of tribal lands, interests in lands, or other tribal assets without the consent of the tribe; and to negotiate with the Federal, State, and local Governments. The Secretary of the Interior shall advise such tribe or its tribal council of all appropriation estimates or Federal projects for the benefit of the tribe prior to the submission of such estimates to the Bureau of the Budget and the Congress.

Sec. 17. The Secretary of the Interior may, upon petition by at least one-third of the adult Indians, issue a charter of incorporation to such tribe: Provided, that such charter shall not become operative until ratified at a special election by a majority vote of the adult Indians living on the reservation. Such charter may convey to the incorporated tribe the power to purchase, take by gift, or bequest, or other wise, own, hold, manage, operate, and dispose of property of every description, real and personal, including the power to purchase restricted Indian lands and to issue in exchange therefore interests in corporate property, and such further powers as may be incidental to the conduct of corporate business, not inconsistent with law, but no authority shall be granted to sell, mortgage, or lease for a period exceeding ten years any of the land included in the limits of the reservation. Any charter so issued shall not be revoked or surrendered except by Act of Congress.

Sec. 18. This Act shall not apply to any reservation wherein a majority of the adult Indians, voting at a special election duly called by the Secretary of the Interior, shall vote against it application. It shall be the duty of the Secretary of the Interior, within one year after the passage and approval of this Act, to call such an election, which election shall be held by secret ballot upon thirty days' notice

Sec. 19. The term "Indian" as used in this Act shall include all persons of Indian descent who are members of <u>any recognized Indian tribe now under Federal jurisdiction</u>, and all persons who are descendants of such members who were, on June 1, 1934, residing within the present boundaries of any reservation, and shall further include all other persons of one-half or more Indian blood. For the purposes of this Act, Eskimos and other aboriginal peoples of Alaska shall be considered Indians.
The term "tribe" wherever used in this Act shall be construed to refer to any Indian tribe, organized band, pueblo, or the Indians residing on one reservation. The words "adult Indians" wherever used in this Act shall be construed to refer to Indians who have
attained the age of twenty-one years. Approved, June 18, 1934.

In the aftermath of IRA's passage, Collier, despite the revisions and deletions made in the final bill, Collier could still accomplish the bill's original goals. According to Philip (1977),[275] Collier was certain that applying,

> "undeviating" administrative will he could use it to forge "new collective advantages" for the Indians...that their revived group life would recognize the important sociological principle that society "must be a collaboration of local and unique groups cooperating in order to intensify their significant individualities." This would provide an example for the "directionless" white race, which had become "psychically, religiously, socially and esthetically shattered"....

Implementation of the act would devolve onto a cadre of anthropologists who would institute "scientific government" within these new communities. Collier wrote to this cadre,[276]

> "we are anxious to build upon the potentialities of cooperative economic activity that exist today with the social organization of various Indian tribes and communities with a view of enlarging the tribal ownership of land in lieu of the present system of Indian dual allotments."

The era of allotment and Christian missionization upon federal reservations had come to an end.

In the month following IRA's passage Collier issued a memorandum to all agencies and tribes under their jurisdiction explaining the Act,[277]

---

[275] Philip, Kenneth, 1977, <u>John Colliers Crusade for Indian Reform 1920-1954</u>: 161, University of Arizona Press, Tucson.
[276] NARA Washington D.C., RG 75, Records Concerning the Wheeler-Howard Act, Correspondence File 48994-1934-066 part 9.
[277] NARA Laguna Niguel, RG 75, Mission Indian Agency Records, Correspondence, 1934, July. Notice, Commissioner of Indian Affairs. Interior Document # 90027. Facts About the New Indian Reorganization Act: An Explanation and Interpretation of the Wheeler-Howard Act as Modified, Amended and Passed by Congress.

The Indian Reorganization Act, as approved June 18, 1934, is a very modified, shortened and amended version of the original Wheeler-Howard Bill. While the Indian Reorganization Act contains most of the important provisions of the Wheeler-Howard Bill, certain important provisions were left out entirely and many sections were radically changed...

...The outstanding difference between the Indian Reorganization Act and the original Wheeler-Howard Bill is bought about by the omission of two complete and important titles. The Wheeler-Howard Bill set up a system of Indian self-government by authorizing the creation of Indian communities with power to make laws of their own, to make contracts with the Federal and State Governments, to hire their own employees, to compel the removal of government employees, to condemn land for their own purposes and do many things that a county or city can do...

...The Indian Reorganization Act protects the remaining Indian trust land and tribal land against continued loss; it provides for increasing the Indian land holdings...

...Section 1 stops all further allotment of tribal land...But it also affects the tribes on allotted, broken-up reservations. Any new land which is bought for them cannot be and will not be allotted to individuals. Title will remain in the United States in trust for the tribe, which will assign the land for the use and occupancy of its landless members...

...Section 5 authorizes Congress to make an annual appropriation of two million dollars for the purchase of land for landless Indians or for Indians whose holdings are to small or too poor to enable them to make a living thereon...The title to the land bought under this authority will remain in the United States in trust for the Indian tribe or the individual Indian for whose benefit the purchase is made...

...The Indian Reorganization Act authorizes a revolving credit fund...from which to make loans to Indian tribal corporations which in turn will make loans to the individual members of the tribe...

...When Congress authorized this credit fund, it directed that loans from the fund should be made only to Indian charted corporations which in turn would make loans to individuals or groups. This was done so as to make the chartered corporation as well as the individual responsible for conserving the loan fund...

>...only tribes which vote for the acceptance of the Act and decide to incorporate will have the privilege of participating in the loan fund...
>
>...Like the constitution and by-laws, the charter of incorporation cannot be granted until one third of the members of a tribe petition for it and it is ratified by a majority vote of all adult Indians living on the reservation."

This Act stopped further allotments of Indian lands, prevented the sale of Indian reservation lands to non-Indians, and, following the 1921 Snyder Act, continued federal paternal guardianship over all Indians resident on federally established reservations. Most importantly under the provisions of this Act, Indian tribes, bands, and pueblos could voluntarily reconstitute themselves as self-governing reorganized communities by a majority vote. Those who declined remained complete dependent wards of the government.

Also important, Section 19 of IRA stipulated who could come under the aegis of this Act,

> The term "Indian" as used in this Act shall include all persons of Indian descent who are members of any recognized Indian tribe now under federal jurisdiction, and all persons who are descendants of such members who were, on June 1, 1934, residing within the present boundaries of any reservation, and shall further include all other persons of one-half or more Indian blood.

Section 19 explicitly defined and limited what constituted a "tribe" under IRA,

> The term "tribe" wherever used in this Act shall be construed to any Indian tribe, organized band, pueblo, or Indians residing on one reservation.

Collier elaborated upon these requirements in a Circular dated March 7, 1936,[278]

---

[278] Circular # 3134, Enrollment under the Indian Reorganization Act, March 7, 1936. NARA Laguna Niguel, RG 75, Mission Indian Agency, Records Pertaining to IRA, Box 249.

...The language "as used in this Act" is construed to mean "for the purpose of sharing in the benefits provided by the Act", as distinguished from tribal rights generally. Thus, if a person of Indian descent belongs to a recognized tribe which was under Federal jurisdiction on the date of the Act (Class 1) or is a descendant of such a member residing on a reservation June 1, 1934, (Class 2), he is entitled to participate in the benefits of the Act regardless of his degree of Indian blood; and, likewise, a person of one half or more of Indian blood (Class 3) is eligible therefore irrespective of tribal membership or residence on a reservation...

Collier made it clear that those Indians organizing under the Class 3 category were not, based upon the definition of tribe in Section 19 of IRA, considered to be tribes, but merely organized IRA communities.

A critical distinction was made by the Interior Department on the basis of the three classes. This critical differentiation was between "historic" and non-historic IRA Indian groups. Historic groups were those "Class 1" tribes under federal jurisdiction at the time of IRA who had a previous treaty-based relationship with the Federal Government. Non-historic were those Indians (Class 2 and Class 3 under Section 19 of IRA) who were residing upon a federally-established reservation but had no previous federal relationship at the time of IRA's enactment and/or were landless Indians, such as some California Mission Indian groups and rancherias, having one half blood quantum or more.

In an important solicitor's opinion dated April 15, 1938[279], Solicitor Nathan Margold wrote regarding an issue involving two such non-historic Indian communities, Lower Sioux and Prairie Island. What Margold posited was that Class 2 and Class 3 were not considered tribes and had less "powers" than those of a tribe (Class 1),

---

[279] Opinions of the ‚Solicitor :813-814, April 15, 1938, "Powers of Indian Group Organized Under IRA But Not As Historical Tribe."

Neither of these two Indian groups constitutes a tribe but each is being organized on the basis of their residence upon reserved land. After careful consideration in the Solicitor's Office it has been determined under section 16 of the Indian Reorganization Act a group of Indian which is organized on the basis of a reservation and which is not an historical tribe may not have all the powers enumerated in the Solicitor's opinion on the Powers of Indian tribes dated October 25, 1934. The group may not have such of those powers as rest upon the sovereign capacity of the tribe but may have those powers which are incidental to its ownership of property and to its carrying on of business, and those which may be delegated by the Secretary of the Interior.

Additionally, Solicitor Margold in his August 31, 1936 opinion[280] added a further dimension to those landless Indians organizing under IRA as Class 3 groups, "Moreover, these Indians may be organized under the provisions of the Wheeler-Howard Act after land has been acquired for them." Unlike historic tribes residing upon federal reservations, land had to be taken into trust for the group by the Federal government before these Indians could participate in IRA. No land, no IRA participation.

Under Section 16 of the act, Indian groups seeking to organize under the Act in order to be considered a "reorganized tribe" were required to create and vote into effect, via a referendum, a tribal constitution,

> Sec. 16. Any Indian tribe, or tribes, residing on the same reservation, shall have the right to organize for its common welfare, and may adopt an appropriate constitution and bylaws, which shall become effective when ratified by a majority vote of the adult members of the tribe, or of the adult Indians residing on such reservation, as the case may be, at a special election authorized by the Secretary of the Interior under such rules and regulations as he may prescribe. Such constitution and bylaws when ratified as aforesaid and approved by the Secretary of the Interior shall be revocable by an election open to the same voters and conducted in the same manner as hereinabove provided.

---

[280] Opinions of the Solicitor, August 31, 1936:668-669, "Purchases Under Wheeler-Howard Act."

At this point in time, the organizing group, having a constitution or articles of organization approved by the Secretary of the Interior, would come under the auspices of IRA.

The process described in Section 16, as well as Section 17, was the work of Felix Cohen. Although not well versed in the many Indian cultures, he nonetheless realized that flexibility, rather than a solid boiler plate, was needed in the application of IRA to the various tribes, thereby ending both staff, anthropological, and Indian apprehensions over the proposed legislation. Each group or tribe voting to come under IRA was free to create its own constitution and mode of governance based upon its own socio-cultural environment, although the paternalistic attitude was still present by the requirement that the Secretary of the Interior had final approval over such an organizational document.

What did IRA mean by organize? Collier testified to the House Indian Affairs Committee in 1935 to the effect, "…in a great many Indian reservations-more than half of them- the tribal relations have been dissolved, and elsewhere the tribal customs are so vague that nobody knows what they are"[281] Collier addressed the urgent need to organize in his August 18, 1935 Department of Interior Circular (#3095) on "Group Organization."[282] Collier talked of group organization based upon "natural social groups" of varying configurations based upon "community interests" be they kin-based or through shared economic interests. Clearly Collier was not speaking of tribal organization. His Circular spoke of various interest groups within the bounds of a reservation as the organizational principle. Councils would be organized on the basis of these

---

[281] Rusco, Elmer R., 2000, A Fateful Time: The Background and Legislative History of the Indian Reorganization Act :153, Reno, University of Nevada Press.
[282] US Department of the Interior Circular # 3095, RE: Group Organization. NARA Laguna Niguel, RG 75, Mission Indian Agency, Records pertaining to IRA, Box 249.

interest groups. The Indian group present upon a reservation would reorganize itself following these principles. Organization under IRA varied with each reservation and the interest groups so-noted residing upon them. The process required the reorganized community to create a constitution or articles of organization agreeable to the Secretary of the Interior. At that time the community would come under the aegis of IRA. Some tribes took over thirty years from the time of their initial IRA vote to the submission of such an organizational document or charter. As Collier noted, "these are not matters determined by the Act. Nor does the Indian Office determine them."[283] The ultimate goal of Indian policy for Collier was that an Indian community would achieve political stability and economic viability to the point that federal guardianship could cease. Termination of a federal government-to-government relationship was the ultimate goal of Collier's plan. As we shall see, by 1945 Collier was calling for the termination of federal guardianship for a number of reorganized tribes and Mission Indian bands.

The Act also provided for the acquisition and establishment of new reservations for landless Indians (Collier's Class 3 Indians) in order to form new reservation non-tribal communities under the Act. Section 7 noted,

> Sec. 7. The Secretary of the Interior *is hereby authorized to proclaim new Indian reservations on lands* acquired pursuant to any authority conferred by this Act, or to add such lands to existing reservations: Provided, that lands added to existing reservations shall be designated for the exclusive use of Indians entitled by enrollment or by tribal membership to residence at such reservations.

An Indian group or community seeking to come under this act had to meet not only the definitions as stated above in Section 19, but also hold a referendum vote

---

[283] NARA Washington D.C., RG 75 John Collier Reference File 1939-45, June 15, 1935

whether to come under the Act as depicted in Section 16.[284] Following such a referendum, the Indian community had to create, vote upon, and submit for approval, a constitution or by-laws to the Secretary of the Interior. According to the Interior Department's Solicitor there were two types of referendums:

> In the first place, it [the IRA] authorizes the members of a tribe (or of a group of tribes located upon the same reservation) to organize as a tribe without any regard to any requirements of residence. In the second place, this section authorizes the residents of a single reservation (who may be considered a tribe for purposes of this act), under Section 16 to organize without regard to past tribal affiliation.

Only upon acceptance of this governing document by the Secretary was the community considered to be "reorganized" under the Indian Reorganization Act. A third optional step was for the community to seek a charter of incorporation from the Secretary,

> ...Under the proposed plan of Indian self-government, Indian municipal corporations will be chartered by the Secretary of the Interior, subject to ratification by the Indian community, and these corporations will be endowed with the powers which, in the opinion of the Secretary of the Interior, they are competent to discharge The bill proposes a progressive and experimental delegation of powers...[285]

Indians organizing under Class 3 (blood quantum irregardless of tribal affiliation or residence) first had to have land provided for them before they could organize. A 1936 Solicitor's Opinion[286] authored by Nathan Margold mandated this. In part this opinion read,

---

[284] Solicitor's Opinion M-27810 December 13, 1934, cited in Letter of January 14, 1994, Wyman D. Babby, Acting Assistant Secretary-Indian Affairs to Congressman George Miller, Chairman, Committee on Natural Resources, House of Representatives.
[285] 1934, February 13, Department of the Interior, Memorandum to the Press. Proposed Wheeler-Howard legislation.
[286] August 13, 1936, "Purchases Under the Wheeler-Howard Act

The Wheeler-Howard Act, however, authorizes the purchase of land for Indians and defines the term "Indian" to include those persons of one half or more Indian blood regardless of membership in a recognized tribe under Federal jurisdiction and regardless of residence on a Indian reservation...Moreover, these Indians may be organized under the provisions of the Wheeler-Howard Act after land has been acquired for them....

How was IRA explained to the tribes?[287]

"...The bill rightly starts with a long section prescribing ways and means and methods by which an Indian tribe may obtain self-government, may reach in the course of time the right to run its own affairs in its own way...This title prescribes how a tribe or how part of a tribe may apply for a Federal charter, what this charter may contain, what powers it confers upon the Indian community organized under such a charter...

...A chartered community does not mean necessarily an entire tribe or a single reservation. It means that a certain territory is set aside, is delimited, and that the residents within that territory by their own initiative, under their own steam, and through the petition of 25% of the resident population for a charter and a vote of 3/5 of that population in favor of that charter may broach the matter to the Department. All the enrolled members living within this territory which it is proposed to organize into a community are eligible as members of the community, and are entitled to vote and say whether they want a community or not.

The enrolled members within the area must petition for a charter, they must negotiate with the Secretary of the interior for the powers, functions and kind of community organization they want to have...

...No. The Secretary of the Interior has a wide authority in determining whether community will be chartered and what powers will be granted, but once specific terms are fixed the Secretary has no final authority...

...When there are two factions on a reservation, may they be given charters as separate communities...

---

[287] 1934, March 17/18. Discussion of proposed Wheeler-Howard Bill. Department of the Interior Document #83144. Proceedings of the Conference for the Indians of Southern California held at Riverside, Cal. (California Indian Congress)

> The Act gives authority to the Secretary of the Interior to charter those factions as separate communities, and gives authority to buy new lands for both factions...
>
> ...If the tribe wants to organize under a constitution or a charter or a set of by laws, - called charter here- they will be able to do so if this legislation passes...If a tribe voluntarily wants to do that and the charter is prepared by you and by the Indian Office together, accepted by the Secretary of the Interior, before it can be put into effect, 60 out of every 100 adults must vote in favor of it...
>
> ...That constitution which you speak of not in force as a charter until the Secretary approves it and 60 percent of the Indians approve of it.
> [emphasis added]

Collier spoke of Indian communities emerging out of this IRA process, not tribes. For instance, a class 3 group that acquired land from the Federal government after having voted to participate in IRA did not emerge as a tribe from the process. Such a group was designated an Indian community, not a tribe, band or Pueblo. A Class 1 historic tribe (or portion thereof) under federal jurisdiction that voted for IRA emerged as a reorganized Indian community. Re-establishing or affirming tribalism did not apear to be a goal of IRA.

How did Collier explain IRA to the public? The following is his press statement concerning IRA,[288]

> "...The bill is aimed primarily at stopping the rapid draining of Indian lands and other natural resources into white ownership through the allotment system, and at curbing the hitherto almost autocratic powers of the Office of Indian Affairs over persons, property, and institutions of the Indian by granting to them the elementary powers of self-government...

---

[288] 1934, February 13, Department of the Interior, Memorandum to the Press. Proposed Wheeler-Howard legislation.

>...It seeks to give to the Indians the simple right...of establishing an elementary form of self-government, organizing for collective action, and taking part in the management of their own affairs. This bill thus strikes a double blow at the two fatal weaknesses of Indian administration across a whole century: first, the dissipation of the Indian estate and the progressive pauperization of the Indians, and second, the suppression of Indian tribal and social and religious institutions and the steadfast failure of the Government to organize any effective plan of collective action by which the Indians could advance to citizenship and protect their rights...[emphasis added]
>
>...While the bill provides various devices of relinquishment, purchase, and exchange, for restoring allotted and inherited lands to community ownership, it carefully safeguards the vested rights of Indian allottees and heirs. As pointed out by Commissioner Collier, the white man's system of fee patent ownership has not worked with the Indians...
>
>...Under the proposed plan of Indian self-government, Indian municipal corporations will be chartered by the Secretary of the Interior, subject to ratification by the Indian community, and these corporations will be endowed with the powers which, in the opinion of the Secretary of the Interior, they are competent to discharge The bill proposes a progressive and experimental delegation of powers..."
>[emphasis added]

The above contains some peculiar language, "Indian municipal corporations, Indian community vis' a vis' tribe, progressive experimental delegation of powers." What did Collier mean? What were his intentions?

Visions of Red Atlantis

What was Collier's real intent of this Act? It was certainly not the creation of new "recognized" tribes. His intent was the creation of reorganized Indian communities with powers of self-government. In his 1943 "Circular"[289] to all

---

[289] Circular No. 3537, United States Department of the Interior, Office of Indian Affairs, November 15, 1943. RG 75, Mission Indian Agency, Letters Sent, NARA Laguna Niguel.

"Superintendents, Tribal Councils, All Indian Service Personnel and all Indians" John Collier, explained the purpose of IRA.

Collier's main thesis in this document was that IRA was devised to promote "the development of Indian democracy and equality." Given the apparent failure of attempting to integrate and assimilate the individual Indian under the Dawes Act, the focus of IRA was, according to Collier, to allow for the gradual dissipation or "diffusion" of tribal governments and the emergence of self-governing assimilated communities "in the modern democratic sense." Collier went on to state'

> During this transitional period (however short or long it may prove to be) the Federal Government is forced both by the fact of law and the fact of self-interest to continue to give a friendly guiding and protective hand to Indian advancement...
>
> But the government's relationship to Indians is itself in transition. The Indian Reorganization Act made that inevitable. The Indian Office is moving from guardian to advisor, from administrator to friend-in-court. In this transition, many powers hitherto exercised by the Indian Service have been transferred to organized Indian tribes...
>
> This means more than consulting the tribal Council. It means in addition to these things, that separate communities, as the primary group within the tribe, must be organized for planning...It is our function to help Indian communities to understand their own situation, to be conscious of their own needs, to appraise their own interests and their own resources...
>
> This is why I stress that community organization as the key to planning as social action....

Collier made it clear that the IRA's goal was to let tribal organization 'whither on the vine' out of which were to emerge agrarian based Indian communities. To Collier, the term "tribe" held "primitive and atavistic connotations..." which "is the only presently feasible type of local civic self-government they can share in and use for their advancement"²⁹⁰ The Federal government's focus was to be on the political and economic development of Indian communities, not tribal entities. Interestingly, this view reflects the intent of the March 3, 1871 proviso, to reduce tribes to "domestic communities."

"making Reds of the Indians"

The Indian Reorganization Act, according to Felix Cohen, the principal drafter of the Act, was not intended to create new tribes, but reorganize them in such a manner that these "village" communities would serve as a model for the social reconstruction of American society in such a way "that would usher in a socialist democracy to replace the chaos of capitalism."²⁹¹ Collier, in turn, was deeply influenced by the utopian writings of the Russian anarchist and neo-evolutionist, Prince Petr Alekseevich Kropotkin and his writings as presented in his book titled, "Mutual Aid: A Factor of Evolution " and those parallel ideas of the communist theologian Frederick Engels. The agrarian rural village community was central to Kopotkin's view of an ideal society. In chapter 8 of his writing Kopotkin stated,²⁹²

> When we examine the every-day life of the rural populations of Europe, we find that, notwithstanding all that has been done in modern States for the destruction of the village community, the life of the peasants remains honeycombed with habits and customs of mutual aid and support; that important vestiges of the communal possession of the soil are still retained; and that, as soon as the legal obstacles to rural association were lately removed, a network of free unions for all sorts of economical purposes rapidly spread among the peasants -- the tendency of this young

---

[290] 1943, November 15, Department of the Interior, Office of Indian Affairs circular # 3537. John Collier to Superintendents, Tribal Councils. All Indian Service personnel and all Indians. Planning. RG 75, NARA Laguna Niquel
[291] Philip, Kenneth R. 1999, <u>Termination Revisited: American Indians on the Trail to Self-Determination, 1933-1953</u>:4, University of Nebraska Press, Linclon.
[292] Kopotkin, Petr, Alekseevich, 1902, <u>Mutual Aid: A Factor of Evolution.</u>

movement being to reconstitute some sort of union similar to the village community of old.

Collier's Indian community adaptation of Kropotkin's village communities was presented in his August 8, 1935 Circular.[293] In this circular Collier instructed his "Superintendents and Other Field Officials" to utilize the "natural social group or community" as the "basic representation unit on the various reservations involved." Collier continued by stating such natural, "groupings or divisions" should be "based on actual community interests and needs" utilizing "older political groupings", "remote kinship affiliations" or "equally often today, on common economic activities such as farming groups in one portion of the reservation and stock-raising groups in another." Collier also advocated, "…tribal councils composed of delegates elected from socially significant districts will be more representative of the actual interests, economic or otherwise, present on the various reservations…." Traditional Indian kin-based clan or lineage councils were to be discouraged. The preferred emphasis was to be upon a socialist economic-based "Mutual Aid" collective community model.

As noted earlier, aiding Collier's effort was Nathan R. Margold, the Interior Department's solicitor and former American Civil Liberty Union attorney who devoted his talents towards Indians and Blacks, and his assistant Felix S. Cohen. It was Margold who first advanced the legal notion that Indian tribes retained limited, or inherent sovereignty. This assertion was later elaborated upon by Cohen under the concept of inherent sovereignty.

Both Cohen and Margold were deeply influenced by the writings of Cohen's father, Morris Raphael, a professor of philosophy at City University of New York.

---

[293] US Department of the Interior Circular # 3095, RE: Group Organization. NARA Laguna Niguel, RG 75, Mission Indian Agency, Records pertaining to IRA, Box 249.

The elder Cohen encouraged both his son and Margold to utilize "Marxist and Hebraic perspectives to point out the flaws of capitalism, militarism, and nationalism." Felix Cohen, who described himself as "Bolshevik",[294] writing in the American Socialist Quarterly, expressed his belief, a belief that was to influence his later legal writings, "that a revolutionary interpretation of existing legal forms would destroy the foundations of capitalist law that resulted in oppression and class violence."[295] Cohen, commenting on the forthcoming IRA legislation noted, they were "…making Reds of the Indians."[296] Under the sympathetic aegis of Harold Ickes, the Secretary of Indian Affairs, the three were allowed to devise a law that in essence was a socialist experiment in which the Indians were their guinea pigs.

Collier pursued this experiment to create what he termed his "Red Atlantis" despite warnings "from anthropologists and Indians who feared that his proposal would prove difficult to accomplish".[297] Most of all Collier, in pursuit of his socialist romanticist notions, ignored the desires of those Indians, Indian Bureau personnel, and members of Congress who favored continued assimilation. "They viewed the reservation either as a backwater where segregation and poverty flourished or as a temporary way station for full-bloods, but not as a base for social achievement."[298] In retrospect, these critics were correct.

Nonetheless, Collier was determined to see his experiment succeed.

---

[294] Mitchell, Dalia Tsuk, 2007, <u>Architect of Justice: Felix S. Cohen and the Founding of American Legal Pluralism</u>, London, Cornell University Press :34.
[295] Philip, Kenneth R., 1977, <u>John Collier's Crusade for Indian Reform 1920-1954</u>:4, The University of Arizona Press, Tucson
[296] Mitchell, Dalia Tsuk, 2007, <u>Architect of Justice:, Felix S. Cohen and the Founding of American Legal Pluralism</u>, London, Cornell University Press :75.
[297] Philip, 1977:159
[298] Philip, 1981:160, paraphrasing Hertzberg, Hazel W., <u>The Search for an American Indian Identity, Modern Pan Indian Movements</u>:315-316, Syracuse University Press, Syracuse.

Approval at Any Cost

To what degree were Collier, his associates, and field agents willing to go to succeed in having Indian tribes and individuals come under the transformative aegis of the Indian Reorganization Act? Collier realized that his plan's success was ultimately at the mercy of Indian voters. While searching for the answer to this question, two events came to light that were indicative of how far this willingness was to go. One event transpired on the agency level, the other, on the administrative level within the Offices of Indian Affairs and its solicitor. The two depict a disturbing pattern which calls into question the overall validity of IRA votes held amongst the many Indian reservations and groups.

In his March 7, 1936 Circular (#3134) [299] mentioned earlier, Commissioner Collier, after discussing the three class divisions of Indians eligible to participate in IRA, went on to discuss both Class 2 and Class 3 enrollments and the need to create registers of enrollees,

> There will not be many applicants under Class 2, because most persons in that category will themselves be enrolled members of the tribe, except where a final roll has been made, and hence included under class 1. The main use of the form, therefore, will be to obtain a register of class 3, - persons having one-half or more Indian blood who are neither enrolled members of a tribe (Class1) nor unenrolled descendants of such members

---

[299] Circular # 3134, Enrollment under the Indian Reorganization Act, March 7, 1936. NARA Laguna Niguel, RG 75, Mission Indian Agency, Records Pertaining to IRA, Box 249.

residing on a reservation June 1, 1934, (Class 2). However, the form has been so prepared that it is equally applicable to Classes 2 and 3.

In addition to the need to create registers, especially for Class 3 blood quantum applicants, Collier needed positive outcomes from Indian groups who held IRA referendums, especially among those landless Class 3 applicants for whom land would be acquired by the Interior Department and held in trust for their use. The Rancheria system and the present-day reservations of many Southern California Mission Bands were so formed from this Class 3 group. They were not historic tribes who, according to Margold, retained "inherent sovereignty", but post-IRA created communities having only limited land rights. The problem for the Indian Office was the minimum threshold of one half Indian blood that was required. Finding and acquiring such applicants were a problems for the local or regional agencies whose responsibilities were to organize a referendum. IRA could not succeed without a significant number of positive votes. Thus, the political pressure to find suitable applicants and to produce positive votes was substantial. This led to two problems: one at the agency level, the second was to emerge at the departmental level.

As an example of the first problem, there was a Class 3 entity that was to become the Santa Ynez Band residing on privately-owned land near the former Catholic Mission of Santa Ynez in Santa Barbara County, California. Since 1902 the Federal government had been trying to take fee ownership of the lands upon which they resided from both the Roman Catholic Church and a local land development company. Numerous legal difficulties had, up until the time of IRA (1934) prevented this taking. In 1940 these issues had yet to be resolved and no federal reservation had been established for the Santa Ynez. As a result, the Santa Ynez community was not residing on a reservation or public fee-held lands, but resided as tenants at will on the lands of private fee owners. Since the advent of the twentieth century there had been a constant influx of non-Indian Mexicans and non-Santa Ynez Indians of varying degrees of Indian ancestry onto the former Santa Ynez mission lands. The 1930 federal census reported that there were thirty-two individuals residing at Santa Ynez. According to this census, over half of the Santa Ynez community population was enumerated as "Mexican." In 1934, this group still formed the majority community population at Santa Ynez. The Riverside Indian Agency conducted a yearly census at Santa Ynez, but for unknown reasons, these censuses did not provide the ethnic identity of the individual or family group enumerated. If Santa Ynez were to come under the aegis of IRA, a suitable one half blood (Class 3) voting population had to be constructed and registered. This led to some sleight-of-hand actions by the Riverside Indian Agency which was responsible for organizing an IRA vote at Santa Ynez.

An analysis of the Riverside Indian Agency IRA-related documents reveals dubious actions which allowed individuals who did not meet the one half blood requirement to vote as Class 3 applicants.

Section 19 of IRA required that to be considered eligible to enroll as a voter in the IRA election, an individual must have been at least twenty-one years of age, and a member of, or a descendant of a recognized tribe residing upon an established federal Indian reservation. Barring these requirements, an individual must have at least one half Indian blood quantum to register. Santa Ynez was not descended from an historical tribe, nor was it residing upon a federal Indian reservation at the time of IRA.

Prior to the Santa Ynez IRA December 15, 1934 vote, on April 1, 1934, the Bureau of Indian Affairs conducted a census of Santa Ynez.[300] The total enumerated population at Santa Ynez was "90". Later that year, on December, 15, 1934, a vote was undertaken by the adult members of the Santa Ynez band in order to decide whether to come under the aegis of the Wheeler-Howard (Indian Reorganization) Act. The registered results were:[301]

> California: Mission Agency; Santa Ynez
> Voting Population 90, Yes Votes 48, No votes 20. December 15, 1934

Among the listed voters there were only twenty who actually cast ballots (this discrepancy will be discussed below) and whose names were noted on a copy of the voter eligibility list. This list, along with the cast ballots were found in the Mission Indian files at NARA Laguna Niguel.[302] When the names of those who voted were compared to the 1933 BIA census after-the-fact hand-written alterations to the blood quantum were noted on this census to the names of nine of the twenty voters. Previous to the 1933 census they all were listed as having less than one half blood quantum. These changes occurred subsequent to the April 1, 1933 census and prior to the December 18, 1934 IRA vote.

Two of these voters for example, Florencia Armenta and Eulalis Armenta were mixed Indian-Mexican descendants of migrants from Senora Mexico. The two were apparently satisfied during preceding years to be identified at a lower one eighth to one quarter blood quantum level. A sudden 'up-tick' via inserted hand written "claims" on the April 1934 BIA census appeared which allowed

---

[300] 1934, April 1, Indian Census Roll, Santa Ynez reservation of Mission Indians, NARA Laguna Nigel, Microfilm copy.
[301] 1934, December 15, Vote by the Santa Ynez band to come under IRA. From Hass, Theodore H. 1947, Ten Years of Tribal Government Under I.R.A. US. Dept. of the Interior.
[302] 1934, November 24, Voter eligibility list, NARA Laguna Nigel, RG 75, Mission Indian Records, Box 258.

them to vote in the IRA referendum. Similarly, it was noted that voter registration list contained the names of seven other persons who actually cast IRA ballots at Santa Ynez that were similarly not qualified to vote. Additionally, both Florencia and Eulalis were not members of the Santa Ynez band, but were, according to census and agency records, children of a family from Senora, Mexico.

In this situation, the blood quantum of all these individuals was arbitrarily raised from either "one eighth" or "one quarter" to "one half". As noted earlier, one half was the minimal Class 3 blood quantum requirement for individuals, not members of tribes under federal jurisdiction, and not residing on a reservation to vote on Indian reorganization.

A comparison of the 1933 Interior Department/BIA Santa Ynez census roll to those of the 1930, 1931, and 1932, Interior Department/BIA Santa Ynez census records confirms the lower one quarter blood quantum numbers for these persons for those years. For instance, on the 1930 census, Florencia (Pena) Armenta and her daughter Eulalia were both cited as having one quarter blood quantum.[303] The same appeared for both on the 1931 and 1932 census'.[304] However when the April 1934 census is reviewed, both mother and daughter had "one half" blood quantum.[305] Of interest to note was that on the April 1, 1934 census, Florencia was cited as having one half blood degree, but another handwritten notation on that census document states "*claims F*" (full). During two BIA census cycle's she went from one quarter blood to full blood. Upon what evidence was her claim

---

[303] NARA Laguna Niguel, Microfilms M 595, Roll #12 (1931).
[304] NARA Laguna Niguel, Microfilms M 595, Roll #12 (1932).
[305] A March 19, 1965 memorandum from the Riverside Field Office to the Sacramento Area Office purportedly contained a listing of Santa Ynez Indians who were registered in 1933 as California Indians. On this listing Florencia Armenta was cited as "4/4 Mission Santa Ynez" blood degree (NARA Laguna Niguel, RG 75, Southern California Agency, Tribal Government Files, Enrollment/Adoptions, Box # 13). .

based? It was certainly not based upon the historical and genealogical record. It clearly did not support this assertion.

The second issue, also involving IRA votes, had even more far-reaching implications. It emerged in the aftermath of the passage of IRA as a serious dispute between Commissioner Collier, Interior Solicitor Margold and both the House and Senate Committees on Indian Affairs. Again, the issue centered around the question of IRA votes and Collier's and Margold's interpretation of Section 18 of the Act, most specifically, the tallying of a band's votes in its referendums to either come under IRA or to reject it. The pertinent section read as follows,

> ...This Act shall not apply to any reservation wherein a majority of the adult Indians, voting at a special election duly called by the Secretary of the Interior, shall vote against its application.

This dispute centered upon conflicting interpretations of the above, due to the presence of a comma between "Indians" "voting." This controversy not only called into question all 277 IRA votes undertaken during 1934-1935, it also eroded congressional political support for later funding of IRA leading to its eventual failure. This issue led Congress to amend the Act in 1935.

"there was some change in punctuation"

This controversy first came to light when several Mission Indians from California brought to Congress's attention an incident which occurred as a result of an IRA referendum vote held at the Santa Ysabel Mission Indian reservation. It appears, based upon a direct numerical counting of the votes (14 for, 47 against), that the Indians at Santa Ysabel voted not to come under IRA. Collier and company insisted they did. How the Indian Office arrived at this conclusion ranks amongst the annals of bureaucratic finesse.

In hearings held between February 11- 13, 1935, their complaint was bought before a House Subcommittee of the Committee on Indian Affairs.[306] The issue at hand was fully articulated by Winslow Couro, one of two delegates representing the Mission Indians of California to a highly incredulous House committee. At that time, he presented to the Committee a statement from the Mission Indians of California. In part it read,

> ...Whereas through the unfair and un-American methods used by the Superintendent of the Mission Indian Agency and the Commissioner of Indian Affairs, against the best judgment and interests of Indians living upon the various reservations; and
> Whereas it was the unanimous opinion of the conference duly called and assembled that it was for the best interests of all the Mission Indians represented to send delegates to Washington with authority to appear before Congress or other official body or individual, and ask for repeal of said bill [IRA] and to urge the removal of Commissioner John Collier, Supt John W. Dady, and certain other Bureau employees....

Couro then proceeded articulate the Santa Ysabel reservation's complaint.

[:59]**Statement of Winslow Couro**, A Delegate from the Mission Indians of California and Spokesman for the Santa Ysabel Indian Reservation.
Mr. Couro, On December 19, 1934 a referendum was held under the Indian Reorganization Act at the Santa Ysabel, California, Reservation, Riverside, California.

The superintendent of that agency appointed three judges to take charge of the election. He appointed the Indian policeman John Leo as teller, and John Beresford, the Indian school bus driver, and myself. Mr. Beresford and I were the judges and John Leo was the teller.

The superintendent submitted a list of names of those, he said, eligible to vote, and his instructions to the teller were that if anybody came to the

---
[306] 1935, February 11, Indian Conditions and Affairs. Hearings before the Subcommittee on General Bills of the Committee on Indian Affairs House of Representatives, 74th Congress, first session on H.R. 7781.

polls and his name was on the list he should be allowed to vote. Examining the list we found the names of eight Indians of whom we have never heard of, and they had never resided upon the Santa Ysabel Reservation. Eighteen Indians did not vote; 44 non-resident Indians did not vote; 52 Indians voted on the bill. The list contained the names of 15 Indians who were never accepted into the reservation by the people, but they had resided there from 15 to 45 years, and according to the rules, they voted. Forty-three names on the roll had been gone from the reservation from 2 to 45 years and many of them had not been heard from in a great many years. One name was on that list, and yet the Indian had died a week previous to the election. Forty-three voted against the bill, nine for it.

I sent a notice to the superintendent asking the reason he submitted the names of Indians who did not live on the reservation and why we had to reject Indians who were members of our tribe, some of whom had lived there for 70 years. They were not allowed to vote. He did not answer....

Couro then placed several documents into the record. Among them was the official vote tally provided by Agency Superintendent Dady, "At Polls 9 for, 47 against, Absentee votes by mail, 5 for, 0 against, Total 14 for, 47 against, Eligible voters on reservation census roll 122"

[:62] "...**Mr. McGroarty.** What was the result of the election?
Mr. Couro. Forty-three voted against the Wheeler-Howard bill and nine voted for it...
[:63]**Mr. McGroarty.** That letter [from Superintendent Dady] says that 9 voted for it at the polls, 47 against it and there were 5 absentee ballots that favored it, making 14 for and 47 against. *Therefore the bill was defeated.*
Mr. Burdick. No; it was not.
Mr. McGroarty. *They counted 122 that did not vote as being for the bill.*
Mr. Couro. And the dead man, we buried him a week before the election...
Mr. Werner. The vote is in accordance with the interpretation placed upon the act by the Department [Interior] is it not?
Mr. Murdock. The determination of the results of the election conforms to the construction placed upon section 18 by the Department.
Mr. Werner. But it does not conform with section 18 as written by the committee and passed by Congress...

> Mr. Werner. It seems that there was some change in punctuation, or the addition of some punctuation in connection to the act after the bill passed Congress.
> Mr. Murdock. It seems Mr. Margold [DOI solicitor] places great emphasis on the punctuation of the act.
> [:64] Mr. Werner. I think that this committee in the last session of Congress had a clear-cut idea of what we were trying to do; but the Department has apparently overridden the committee…
> [:65] Mr. Ayers. I have, unfortunately, not been able to be here at the meetings of the subcommittee, but I should like to know where the Department [Interior] gets this authority-
> Mr. Collins. I may say that Mr. Margold, the Solicitor of the Department of the Interior, will be here to testify.
> Mr. Murdock. You do not know where the Department gets the authority to construe the act as it has?
> Mr. Ayers. I do not…"

The Riverside Indian Agency, the agency having jurisdiction over the Mission bands that came under the 1891 Mission Indian Relief Act, together with the Indian Bureau, counted as positive votes those votes not actually cast by eligible voters (61 votes). This assured a positive IRA vote by the band, despite the fact that the actual votes cast refuted the Act. This action appears to have been against the original intent of Congress when it passed the Wheeler-Howard Act.

According to later testimony given by Commissioner Collier, seventeen other Mission bands and reservations had their votes manipulated in the same manner. In his later testimony[307] before the House Committee on Indian Affairs, Purl Willis, co-representing the Mission Indians with Winslow Couro, provided further testimony on the Santa Ysabel vote controversy. Willis testified to the Committee the following,

---

[307] 1936, Conditions of Indians in the United States, Hearings before the Committee on Indian Affairs, House of Representatives, 74th Congress, 2nd Session on H.R. 8360, part 2. :67-68, Statement of Purl Willis, Representing California Indians.

...The Mission Indians, numbering some 3,000, did not approve the Wheeler-Howard bill. The intensive campaign and propaganda used to get them to endorse this bill has been put in the record..."

Taken to the Woodshed

Purl Willis, still representing the California Mission Indians, was again called to testify before the House hearings.[308] Willis' testimony contained previous Senate testimony and Interior Department correspondence in which Commissioner Collier seemingly contradicted his prior statements made to a Senate committee on this controversy,

> [:69] **Mr. Willis.** I did receive letters from Mr. Collier saying that he was for the things that the Mission Indian favored...
> [:70] ...Also I have a short brief that recites facts and quotes Mr. Colliers statement before the Senate Committee on Indian Affairs. I want to quote from page 93 of Senate hearings of April 26, 1934, as follows:
>
> ***The Chairman,*** *Suppose you do not have an election at all. Would they all automatically come under the bill? And then it would take a majority to get them out.*
> ***Commissioner Collier,*** *If the majority of the tribe voted to have this bill apply to them, it would apply to them. If a majority at the election voted that they wanted the bill to apply, it would apply. If a majority voted that they do not want it to apply, it would not apply.*
>
> *[:72]****Senator Thomas of Oklahoma****. You just stated that it would take a majority of the Indians voting against it to keep it from passing.*
> ***Commissioner Collier****. A majority of the vote at the election cast against the application would cause it not to be applied...."* [emphasis added]

Here Commissioner Collier was suddenly concurring with the Committee and contradicting Solicitor Margold's testimony that a majority vote "at the election cast" would determine the outcome of the referendum. Yet, despite this assurance

---

[308] 1935, February 11, Indian Conditions and Affairs. Hearings before the Subcommittee on General Bills of the Committee on Indian Affairs House of Representatives, 74th Congress, first session on H.R. 7781

to the Committee, Willis noted that Collier sent out the following to John Dady, the Superintendent at the Mission Indian Agency at Riverside,

> [:72-73]**Mr. Willis**. The following are the words of the Indian Office in a letter sent out to "the Indian spokesmen and leaders of the Mission Indians Reservation the Mission jurisdiction" by Superintendent Dady at Riverside on December 3, 1934:
>
> " *In this connection Indian Office letter dated October 27, 1934, advises as follows"*
> *Section 18 gives the Indians on all reservations the right to exclude themselves from the application of the act. This exclusion can be brought about only if a majority of all the adult Indians on the reservation cast their ballots against the application of the act.* ***If less than a majority vote against the act, even if the negative votes should outnumber the affirmative ones, the act still applies."*** [emphasis added]

It appears in the following that an opinion issued by the Interior Solicitor was at the heart of the controversy. The Committee called Nathan R. Margold, the Interior Department's Solicitor, to testify upon this issue. His extensive questioning and lengthy, sometimes arrogant, testimony cast significant doubt upon the validity of the votes taken amongst the Mission Indian bands under the California Agency, and cast a serious pall over all the IRA votes held in general.

> **Mr. Murdock.** The purpose of calling you here this morning is due to the fact that the committee as a whole, I think, with possibly one or two exceptions, do not agree with the construction of the Indian Bureau or the Indian Office of section 18 of what is commonly known as the "Wheeler-Howard Act" Public, 383, Seventy-third Congress, I understand that you rendered an opinion in December 1934 on the request of the Indian Office as to the proper construction of that Section 18.
> **Mr. Margold.** That is correct…
> [:77] **Mr. Murdock.** Let me ask this question: Was your reconsidered opinion of February 5, 1935, made by you after a very thorough briefing of the question submitted?
> **Mr. Margold.** It was made after a memorandum was prepared, which is in large measure embodied in the opinion, and personal discussion with two

of my assistants in regard to the matter, which assistants had done the preliminary work for me.

Mr. Murdock. As I recall, in the reconsidered opinion there are not to exceed three cases referred to, all of those cases having to do solely with pronunciation?

Mr. Margold. That is correct,...

...**Mr. Murdock.** The section in question and which you set out in your reconsidered opinion, the language of the statute upon which you must depend for construction of that part of the act reads as follows:
This act shall not apply to any reservations wherein a majority of the adult Indians, voting at a special election duly called by the Secretary of the Interior, shall vote against its application...

[:78]**Mr. Margold.** That is correct.

Mr. Murdock. Your construction of that, as the committee understands, is this: That the Wheeler-Howard Act (Public 383, 73d Cong.) applies to all Indian reservations wherein a majority of the adult population of the reservation have failed to vote against application of the act to that particular reservation.

Mr. Margold. That is correct: or, I should say, it applies unless or until within a year that a majority do vote against it. I have in an opinion rendered held that if we have an election and a majority fail to register and vote against the act, it is within the discretion of the Secretary to call a second election and afford a second opportunity to vote.

Mr. Murdock. By a majority do you mean a majority of the votes actually cast or a majority of the entire membership of the reservation or tribe?

Mr. Margold. The latter.

Mr. Murdock. And not the vote actually cast?

Mr. Margold. That is correct...

Mr. Murdock. In this particular instance, which of your assistants, if you recall, covered that?

[:79]**Mr. Margold.** The law was searched by Mr. Cohen, who prepared an opinion....

The tortured nature of reasoning utilized by Margold to arrive at his interpretation of Section 18 of IRA was demonstrated in the following. Margold was asked by Senator Wheeler, one of the sponsors of IRA, to re-examine his initial October 23, 1934 opinion.[309] Wheeler did so on the basis that the Senate's legislative counsel

---

[309] Solicitor's Opinion M-27810 (approved October 23, 1934, reaffirmed December 13, 1934)

disagreed with Margold's interpretation of Section 18 of IRA as expressed in his Opinion, then being considered for passage by the Senate.

> **Mr. Murdock.** On page 2 of your opinion of February 5, 1935, you say that, [in response to Senator Wheeler]
> *You requested me to reconsider this opinion...*
> **Mr. Murdock.** Further in this opinion this language is used in paragraph 1:
> *Unless the punctuation of the phrase in question be entirely, the word "majority" would appear to refer to the following words: "of the adult Indians"; and the succeeding phrase, set off from the rest of the sentence by commas, would appear to be parenthetical and nonrestrictive, indicating simply the manner in which "a majority of the Indians* * *shall vote against its application.*
> **Mr. Murdock**...As I construe the first sentence, the punctuation has not been entirely disregarded, but emphasis has been given to it. I may not understand; I may be dumb; but I cannot follow that reasoning...
>
> [:82] **Mr. Murdock.** Coming back to section 16, the language of which I shall not read, there is no question is there, Mr. Margold, but what under your construction, in order to adopt the constitution and by-laws, and so forth, it does require a majority vote in favor of the constitution and that "majority" refers to the entire adult membership of the tribe rather than to those actually voting?
> **Mr. Margold.** That is correct.
> **Mr. Murdock.** Passing to section 17 we find that-
> *The secretary of the Interior may, upon petition by at least one-third of the adult Indians issue a charter of incorporation to such tribe: Provided. That such charter shall not become operative until ratified at a special election by a majority vote of the adult Indians living on the reservation.*
> **Mr. Margold.** That is correct.
> **Mr. Murdock.** Do you not, Mr. Margold, distinguish between the language of those two sections and the language of section 18?
> **Mr. Margold.** I see no basis for making that distinction, in view of the insertion of the commas. Without the commas, I should have reached the opposite conclusion. In section 18, if there were no comma after the word *Indians* and no comma after the word "*Interior*", that provision would require merely a majority of those voting rather than a majority of the adults...

Mr. Murdock. You, of course, gave no effect whatever in your opinion to the hearings on this particular matter, as those hearings occurred in the Committee on Indian Affairs.

Mr. Margold. I would say this-

[:83]**Mr. Murdock.** Please answer yes or no.

Mr. Margold. In reaching the conclusion I gave no effect to them. I should have reached the same conclusion regardless of those hearings.

Mr. Murdock. So that the conversations and interrogations carried on by members of the committee meant nothing to you in construing that particular act.

Mr. Margold. They did not, because the rule on construction is that if the meaning of a statute is clear the legislative history cannot be referred to. I thought the meaning was clear, and the legislative history would not have influenced me...

Mr. Murdock. Notwithstanding that, you think that the commas should be given weight as against all other evidence?

Mr. Margold. Yes, because that represents the final version as the bill came out of committee.

[:92] **Mr. Murdock.** You knew Mr. Collier's position was at the time of these hearings?

Mr. Margold. Yes.

Mr. Murdock. And you knew that the construction placed on this section by you and for the administration of the act was clearly contrary to his views at the time?

Mr. Margold. Yes, sir.

Mr. Murdock. Did he ever tell you that your opinion was wrong?

Mr. Margold. He did not.

Mr. Murdock. But he did come back for another opinion?

Mr. Margold. He did not.

Mr. Murdock. He did not?

Mr. Margold. No, sir.

Mr. Murdock. Did he ever indicate to you that he thought that administration of the law under your construction would be unfair and inequitable?

Mr. Margold. He did not...

Mr. Murdock. And do you not assume that the Indians had beaten you to this construction of the act and they already had knowledge of the fact that they did not have to vote to express themselves as being in favor of the act? You say that in your opinion.

Mr. Margold. I say that was their impression and they may have relied upon it.

Mr. Murdock. Where did you get that?

Mr. Margold. I inquired about it.
Mr. Murdock. Of whom?
Mr. Margold. My assistant, when this case was before him.
[:94] Mr. Murdock. Do you refer to Mr. Cohen?
Mr. Margold. Yes.
Mr. Murdock. What was his information?
Mr. Margold. He stated that a memorandum had been circulated, as I recall.
Mr. Murdock. A memorandum had been circulated by whom?
Mr. Margold. By the Indian Office, which memorandum indicated that view. That is my best recollection.
Mr. Murdock. If the Indians wanted the act to apply they did not need to appear?
Mr. Margold. *The statement was that the majority of the adult Indians on the reservations would be required to vote against it to reject it.*
Mr. Murdock. Do you think all the Indians were familiar with that?
Mr. Margold. I do not know. I mentioned the fact that the statement had been sent out.
Mr. Murdock. Reading from page 4 of your statement, I find you saying that-
As a matter of fact the statutory provision permitting Indians of a given reservation to nullify an act of Congress is so exceptional that it can scarcely be supposed that Congress would wish to give this power to what might be a very small group of actual voters on a reservation.
You could not have arrived at that conclusion from the discussions of this subject before the Committee on Indian Affairs...
Mr. Murdock. It is more natural to assume that Congress -are you basing this statement on your own knowledge of the law or just knowledge of the Committee on Indian Affairs and Congressmen generally?
Mr. Margold. This is a general reference from the situation.
Mr. Murdock. It really has no part in a legal discussion of the act?
Mr. Margold. That is correct:
I t is more natural to assume that Congress having adjudged the provisions of the Wheeler-Howard Act to be beneficial to the Indians of the Nation generally should have required a very definite expression of dissent to render the act inapplicable to any reservation.
To consider an actual example, the Commissioner of Indian Affairs reports that on the Walker River Reservation, out of 301 eligible voters only 41 [:95] actually voted to reject the act, while 37 voted to continue the act in force, and 223 failed to vote at all. It is quite possible that many Indian refrained from voting because they had been informed that rejection of the act could be accomplished only by a majority of eligible

voters. That meant, in effect. That voting in favor of the act had no different effect than refusing to go to the polls.

We see in Solicitor Margold's testimony, the radical position expressed previously by Felix Cohen in the American Socialist Quarterly, "that a revolutionary interpretation of existing legal forms would destroy the foundations of capitalist law that resulted in oppression and class violence." We also note a willful ignoring of congressional intent by Collier, Margold, and Cohen. Most disturbing of all was their efforts to subvert the democratic rights of the Indians by a deceptive nullification of the rule of majority vote. In addition the comma issue, a situation in which the comma in question did not appear on the bill draft, but subsequently appeared on the printed copies of the Act that came out of the Government Printing Office (a possible printers insertion?), two other factors make this issue even more disturbing. First, there is the Dady memo of October 1934 to the Mission Indian reservations wherein,

> In this connection Indian Office letter dated October 27, 1934, advises as follows"
> Section 18 gives the Indians on all reservations the right to exclude themselves from the application of the act. This exclusion can be brought about only if a majority of all the adult Indians on the reservation cast their ballots against the application of the act. *If less than a majority vote against the act, even if the negative votes should outnumber the affirmative ones, the act still applies.* [emphasis added]

In addition to problems in notification, physical distance from the reservation and transportation issues, by this memorandum, off-reservation voters were discouraged to vote and encouraged to stay away from the election site. At the same time, we have the testimony before the Committee at the same hearings by Commissioner Collier. Here he testified to the Committee that the voter eligibility rolls were not prepared by the bands, but instead by the Agency which utilized a very loose criteria for inclusion, possibly to inflate the lists to make a negative majority vote difficult, if not impossible,

[:105]**Commissioner Collier**…The instructions given to the superintendent with reference to making up the roles of eligible voters for the referendums are that, first, the Indians resident on the reservation, enrolled at and resident of the reservation, shall be eligible; next, that those who are constructive residents, those enrolled there but who are still *keeping up some sort of relationship* with the place who may reasonably be expected to make it their homes, or who are keeping up a permanent connection, shall be eligible. That may consist of a property interest in the reservation, and the Indians might be living in some town far or near making a living.

Only one California reservation managed to garner sufficient votes cast to achieve a negative decision, that reservation was Rincon.[310]

As a result of these hearings and the voter abuse uncovered during the hearings, six attempts were made in Congress to repeal IRA.[311] One of these attempts was made by Senator Burton Wheeler, one of the original sponsors of the original 1934 Wheeler-Howard Act,

> The senator admitted that he sponsored this legislation because he favored letting the Indians "carry on their own affairs." But he soon became disillusioned after Collier sent a "lot of uplifters" from Chicago and New York, who never saw an Indian except in a moving picture show, to impose their social theories on the Indians. When the tribes objected to these policies, Collier continued "the same old practice of controlling Indian councils that was in vogue under the Harding Administration…many Indians resented "being herded like cattle" on to reservations where the Bureau treated them like "some special kind of creature.[312]

---

[310] Philip, Kenneth, R. 1981, John Collier's Crusade for Indian Reform 1920-1954:157,University of Arizona Press, Tucson.

[311] 1937, April 28, Report of The Secretary of the Interior on Senate Bill 1736, to Repeal The Indian Reorganization Act of June 18, 1934 (48 Stat. 984). 1937, March 4, Department of the Interior document # 131868. Statement by Commissioner John Collier: Six Efforts in Congress to destroy the Indian Reorganization Act.

[312] Philip, 1981:198-199

Atlantis Sinking

In the end, on June 15, 1935,[313] Congress passed an act amending Section 18 of IRA. This section was amended to state that any such IRA election would require no less than 30 percent of the total eligible voters in order to be valid. By doing so, Congress repudiated the actions of Collier and Margold's opinion.

Following the above hearings there were six attempts to repeal the Indian Reorganization Act. Collier, reacting to one such effort sponsored by both Senator's Wheeler and Frazier depicted Wheeler's actions as "mystifying".[314] Collier continued by stating that,

> Senator Wheeler is quoted as objecting that features stricken from the original Wheeler-Howard Bill are nevertheless being put into effect by the Secretary of the Interior through constitutions granted to the tribes which have organized under the Act.

If Collier and Ickes could not get what they wanted in the initial legislation, they found non-legislative avenues to achieve their goals. Needless to say, when Congress became aware of this circumvention, action was taken. Collier, not denying what he was attempting to do countered Wheeler by claiming that IRA gave the Secretary of the Interior the power to do so,

> But the Act expressly states that the powers vested in Indian tribes through their constitutions may be not only those specified powers named in the Act but "in addition, all powers vested in any Indian tribe or tribal council by existing law." The "existing law," as it stood before the Indian Reorganization Act was signed, gave to the Department certain powers to vest authority in tribes, and directly vested certain authorities in tribes. The Indian Reorganization Act extended these authorities and limited the authority of the department.

---

[313] 49 Stat. L.378

[314] NARA Laguna Niguel, RG 75, Riverside Indian Agency, Indian Reorganization Act Correspondence. Document # 131778. "Statement By Commissioner John Collier, To The Associated Press, On The Attempted Destruction Of The Indian Reorganization Act By Senate Bill 1736, March 3, 1937

Collier concluded his defense by stating,

> Why has it been wrong for the Secretary of the Interior to obey the express language of the Indian Reorganization Act, and to vest the tribes with all those authorities given by prior acts as well as by the Reorganization Act?

As in the "comma" interpretation of Section 18 of IRA, Collier was again attempting to circumvent the original intent of Congress. When Congress deleted the proposed independent Indian judiciary section of the bill, Collier resorted to circumvent the will of Congress by inserting language within the organizational constitutions of Indian groups that voted to come under IRA that gave them the authority to do so.

Collier also reacted strongly to other attempts to repeal IRA. He blamed such attempts on two distinct groups.[315] The first group he referred to as "White operators" who, in his opinion, were trying to exploit Indian range lands, forest lands, and timber resources. The second group he described as protectors of Indian property rights, "yet who dislike the Reorganization Act because they think they find it a romantic, even an alien element."

Collier continually attempted to gain powers for reorganized Indian communities that were struck by Congress in the initial legislative draft. Surely these actions, his confrontational style, the IRA vote scandal, and his tactics of administrative subterfuge did not gain him or IRA any political support in either house of Congress. At the same time, Indian political groups such as the American Indian Federation (AIF) attacked IRA and Collier, going so far as to ask the House Indian Affairs Committee to remove Collier as Commissioner of

---

[315] NARA Laguna Niguel, RG 75, Indian Reorganization Act correspondence, Document #131868, March 4, 1937, "Six Efforts In Congress To Destroy The Indian Reorganization Act."

Indian Affairs. Their reason for doing so, as stated to Congress[316] was that Collier "insulted Indians in magazine articles, misrepresented their attitude toward the Wheeler-Howard bill, retained incompetent superintendents, and consistently advocated measures which created tribal divisions." Collier's response to the House Committee was to call these charges "an audacious humbug." In response, Collier's attitude and comments further provoked hostile responses from the Committee's members. Some members advocated the abolishment of the Bureau, that the IRA was unconstitutional, They demanded to know if tribal trust funds were still being used to fund Bureau of Indian Affairs operations?, whether IRA was founded on the theory of communistic administration, and accused Collier of being a member of the American Civil Liberties Union, an accusation he did not deny, but stated he could not remember if he was.[317]

On the budgetary side, Collier had already made a powerful enemy of Representative Jed Johnson of Oklahoma, Chairman of the House Indian Appropriations Subcommittee. The Committee slashed funding for IRA related activities stymieing the Bureau's efforts to carry out IRA's agenda, especially land acquisition provisions for Class 3 IRA groups. Johnson continually cut Indian appropriations, going as far as a 25% decline in fiscal year 1943. Another land-related problem was the reluctance by Indians who had received land allotments prior to IRA to return them to community common lands upon the various reservations, especially where those Indian social systems valued individualism. Again, warnings of potential application problems of IRA on reservations by many ethnologists that were ignored by Collier, coupled with his own limited experience with these Indian tribes and his ideological blindness,

---

[316] House Hearings on HR 7781, Indian Affairs Committee, 1935, An Act to Repeal the Wheeler-Howard Act, 74th Congress, Session 1:14-21.
[317] Philip, Kenneth, R. 1981, <u>John Collier's Crusade for Indian Reform 1920-1954</u>:174,University of Arizona Press, Tucson.

created further problems for IRA that impeded its chances of success. As for the Indians themselves, IRA was compelling them to participate in seemingly schizophrenic behaviors. On the one hand IRA was propelling Indian communities towards progressive modernization, and on the other, these same communities were being compelled to retain or recreate traditional tribal community norms and values. Neither Collier nor IRA was able to rectify these two conflicting tensions.

Perhaps the ultimate point of conflict was with Collier himself and his seemingly obsessive compulsion to recreate a socialist utopian society, his Red Atlantis if you will, that in fact never existed. His own efforts represented an extreme form of paternalism by forcing his notions of political self-governance upon Indian communities whose own institutional memory was based upon treaty formed dependency or of pressuring land allotment holders who had adjusted to the concept of private ownership and self responsibility into backpedaling to communal ownership and political governance with little thought of individual rights.

Collier apparently loathed volunteer-based community organizations such as the Mission Indian Association or the American Indian Federation. They did not fit his limited romanticized vision of traditional Pueblo kinship-based activities.

Collier never voiced his support for Indian voting rights. Such a democratic institution poised a threat to his program. His willingness, along with his ideological associates (Margold, Cohen, and Ickes) to participate in the manipulation of IRA voting perhaps was indicative of how he viewed such activities as a threat to IRA and himself. In matters of Indian education, the Indian Office, under Collier, was more concerned with teaching Indian children about traditional tribal values than in preparing these children to be able to function in the mainstream. Paternalistic as ever, the Indians were not allowed by the Indian Bureau to have a say in reservation school curriculum. Again Collier's ideological concerns came to the forefront. Teaching children the values of citizenship and rights, despite the presence of the 1924 Indian Citizenship Act, were a threat to Collier's utopian communal notions.

Collier, through the enactment of IRA, did succeed in ending land allotment under the Dawes Act. He also changed the nature of the reservation Indian's relationship with the outside world. The Indian community, rather than the individual would gradually cross-accommodate and economically integrate itself to the outside society. On many reservations functioning Indian government was almost non-existent. Herein lies IRA's greatest legacy, the required establishment of the tribal councils via approved constitutions or articles of organization as a means of local self-government. Slowly the autocratic powers of the Indian Agent, many of whom felt threatened at the prospect of IRA's success, were whittled away. In time, and that which was the goal of IRA, the federal relationship, oversight and responsibility would be terminated. Under IRA and New Deal programs, reservation lands and resources were renewed and husbanded, roads and irrigation systems constructed.

Yet, IRA was fatally flawed from its very inception, because the driving ideology behind it was equally flawed. It failed to fully take into account the cultural and political diversity present amongst American Indian populations. President Roosevelt came to that realization in 1941 that IRA relied too much on data derived solely from the Southwest Indian tribes.[318] Atlantis was sinking.

---

[318] Harold L. Ickes Papers. Library of Congress. Diary, Reel 5, February 15, 1942:6345-6346

Atlantis' Inundation

Continued congressional hostility to Collier and IRA, as well as the demands placed upon the national budget by the onset of World War II, further affected implementation of IRA. In 1941 President Roosevelt sought in part to ease tensions between the Indian Bureau and Congress by removing the Bureau to Chicago. During this same time period, Congress began to reassert its powers over Indian affairs, powers that Congress, since the 1934 Johnson O' Malley and Indian Reorganization Acts, had increasingly informally delegated to the Interior Department. Solicitor Margold's controversial October 25, 1934 eighty-seven page opinion, "Powers of Indian Tribes"[319] served as a catalyst for opposition to IRA. This "Opinion" was viewed by some in Congress as an attempt to restore sovereign powers to Indian tribes that they held prior to the March 5, 1871 proviso ending tribal sovereignty and treaty-making with Indian tribes. Margold argued that not only did tribes hold "unrestricted powers to self-government", but also powers associated with inherent sovereignty, that is, any powers not explicitly surrendered to the Federal government. This notion appears to have been conceptually derived from Article X of the federal Constitution,

> The powers not delegated to the United States by the Constitution, nor prohibited by it to the states, are reserved to the states respectively, or to the people.

A counter argument to Margold's notion is based upon legislative original intent as expressed in Congressional hearings on the 1871 Proviso ending tribal sovereignty. It was understood that treaty tribes (Margold's "Historic Tribes")

---

[319] Opinions of the Solicitor, 55 ID 14, October 25, 1934: 426-478

would no longer be considered sovereigns, but domestic dependent communities, wherein specific obligations present in negotiated and ratified treaties would still be honored by the Federal government,[320]

> The result will be that in the future our dealings with them will be as mere domestic communities, with whom we may contract, but only with the approval of Congress. They will be contracts, not treaties. Of course, such withdrawal of our recognition would not affect the validity of any treaties already lawfully made, but there is propriety in the distinct reaffirmance of our adherence to all our treaty obligations.

Margold, in turn, utilized Justice John Marshall's 1832 *Wooster v. Georgia* opinion to argue against the notion that tribal powers were delegated by Congress, but were inherent powers not surrendered to the Federal government,[321]

> All these acts, and especially that of 1802, which is still in force, manifestly consider the several Indian nations as distinct political communities, having territorial boundaries, within which their authority is exclusive, and having a right to all the lands within those boundaries, which is not only acknowledged, but guaranteed by the United States. The treaties and laws of the United States contemplate the Indian territory as completely separate from that of the States; and provide that all intercourse with them shall be carried on exclusively by the government of the Union   The Indian nations had always been considered as distinct, independent political communities, retaining their original natural rights, as the undisputed possessors of the soil, from time immemorial, with the single exception of that imposed by irresistible power,

In this case, Justice Marshall's opinion is expressly addressing those tribes or "nations" residing outside the boundary of any state. Margold's "Powers of Indian

---

[320] The Congressional Globe containing The Debates and Proceedings of the Third Session Forty First Congress Embracing the Laws passed at that Session 1871:1812, "Debate on House of Representatives Resolution 502: To Restrain the making of Treaties with Indian Tribes, March 1, 1871."
[321] United States Supreme Court, Worcester v. Georgia, 1832, 31 US. (6 Pet.) 515. Justice Marshal's opinion: 516,:519,:17.

Tribes" did not identify this context. These were pre-1871 tribal groups considered by the Federal government to be sovereign tribes.

Regarding tribes residing within the boundary of a state, that is those subject to an "irresistible power", Justice Marshal opined,

> …it may well be doubted whether those tribes which reside within the acknowledged boundaries of the United States can, with strict accuracy, be denominated foreign nations. They may, more correctly, perhaps, be denominated domestic dependent nations. They occupy a territory to which we assert a title independent of their will, which must take effect in point of possession ceases. Meanwhile they are in a state of pupilage. Their relation to the United States resembles that of a ward to his guardian.

At the time of IRA, all Indian tribes were residing within the boundaries of states and were therefore domestic dependent nations, no longer able to assert any attributes of sovereignty. The complete political domination over Indian tribes by the Interior Department attests to this fact. As was presented, on the basis of the historical sources in Chapter 1, sovereignty is an absolute. There may be attributes of sovereignty that are present within a tribal group or community, but they are present either on the basis of a treaty stipulation that has been acceded to by the Federal government, or by rights given legislatively by Congress by virtue of Congress' plenary powers over Indian tribes. Certainly Class 2 or Class 3 groups under IRA could not hold such attributes.

According to Margolds' thinking, IRA's enactment merely affirmed these existing inherent powers, especially self-government and the administration of justice. These inherent powers, according to Margold in a subsequent opinion,[322]

---

[322] Opinions of the Solicitor, April 14, 1938:813-814, "Powers of Indian Group Organized Under IRA But Not As Historical Tribe."

were restricted to "Historical Tribes" that is, those IRA Section 19 Class 1 recognized tribes who were under federal jurisdiction at the time of IRA's enactment. These were the so-called "treaty tribes." IRA Class 2 and Class 3 entities organized under IRA had legislatively-derived powers only "incidental to its ownership of property...."

The Indian Bureau used Margold's two opinions as guidelines for creating IRA constitutions. Yet the Interior Department set up a contradiction on this issue. It utilized Margold's opinion, especially the notion of inherent sovereignty as it pertains to Indian self-government, but at the same time required the Secretary of the Interior to have the final say in accepting Indian governing constitutions. The Interior Department wanted the Indians to be free from congressional oversight, but not from Interior's inherent paternalism. Needless to say, Margold's position that tribal rights are not delegated by Congress was not well received within Congress. His opinion on behalf of the Indian Bureau was a direct challenge to Congressional oversight.

In 1943, the Senate Subcommittee on Indian Affairs issued a report[323] condemning the Indian Reorganization Act as legislation that relegated Indian communities to perpetual federal ward-ship. The report went on to recommend the abolishment of the Indian Bureau, an end to federal trust over Indian lands, and to transfer to the states the responsibility for the education of Indian children. The first two recommendations were in response to Marigold's "Power of Tribes" opinion. The last provision was an attempt to end Collier's idea of educating Indian children in native traditional ways and allowing such children to learn the ways of the dominant society.

---

[323] Senate Report 310, 78th Congress Sess 1. (June 11, 1943:1-22, "Analysis of Statement of Commissioner of Indian Affairs in Justification for Appropriations for 1944 and Liquidation of the Indian Bureau."

That same year, Collier issued a circular[324] to all Indian Service personnel instructing them to begin considering what functions could be assumed by organized Indian communities, "…and how best the advisory function reduced…what additional services might be assumed by State, county or municipal agencies." As Collier noted, "…But the government's relationship to Indians is itself in Transition. The Indian Reorganization Act made that inevitable. The Indian Office is moving from guardian to advisor, from administrator to friend-in-court…We can begin, I think, by agreeing that in the process of assimilation to American life, the Indians need political experience and economic experience…" Collier had changed direction, his vision of a Red Atlantis that was to serve as a model for the reconstruction of American Society was no more. Accommodation and assimilation was the new reality.

"edging towards termination"

Termination of federal oversight and services was the ultimate goal of IRA. Federal Indian policy was to enter its final stages as Indian communities under IRA ceased being the subject of congressional plenary powers as a result of achieving economic and political self-sufficiency. Collier noted that 258 IRA elections had been held by 1944 in which 192 tribes had voted to come under IRA. On the surface the numbers looked encouraging, but during World War II an estimated forty-three thousand Indians migrated off reservations assuming employment in urban war industries. An additional twenty thousand served in the armed forces. That amounted to twenty-five percent of the total Indian reservation

---

[324] NARA Laguna Niguel, RG 75, Documents pertaining to IRA, Box 15, Circular No. 3537, November 15, 1943. "To Superintendents, Tribal Councils, All Indian service personnel and all Indians." "Planning".

population.[325] These figures in combination with increasing budgetary cuts, and the hostility by members of Congress towards Collier and Margold in part set the stage for a re-evaluation of IRA. The House Committee on Indian Affairs wanted to know from Collier as "to how and when the American Indian would reach the point where he would no longer be dependent upon the federal Government for support?" Collier admitted to this House Committee that reorganizing tribes under IRA was proving to be more difficult than planned and also to problems in acquiring and providing federal lands for seventy-five thousand landless Class 3 IRA Indians.[326] Collier, surprisingly requested that the Committee review the federal Indian trust policy with an eye towards terminating federal supervision of certain qualified Indian groups. This request was viewed favorably by the assimilationists on the Committee. Collier prepared a plan for the Committee to terminate the federal relationship with selected Indian groups, that, in his opinion were significantly progressed into the American mainstream[327],

> At congressional hearings about terminating the California Indians in 1944, Collier himself seemed to be edging towards termination. He recommended that Congress, in the future, concentrate its efforts on the needs of fewer tribes and told committee members that over 100,000 tribesmen could be "shed-off" or "relieved of federal supervision" because they were either mixed bloods or assimilated individuals who for the most part, had lost their tribal identity. To make this point, Collier classified the Indian population into three categories: (1) 93,000 predominantly "Indian" persons, (2) 124,000 semi-acculturated tribesmen, and (3) 150,000 acculturated individuals.
> In order to meet the needs of this diverse population, Collier recommended that Congress create a special commission or tribunal that included Indians to settle all tribal claims and to help the federal

---

[325] Philip, Kenneth R., 1999, <u>Termination Revisited: American Indians on the Trail to Self-Determination, 1933-1953</u>:11, Lincoln, University of Nebraska Press.

[326] Seventy-eighth Congress, Session 1, Hearings on H.R. 166, Part 1:2, 16-21. House Committee on Indian Affairs

[327] Philip, Kenneth R. 1983, "Termination: A Legacy of the Indian New Deal", <u>The Western Historical Society Quarterly</u>, Vol.14, No. 2:165-180. Mission Indian Agency, Termination Plans, House Committee on Indian Affairs, 78th Congress, 2nd Session, Part 2:51-52.

government move "toward the final solution and terminating of the Indian problem." Congress would respond to Colllier's testimony by establishing the Indian Claims Commission, creating a relocation program, lifting restrictions on allotments, and by drafting termination plans for many of the tribes listed under Collier's category of a predominantly acculturated Indian population…

"the United States has not yet discharged its obligation to the Indian"

In the aftermath of the hearings on H.R. 166, in particular Collier's recommendation for the formation of a tribunal to hear and settle issues of Indian land claims, the House Indian Affairs Committee concluded that it would be better to enact legislation directed towards the settlement of such claims rather than to provide the Interior Department with enhanced guardianship powers. [328] On the basis of further investigations, including the creation of a House delegation that met with 250 Indian leaders, the House Committee concluded that the best course, and one that followed Congress's present policy of reestablishing its prerogative in Indian Affairs, was to provide a legislative remedy for such claims and to address the question of termination. This recommendation was published in House Report 2091.[329] In part, this report, the product of a special subcommittee, concluded at the present time (1944), "…that the American Indians as a group are not ready to be turned loose" and that "…the Government of the United States has not yet discharged its obligation to the Indian to the point where the Indian Office can be abolished and the various necessary services to the

---

[328] Seventy-eighth Congress, Session 1, Hearings on H.R. 166, Part 1:48. House Committee on Indian Affairs
[329] Report 2091 Pursuant to House Resolution 166, 78th Congress, 2nd sess.:2, :8. " A Resolution Creating a Select Committee of the Indian Affairs Committee to Make an Investigation to Determine Whether the Changes Status of the Indian Requires a Revision of the Laws and Regulations Affecting the American Indian."

Indian can be discontinued." The settlement of Indian land claims was a prelude to the discharge of federal obligations to the Indians as well as to facilitate a downsizing of the Indian Bureau.[330] Most importantly, the Commission in its report advocated the creation of a claims commission to adjudicate any land claims. If a given claim was found to be valid, the claimants would receive appropriate monetary compensation from the Federal government.

The result was the introduction of House Resolution 4497 on May 26, 1946 calling for the enactment of legislation to act upon Indian land claims. During Senate hearings held on the bill, Commissioner of Indian Affairs William Brophy stated that he viewed such settlements as part of the process of the withdrawal of federal services to, and oversight of, Indian communities[331] Felix Cohen at the direction of Secretary Ickes, introduced several amendments to the bill. Among them was an amendment requiring the commission to hear "claims of whatever nature which would arise on a basis of fair and honorable dealings, even though not recognizable by any existing rule of law or equity." [332] Additionally, one other amendment emphasized that the commission, with its own investigative arm, was to be under congressional jurisdiction and not be considered an independent entity. The bill was intended to cover claims brought by all three classes of Indian entities as stated in Section 19 of IRA. This bill with the new amendments, passed unopposed in the House.

"Congress can expect no constructive advice and assistance from the Bureau of Indian Affairs"

---

[330] Armstrong, Oliver K., 1948, "Let's Give the Indians Back to the Country" <u>Readers Digest</u> vol. 47: 15-17, (April 1948)
[331] Senate Committee on Indian Affairs, Hearings on H.R. 4497. A Bill to Create Indian Clams Commission:15
[332] House Hearings on H.R. 1198 and H.R, 1341:112-33.

When H.R. 1198 came for Senate consideration, the Justice Department presented to the Senate Indian Affairs Committee a number of objections to sections within the House bill. Among them were the elimination of certain Indian groups such as the non-treaty California rancherias and Mission bands. The Commission was to rely upon the 1941 U.S. Supreme Court's "*U.S. v. Santa Fe Railroad Company*"[333] decision wherein the Court opined that "that tribal use in a definable territory from time immemorial" was the criteria for establishing tribal possessory rights. Justice also opposed the proposed commission's "judicial character." Also eliminated were claims based upon the taking of lands without compensation, lands taken under duress or by fraud or misunderstanding. Additionally, Justice wanted the removal of a claimant's ability to appeal decisions to any court of claims or to the U.S. Supreme Court. Lastly, Justice also insisted on removal of language creating the commission's own investigative arm.[334]

The House Committee on Indian Affairs objected to these proposed changes. In a joint conference committee most of the Justice Department amendments were removed. The Indian Claims Commission Act[335] became law on August 13, 1946. A major part of the termination process had been addressed. Congress, now having reasserted its authority would decide as to when and how claim payments would be made.

On January 19, 1945, Collier submitted a letter of resignation to President Roosevelt. His resignation was forced by his old arch enemy, Congressman Jed

---

[333] 314 US 339(December 8, 1941)
[334] NARA Washington D.C. RG 75, Correspondence of the Commissioner of Indian Affairs, Memorandum, Assistant Solicitor Felix s. Cohen to Commissioner William A. Brophy, April 27, 1926
[335] "An Act to Create an Indian Claims Commission, to provide for the powers, duties, and functions thereof, and for other purposes." 60 Stat.1049, Seventy-ninth Congress sess.II., August 13, 1946.

Johnson, Chairman of the House Appropriations Subcommittee on Interior Appropriations. Johnson threatened that unless Collier resigned, Interiors 1946 appropriations would be drastically reduced.[336] The House was intent upon reducing Interior's budget by 50%.[337] Collier's successor, William A. Brophy, a middle of the road politician, was informed during his conformation hearing before the Senate Indian Affairs Committee[338] that during his tenure he was expected to be responsive to Congressional Indian policy. Congress was in no mood to have a repeat of the Collier era. The Senate made it clear that Congress, not the Interior Department, was to have the final say in Indian Affairs. Congress had reasserted its authority. During the course of his nomination hearings[339] Brophy was pressed on this very issue,

> **The Chairman.** Would it be your purpose, if you were confirmed as Commissioner of Indian Affairs, to work with Congress, and not around Congress?
> **Mr. Brophy.** Well, sir, I look at it-I do not know whether I am right or not-as sort of a partnership, when you get right down to it because Congress makes the policies, and they have to be carried out; if an executive does not carry them out, he ought to be fired.
> **The Chairman.** Well, would it be your policy to work with Congress?
> **Mr. Brophy.** Oh, of course. Definitely.
> **The Chairman.** And carry out the congressional policy?
> **Mr. Brophy.** Definitely, I do not think a man could take the oath and not do it….

Commissioner Brophy had the daunting task of initiating and maintaining positive relations with Congress, whilst at the same time trying to preserve

---

[336] Kelly C. Lawrence, 1975, "The Indian Reorganization Act: The Dream and Reality" in Pacific Historical Review, vol. 44:306-308.
[337] "Interior Department Appropriation Bill" House Report 1984, 79th Congress, 2nd sess.
[338] Tyler, Lyman S. 1964, "Indian Affairs: A Work Paper on Termination":30, Provo, Brigham Young University, Institute of American Indian Studies. (Mss. copy Interior Department Library, Washington D.C.)
[339] Hearings before the Indian Affairs Committee, 79th Congress, sess 1., February 20-March 1, 1945. Nomination of William A. Brophy to be Commissioner.

remaining Interior Department policy prerogatives that had been delegated in the past to the Department. One month after his congressional confirmation Brophy was warned by Interior Department's Director of Budget and Administrative Management, Vernon Northrup, that Congress would no longer tolerate the excessive monetary expenses and administrative costs associated with the New Deal and IRA programs. What would Congress have thought if it had been aware of the additional funds acquired by the Indian Office to support IRA via extensive raiding of Indian trust accounts by Ickes and Collier? Director Northrup advised Brophy that the only means of reducing these costs was to accelerate the process of termination of Indian responsibilities.[340]

To "...take his place in the white man's community on the white man's level...."

The following year, 1946, Secretary Ickes also resigned. He did so in the aftermath of a presidential appointment dispute with President Truman. Additionally, under the Legislative Reorganization Act of 1946 both the Senate and House Committees on Indian Affairs were eliminated and Indian Affairs was transferred to the Senate Public Lands Committee and the House Committees on Interior and Insular Affairs. Indian affairs were given a subcommittee status in both houses. From that point forward, both Congress and the Executive branch pursued a dual policy within the framework of IRA for both the assimilation of Indians and a final termination of federal relations and responsibilities towards them. Ultimately, the House Indian Affairs Subcommittee concluded that the government's goal was to have the Indian "...take his place in the white man's community on the white man's level with the white man's opportunity and

---

[340] NARA Washington D.C. RG 75, Correspondence, Commissioner of Indian Affairs, Box 14, Indian Office April 27, 1945, Memorandum Vernon D. Northrup to William A. Brophy.

security status." The Subcommittee concluded that IRA as applied was a failure, in terms of Indian education, economic-self-sufficiency, and societal integration. Most significantly, the Committee concluded, "Congress can expect no constructive advice and assistance from the Bureau of Indian Affairs in the solution of the problem."[341] Commissioner Brophy, in response to congressional termination pressures, considered closing four agencies (Grande Ronde, Great Lakes, New York, Tomah) thereby ending federal relations with the Indian groups they serviced. His efforts were stymied due the presence of Indian groups under some of these agencies who had elected to come under IRA and were thus entitled to federal protection of their trust lands. The Federal government would have to transfer that trust, with the Indians permission and congressional approbation, to state jurisdiction and terminate their relationship with the Federal government.

In a Senate hearing held on February 8,1947, Acting Commissioner of Indian Affairs William Zimmerman Jr. (Commissioner Brophy was on a medical leave of absence) presented to the Committee a list of Indian groups indicating their readiness for termination of federal oversight and responsibilities.[342] This list was very similar to one prepared by former Indian Commissioner John Collier in 1944. Zimmerman's list was prepared at the insistence of the Senate Civil Service Committee, many of whose members were anti-IRA and who pointedly informed Zimmerman that Congress alone set Indian policy.[343] Zimmerman was queried about the nature of the criteria he had utilized in constructing his list,

> **Senator Johnson.** What conditions did you use as a measure, so the Committee may have the benefit of that?
> **Mr. Zimmerman.** The first one was the degree of acculturation; the second, economic resources and condition of the tribe; third, the

---

[341] House Committee on Appropriations Report 279, 80th Congress, 1st sess. 1947:15.
[342] Hearings on Senate Resolution 41, Post Office and Civil Services Officers and Employees of the Federal Government, 80th Congress, 1st Session, part 3:547.
[343] Hearings on S.R. 41 Senate Committee on Civil Service 80th Congress, sess. 1:255-257.

willingness of the tribe to be relieved of federal control; and fourth, the willingness of the State to take over....

Zimmerman's list contained the names of those Indian groups whose relationship with the Federal government was being considered either for immediate or future termination. The list was very similar to one produced by former Commissioner John Collier in 1944. In part Zimmerman's list read,

> "Classification Of Tribes Submitted To Committee
>
> In responding to the request of the Senate Committee on Post Office and Civil Service, Acting Commissioner William Zimmerman, Jr. submitted a list of tribes in three groups: Group 1 could be released immediately from Federal supervision; Group 2 in 10 years; and Group 3, indefinite time.
>
> GROUP 1
> Flathead
> Hoopa
> Kalmath
> Menominee
> Mission
> New York
> Osage
> Potawatomi
> Sacramento
> Turtle Mountain
>
> GROUP 2-10 YEARS
>
> Blackfeet
> Cherokee
> Cheyenne River
> Colville
> Consolidated Chippewa
> Crow Fort Belknap
> Fort Peck
> Fort Totten
> Grange Rhonde

Great Lakes
Northern Idaho
Quapaw (in part, Wyandotte Seneca)....
Taholah, Tulalip
Tomah
Umatilla
Warm Springs
Wind River
Winnebago

GROUP 3....

During this same session of the 80th Congress, legislation was introduced to repeal the Indian Reorganization Act as well as to shut down the Bureau of Indian Affairs and to transfer its responsibilities to other governmental agencies.[344] The proposed legislation did not pass. In its stead, Congress passed Public Law 162 that established the so-called Hoover Commission. Section 1 of this legislation authorized the formation of a commission, whose members were appointed by President Truman, the President *pro tempore* of the Senate and the Speaker of the House, to promote "economy, efficiency, and improved service in the transaction of public business...." The Commission's tasking was in conformity with Truman's national fiscal policy of political economy. That is, the restraining and economizing of governmental expenditures including those related to Indian affairs. Politically, the environment was conducive to termination as a means of cost-cutting. Following President Truman's policy of political and fiscal economy, the Committee led by former President Herbert Hoover focused upon the functioning and administrative effectiveness of Indian affairs within the Department of the Interior.

---

[344] Annual Report of the Commissioner of Indian Affairs for the Year 1947: 351-352, US Department of the Interior.

In 1948, this Commission compiled a report of its findings.[345] The Commission concurred with the promotion of self-governance for Indian communities. It considered such self-governance a transitory stage between government paternalism and the Indians full assimilation and participation in the mainstream of American society. In consequence, some of the Commissioners strongly disagreed with the Collier-era educational emphasis on resurrecting tribal institutions that had no effect in assisting the Indians in participating and assimilating into twentieth century America. The Commission cited this as one of the principle factors for the Indians' lack of support for IRA. The Commission proposed that all Bureau-run schools, as well as judicial functions should be transferred to state operation and jurisdiction and therefore state approved curriculums. At the same time, during this transitory period, the Commission recommended that the Bureau of Indian Affairs be transferred from the Interior Department to the "Federal Security Agency" which coordinated activities between the Social Security Administration, Office of Education, the Public Health Service, and state-run services. Other Commissioners were in dissent. They wanted more input from the Indians themselves before these assimilative actions were implemented, especially placing Indian communities under state jurisdiction. Acting Indian Commissioner Zimmerman was caught in the middle of this debate. Zimmerman was steadfast in his belief in the gradual termination of federal oversight and responsibilities. He was against the Commission's advocacy for rapid assimilation and termination. Zimmerman also argued, in concurrence with the original intent of the 1871 proviso, that all treaty obligations should still be honored with those tribes who had such a pre-1871 relationship with the Federal government. As a result Zimmerman steadfastly urged the

---

[345] Commission on Organization of Executive Branch of Government, "Report on Social Security, Education, and Indian Affairs":1-156. Department of the Interior Library, Washington D.C.

Truman administration not to consider many of the recommendations made in the Hoover Commission Report, especially those affecting the Indian Office.

Supporting termination, in 1949, President Truman's Secretary of the Interior Julius Krug argued to Congress that in enacting the Indian Reorganization Act, the Federal government had authorized itself to end its responsibilities towards those Indian tribes and Indian groups who completed the IRA process of instituting self-governance and achieving competency goals.[346] Secretary Krug cited as an example the Saginaw Chippewa who, by the provisions of their IRA charter, limited the authority of the Secretary of the Interior's oversight over their community. Krug envisioned further reductions in the Secretary's authority.

In 1951, Krug's Indian Commissioner, Dillon Myer announced his own bureau policy in support of the termination process. Myer wrote[347] that his long-term objectives were to achieve, "(1) a standard of living for Indians comparable to that enjoyed by other segments of the population, and (2) the step by step transfer of Bureau functions to the Indians themselves or to appropriate agencies of local, state or Federal government." The idea of such a transfer of services from the Federal government was not new or novel. It will be recalled that this was a central component of the 1934 Johnson-O'Malley legislation. Termination, in fact, represented the freeing, not dissolution, of Indian communities from the paternalistic constraints imposed by the Federal government, it was not, as popularly construed, to represent an end to Indian culture or political self determination. Termination of federal supervision did not equate to any sort of termination of tribal or community existence. Termination's only goal was to end the Indians racial, economic, and political segregation from nation.

---

[346] Annual Report of the Secretary of the Interior for the Year 1949:388-389.
[347] Annual Report of the Commissioner of Indian Affairs for the Year 1951:353.

Myer later wrote to Krug expressing his position on continued federal supervision and oversight of Indian communities.[348] Meyer argued that on the basis of Indian self-determination under IRA, the federal trust responsibility had been irrevocably altered from its treaty and statutory foundations. Indeed, Myer further argued that the present Federal Indian policy regarding trust responsibilities set up an irreconcilable dichotomy. In contrast to Indian self-determination, federal trust policy asserted paternalistic governmental protections for the IRA Indian communities which in turn fostered continued Indian dependency upon the Federal government. Thus Indian policy had to be amended or changed.

First proposed in 1951, Secretary Krug authorized in 1952 the creation, within the Bureau of Indian Affairs of a "Division of Programs"[349] that was to "...stimulate guide and assist the development of joint programming by tribal leaders and Bureau personnel looking toward the improvement of the basic economic status of the Indians and a sep-by-step withdrawal of the Bureau from Indian Affairs." The first Indian communities envisioned by the Bureau for complete withdrawal from federal supervision were, the Indian's of California, the Oregon-based Grande Ronde, Siletz, and Klamath, the Paiutes and Utes of Utah, the Menominee of Wisconsin, and the Missouri River Sioux.

Yet Commissioner Myer faced one obstacle to his policy. IRA proscribed that the powers of self-government and the rights of possession that a IRA community held by virtue of its IRA organization charter could only be diminished by congressional legislation. Transferring any jurisdictional matters to a state would

---

[348] NARA, Washington D.C. RG 75, Correspondence of the Commissioner of Indian Affairs, Box 15, file 20. Letter, March 20, 1953, Dillon S. Meyer to Secretary of the Interior Julius Krug.
[349] Annual Report of the Commissioner of Indian Affairs for the Year 1951:389.

require congressional intervention. The House of Representatives stepped into this issue when the House Committee on Interior and Insular Affairs submitted House Resolution 698.[350] Under the authority of this resolution, the House Interior and Insular Affairs Committee requested a report from Commissioner Myers addressing the following,[351]

1. The manner in which the Bureau of Indian Affairs has performed its functions of studying the various tribes, bands, and groups of Indians to determine their qualifications for the management of their own affairs without further supervision of the Federal Government;
2. The manner in which the Bureau of Indian Affairs has fulfilled its obligations of trust as the agency of the federal Government charged with the guardianship of Indian property;
3. The adequacy of law and regulations as assure the faithful performance of trust in the exchange. Lease or sale of surface or subsurface interests in or title to real property or deposition of real property of Indian wards;
4. Name of tribes, bands, or groups of Indians now qualified for full management of their own affairs;
5. The legislative proposals designed to promote the earliest possible termination of all Federal supervision and control over Indians;
6. The functions now carried on by the Bureau of Indian Affairs which may be discontinued or transferred to other agencies of the federal Government or to the States;
7. Names of States where further operation of the Bureau of Indian Affairs should be discontinues;
8. Recommended legislation for removal of legal disability of Indians by reason of guardianship by the federal Government; and
9. Findings concerning transactions involving the exchange, lease, or sale of lands or interests in lands belonging to Indian wards, with specific findings as to such transactions in the State of Oregon.

Myers and his Bureau addressed the Committee's request with a massive response to its queries (1,594 pages). This response became know as House

---

[350] US. House of Representatives, 82nd Congress, sess. 2 (1952).
[351] US. House of Representatives, 82nd Congress, sess.2 (1953) Report No. 2503:2-3.

Report 2503.[352] In this report Commissioner Meyer recommended to the Committee that a total of ninety-one Indian groups were, in his opinion, prepared to handle their own affairs and to have their federal relationships terminated. Congress and the Interior Department were now in concurrence on a policy of termination.

Final actions in this change in Federal Indian policy had to await the next administration. In 1953, the administration of President Dwight Eisenhower assumed office. Commissioner Myer was replaced by Glenn L. Edmonds. At his Senate confirmation hearings Edmonds was pointedly asked by a Committee member about his position on the withdrawal of federal supervision. Edmonds replied,[353] "I think we should see that the Government trusteeship is liquidated just as rapidly as possible." Congress, now more conservative and distrustful of federal control and direction over individual lives, became the driving force for termination. The final act heralding the advent of termination as Federal Indian policy was the passage of a legislative resolution in August of 1953. This was "Concurrent Resolution of the Eighty-Third Congress 108".[354] The resolution, with the support of the Department of the Interior, was introduced in the House by William Harrison of Wyoming, an ardent supporter of desegregation, and in the Senate by Henry Jackson. In part this Resolution stated,

> Whereas it is the policy of Congress, as rapidly as possible, to make the Indians within the territorial limits of the United States subject to the same laws and entitled to the same privileges and responsibilities as are applicable to other citizens of the United States, to end their status as

---

[352] 82nd Congress, sess.2.
[353] Hearings before the Committee on Interior and Insular Affairs, US. Senate, 83rd Congress, sess.1. "On the Nomination of Glenn N. Edmonds to Be Commissioner of the Bureau of Indian Affairs:4-6.
[354] Concurrent Resolution of the Eighty-Third Congress, First Session, August 1,1953, (H. Conn. Res. 108) (67 Stat. B122) Kappler, Charles, 1970, "Kappler's Indian Affairs Laws and Treaties", Vol. VI:614, Government Printing Office Washington D.C.

wards of the United States, and to grant them all of the rights and prerogatives pertaining to American citizenship; and
Whereas the Indians within the territorial limits of the United States should assume their full responsibilities as American citizens: Now, therefore, be it

Resolved by the House of representatives (the Senate concurring), That it is declared to be the sense of Congress that at the earliest possible time, all the Indian tribes and all individual members thereof, located in the States of California, Florida, New York, and Texas, and all the following named Indian tribes and individual members thereof, should be freed from Federal supervision and control and from all disabilities and limitations specially applicable to Indians....

The final goal of IRA as envisioned by its creators and supporters now became a legislative reality. Indian groups were making the final step from dependency and paternalism to equality. The form of these groups was not that envisioned by the Collier, Cohen, and Margold socialist retrogressive cabal, but the possibility of Indian social, economic and political equality with the mainstream became a distinct possibility. The terminated Indian groups could culturally remain so. They could freely choose otherwise, or simply, as individuals depart their communities to seek their future. Tribal or community governments would assume full fee title to their lands. Unlike the days of Dawes, wherein the "tribal mass" was to be "pulverized" and good Christians were to be made of the individual Indian. IRA, despite its many faults prevented that from occurring. However, recall the words of the Omaha Indian elder quoted earlier who said, "the road our fathers walked is gone." New paths are yet to be traveled by both the Indian communities and Federal Indian policy.

Chapter 9.
Summary

What has changed? A quest for regaining sovereignty lost by recognized tribes re-emerged in the 1960's and continues into the 21st century. But the sovereignty they claim is not the sovereignty their ancestors ceded. Congress still asserts plenary powers over these tribes. Confusions exists as to what actually constitutes tribal sovereignty. Nathan Margold and Felix Cohen still haunt us and the legal community with their notion of "inherent sovereignty" a term that Margold himself noted in his "Powers of Indian Tribes" was only applicable to the historic "Treaty tribes." Justice Marshall spoke of tribes residing within a state that retained some attributes of sovereignty, but he made it clear that these tribes were not sovereign political entities. How can non-treaty tribes administratively recognized by the Bureau of Indian Affairs post 1975 without legislative authorization from Congress, claim such neo-sovereign rights? It was certainly not the intent of the framers of IRA. How can these administrative tribes make such claims? How can the Bureau of Indian Affairs claim that they have such rights? What is the Bureau's statutory basis of its authority to administratively recognize tribes in the first place? Congress never legislatively delegated such authority to the Executive Branch to do so. So many questions, so few answers.

The two conflicting claims of sovereignty and plenary authority set up a conflict between the historically-supported concept of sovereignty as an all encompassing absolute, total in all aspects, against the notion of tribes being a little bit sovereign (neo-sovereign), that is, Margold's assertion of treaty tribes retaining aspects of sovereignty, not specifically ceded by treaty. Nathan Margold, in his opinions argued this point as did Felix Cohen. Opinions are just opinions, they are not law. Maintaining some attributes of a sovereign political entity does not make that entity sovereign. Plenary is an absolute term as is sovereignty.[355] Margold had argued that such inherent powers provided tribes with the authority to manage their own affairs as does any American community. The highest court in the land has yet to address this critical question regarding the contemporary notion of "tribal sovereignty" and, by extension its first cousin, "tribal immunity." We hark back to Justice Thomas' observation made at the beginning of this writing, that current federal Indian law is "schizophrenic". Its first symptoms surfaced with the advent of the Indian Reorganization Act with the socialist-based policies of Harold Ickes, John Collier, Nathan Margold, and Felix Cohen. If Red Atlantis was to have a political power base upon which to construct and institute a right to self-governance, a support of sovereignty, no matter how limited in nature, had to be devised. It was upon Margold's kernel of legal opinion as an Interior Solicitor, not settled law, that subsequent legal construction was to build upon. This process has assumed the nature of the mythical eleven-headed Hydra, each head projecting itself into the darkest corners of legal theory and practice.

Through the flow of time we have followed the over-arching trends of Indian policy; sovereignty-paternalism/assimilation-self-governance/paternalism-termination-neo-sovereignty. These trends were not isolates, but followed the political, ideological, and social trends of the dominant society.

---

[355] Plenary: "complete or absolute in force or extent." Onions C. T. ed., 1950 Third Edition, <u>The Shorter Oxford Dictionary on Historical Principles</u>, vol.II:1523, Oxford, Clarendon Press

The British authorities considered the Indian tribes on the borders to be sovereign states. They had to. Collectively these bordering tribes had the military potential to eliminate the emerging colonies. Additionally, these tribes singularly had the political sovereignty to align themselves to whatever European power that they so chose to do. France, Spain, or Great Britain, take your pick. The tribal political alignments present during the French and Indian War was such an example. The newly emergent American republic faced the same geo-political situation, thus the continuation of English policy towards these tribes. These continued security-based concerns of the new national government were expressed in the enactment of the Indian Trade and Intercourse Acts.

As the Republic grew in population, wealth, and territorial acquisition, so did its national sense of confidence. The tribes bordering the republic declined in the same areas, population, wealth, and territory. American sovereignty was maturing whilst that of the tribes in socio-cultural contact with the Anglo-American population declined. These Indian tribes were being viewed as less of a threat more of a social and fiscal burden as the national boundary moved west towards the Mississippi River and beyond.

The idea of assimilation of Indians into the dominant society, an idea that is the hallmark of self-perceived societal confidence and superiority, emerged within states amongst whose populations resided those destitute remnants of former tribes that were now under state jurisdiction. The idea was to provide state-owned lands upon which these remnants could gradually accommodate the ideological norms and values of the surrounding society and gradually assimilate into the social mainstream becoming in the process, town inhabitants. The Federal government in turn adopted this practice and by treaty and legislative removal, settled tribes *en masse* on federally-owned lands west of the Mississippi River.

There, according to national policy these Indians could accommodate themselves and in time assimilate into the mainstream.

Paternalism is the hand-maiden of assimilation. Present in the states was the notion of paternalistic oversight and assistance to these assimilating groups. This same motif emerged as national policy. Whilst Indian remnants within a state were assisted by local church and philanthropic organizations, the Federal government established the position of Indian Commissioner, and an associated Indian Bureau to address this same task on a national level. The end of tribal recognition via treaty-making in 1871 marked the final transition of Federal Indian policy from the era of sovereignty to that of incipient paternalism and assimilation. Tribes were no longer tribes, but were now considered by Congress under its plenary power to be "mere domestic communities."

Over time, the historical record demonstrates that the same types of paternalistic and idealistic church and philanthropic organizations that assisted in state assimilation of Indians appeared on the national scene. Their efforts in conjunction with a friendly political environment, resulted in assimilation of the Indian as the law and policy of the land. Like all policies promoted by idealists, they are doomed by their very nature. Idealism is just that, a mental construct that is not tempered by reality. These liberal-progressive philanthropic and religious-based organizations were so intent in voicing their visions of what the Indian ought to become, they never allowed the Indian to have a similar voice, a voice tempered by reality. The two together could have devised reasonable and workable legislation. Instead, legislation was enacted that cried out to be misused and abused, allotted land-leasing and blood quantum being two such prominent manifestations amongst many.

The advent of the Indian Reorganization Act was an idealistically-based corrective measure. IRA did not end paternalism, nor did it end assimilation. It did end the demise of Indian communities. IRA took both the concepts of paternalism and assimilation in a different direction, that is, the experimental "reorganization" of Indian tribes and groups into socialist-based collective communities that in time would both transform the very nature of American society and assimilate themselves into it. That was the idealistic vision of a "Red Atlantis." As with assimilation, the voice of reality of the Indian was excluded by the cabal of idealistic socialists within the Department of the Interior. Idealistic progressivism that was backed by the plenary authority over Indians vested in Congress was the compelling force of IRA. When compelled to listen to the Indians' reality, these progressives did so with a deaf ear. This represented the zenith of paternalism. As with the federal policy of assimilation, the plan and the goal of IRA was too imaginative and placed too much of a burden upon the national treasury. As the stated goal of IRA was ultimate amalgamation and assimilation, the end result was to be the termination of federal oversight (paternalism) and responsibilities over these reorganized Indian communities. The financial imperatives of World War II, coupled with the growing anti-IRA sentiment in Congress, forced an acceleration of IRA towards the end goal. Additionally, interwar cost cutting and economies under the Truman administration and the advent of the Korean War further compelled this process towards termination. Communism itself bred a wariness in America of not only socialism, but also overbidding government control. Termination, an extension of the prevailing American cultural ethos of itself became the national legislatively-supported Indian policy. The problem here was that many tribes that emerged out of IRA wanted what the process had to offer: self-determination and less governmental intrusion, but not the end goal, termination of federal paternalism.

These tribes still jealously protect federal paternalistic protections and monies of, and for, recognized tribes. Yet, schizophrenically, they claim to be sovereign.

What emerged, with kudos to John Collier, Nathan Margold and Felix Cohen was the reemergence of Indian self-governance, on par with any community within any of the states, along with self-governance re-emerged political self-identity and the re-emergence of the notion of tribal sovereignty, albeit in a much altered form. From this emerged a legal, administrative, and legislative quest for state-tribe sovereignty-based political parity. Whether this quest for a kind of neo-sovereignty becomes a reality, and in what form it be adjudicated, if at all, is one that will be decided in the future by the Federal Courts. Will *Imperium in Imperia* be America's future? One impediment is the inability of recognized tribes to shed the bindings and bondage of federal paternalism. Tribes pay too much homage to that altar of federal monies and services, the Bureau of Indian Affairs. In this sense Federal Indian policy has almost come full circle. How many have simply said, no thank you? Then, and only then, will such an entity begin to walk down that path towards sovereignty, that path their ancient "fathers" used to walk.

The question of tribal sovereignty has again come to the forefront in Indian policy. Will the children of Red Atlantis again rise from the depths of dependency and paternalism? Time will tell.

ABOUT THE AUTHOR

James P. Lynch is the owner and principal of Waterbury, Connecticut-based Historical Consulting and Research Services, LLC.

www.ingramcontent.com/pod-product-compliance
Lightning Source LLC
Chambersburg PA
CBHW051044160426
43193CB00010B/1056